THE LIBERTARIAN ATTACK
AGAINST LIBERTY

THE LIBERTARIAN ATTACK AGAINST LIBERTY

FAKE PATRIOTS AND FALSE GODS

JOSEPH W. BURRELL

Algora Publishing
New York

Library of Congress Cataloging-in-Publication Data —

Burrell, Joseph, 1930–
    The libertarian attack against liberty: fake patriots and false gods / Joseph W. Burrell.
        pages cm
    Includes bibliographical references.
        ISBN 978-1-62894-148-7 (hard cover: alk. paper)—ISBN 978-1-62894-147-0 (soft
cover: alk. paper) ISBN 978-1-62894-149-4 (eBook) 1. Libertarianism—United States.
2. Republican Party (U.S.: 1854–) 3. Capitalism—Political aspects—United States. 4.
Globalization—Political aspects—United States. I. Title.
    JC599.U5B86 2015
    320.51'2—dc23
                                2015027254

Printed in the United States

Table of Contents

INTRODUCTION

A balloon of inequality exists as an inevitable part of a false belief held by almost everyone: that American capitalism is democratic and freedom loving. This book aims to puncture that balloon.

My writing consists of sweeping generalizations. Without ferreting out the minute clues and details of political incursions and contradictions, I seek to distill a lifetime of observation and to articulate some basic points that are mostly left unsaid by this country's experts.

I never set out to write nonfiction books about the political, economic, and religious world. In fact, I never set out to be a writer at all. That was largely an accident. In my early life I toyed with the prospect of being a career military man, and I did serve in the Marine Corps during the Korean War. Then, I briefly taught school but found it uninspiring. Finally, I became a middle manager in the federal bureaucracy. Somehow, the years drifted away, my health declined, and I retired to a life of lost purpose.

I had always been a writer of minor missives and, of course, I did much bureaucratic writing, some of it "creative" with regard to the initiation of new policies and programs concerning the manipulation of structures and organizational functions designed to improve the mission of the bureau in which I worked. As I look back on it now, it all seems trivial, and I regret not having done better and larger work. And so I decided to write something of value in my last years, something I could leave behind that might be interesting and useful to others.

Since I was a child and first learned to use a pencil on scrap paper (all I had since we were very poor), I have been in the habit of writing little essays for my own amusement and in order to define and sort out my vague ideas and feelings.

Writing it down helped me to discover and develop my own beliefs. It also helped me to define what I saw of the world's workings. I never showed the essays to anyone. I simply tossed them away —though I did save a few when I thought them worthy.

I also wrote two novels along the way, but they were never published. After my novels failed, I began to put the remnants of my little essays together and found that I had a fairly well-developed political philosophy of my own. I also realized that my essays pointed pretty much in the same liberal direction and sometimes beyond liberalism and in a more radical and perhaps socialist direction. I found it easy to put the growing number of essays together in a coherent whole and, with the writing of some connective tissue, I found I could make a book that I thought made sense. And thus, I can share my conclusions by making this work available to others.

My books and my ideas are certainly not orthodox. I hope my perceptions help others to focus their views as well. My aim is to advance the cause of democratic liberalism, a philosophy now in decline thanks to Republican hostility, a compliant media, and Democratic Party confusion and cowardice.

I do not think that the prospects for a real, liberal democracy in this country or elsewhere are very good. Democratic government in the United States has already been pretty much destroyed and it is not likely to rise again. The false pretense of most Americans—that we have a system of "democratic capitalism"—is prevalent now. The system we have is, instead, fascist and totalitarian. The goals of the American and French revolutions have been entirely subverted and the corporations and their party—the Republican Party—has triumphed; they are in charge of nearly everything and everybody.

The United States has become a thorough oligarchy, a military garrison, and a police state. The people themselves are helpless and deluded sheep blinded by a corrupt corporate media and a political system so diseased and sickened by Republican lies and manipulations that we have all arrived at a dead end from which there is no escape, short of a violent revolution—a course that I do not recommend. Will democracy rise again without bloodshed? Can it?

PART ONE. FAKE PATRIOTS

Chapter 1. The Libertarian Attack Against Liberty

Origins

The idea that the Libertarian movement is libertarian and the Conservative movement is conservative is as ridiculous as the idea that the Republican Party is republican.

These fraudulent representations are slightly variant covers for absolutism, an absolutism derived from ancient royalism and the divine right of kings. Of them all, libertarianism is the most severely warped and, right now, it dominates the Republican Party and is on the attack against the entire American project. It is a system of extreme individualism cemented onto old style aristocratic conservatism. Libertarians consider property sacred, meaning large-scale property. Thus, their first allegiance is to predatory corporatism. Like today's corporatism, the old royal system was based on unregulated power. Today, thanks to the Enlightenment and the American and French revolutions, aristocratic conservatism does not dare any longer to openly call itself royal or divine. Libertarians claim to believe in certain civil liberties but not civil rights, an odd bifurcation. In fact, they do not even support the civil liberties they claim to cherish when those liberties might threaten or limit the privileges of large property owners.

These days, the beliefs of so-called conservatives are not very different from those of libertarians except that conservatives don't believe at all in civil liberties and are nearly always in favor of war as a solution to economic and political problems. They always act in the interest of large property owners but they usually don't quite claim that property is sacred. They hate democratic government as much as the libertarians do but they also want to shackle government power to religious and commercial power and, unlike most libertarians, they believe fervently in overseas attacks and wars to gain resources and positioning for corporations. Unlike the libertarians, they want to weld the government and the Christian churches together. Libertarians are often atheists and are not comfortable with this meld but they rarely object. They know they need the conservatives to help them gain political room for their untrammeled "individualism." The Republican Party is their umbrella and these two pieces of "Republicanism" converge more than they diverge. There are many internal contradictions but they share a hatred of liberalism and democratic government as well as a love of property and wealthy property owners. Thus, libertarianism is a sneaky kind of corporatist aristocracy without the royal and godly trappings of old and without the outright dedication to wars favored by the conservatives.

In the United States, the fundamentalist Christians and the corporatist Republicans are close allies. Lately, the fundamentalist Christians have taken to calling themselves "free-enterprise Christians." Long ago and in opposition to the hostility of Jesus to rich people and their business successes, Calvinism slanted the Christian religion in the direction of a hard driving commercialism. The Christian attachment to corporatism in this country got its recent impetus, I think, from the rise of rural white people, in the South especially, up to middle class prosperity. This occurred, ironically, because of the New Deal and its liberal support of the working class. Even as they were moving up, these people cast off New Deal liberalism because of its civil rights policies. This soon led the solid South to move from being the racist Democratic Party to being the racist Republican Party. The Southern Strategy of the Republican Party was the trigger. This strategy began in 1876 when Rutherford B. Hayes used it to steal an election; it continued as an occasional tactic until Nixon, Goldwater, and Reagan revived it with a vengeance. It has been at the center of Republican political dominance ever since. The libertarian movement developed from this mélange.

The libertarian movement is a corrupted and greatly reduced form of liberalism. Its attachment to the Republican Party was gratuitous and opportunistic. At first, the libertarian philosophy flourished among a thinly scattered collection of upper-class pseudo intellectuals alienated from liberalism because of its intense support of working people and the poor. In other words, alienated Southern racists and a group of fervent "corporatists" in love with an idealized form of extreme individualism preached by Ayn Rand came together because of a shared contempt for civil rights and a hatred of New Deal governance. This weird marriage was reactive; it was a revolt against what had become the liberal establishment. These racists and classists met on common ground in a Republican Party neutered for a generation by the New Deal. Ever since, the twisted and internally contradictory philosophy of the Republican Party has been largely libertarian. The Southern racists brought nothing with them to the Republican Party in the way of a political philosophy. The result was the melding of traditional conservative and libertarian ideas with Southern bigotry. The right name for this conglomeration is corporatism, otherwise known as fascism.

It may sound odd to say the Republican Party is libertarian and Christian at the same time. After all, many libertarians are atheists. Odd or not, it is clearly true that the libertarians and Christians occupy common ground in the Republican Party. Their shared belief consists of a firm dedication to corporatism and a violent hatred of democratic liberalism and the government of the United States.

Thus, the libertarian movement is at present the most powerful part of the conservative movement; and the Republican Party is the political arm of both. It is a fairly recent phenomenon but its adherents claim (falsely, I think) that its ideas stem from John Locke, John Stuart Mill, Thomas Hobbes, and Adam Smith. In the United States, it got its main impetus from Ayn Rand and the Chicago School of economics that imported the ideas of Ludwig von Mises and Fredrick von Hayek from the Austrian School of economics.

Ayn Rand was an atheist and a fascist, two other things that don't usually go together. Her belief in extreme individualism, even including heroic criminals and violent dictators, and her hatred of altruism and traditional Christian morality suggests something that goes beyond the predatory capitalism routinely boosted by the Republican Party and the conservative movement. She claimed to be the greatest philosopher of all time and quite a few Republicans believed her. She should certainly be considered the mother of libertarianism. She also claimed to be a complete rationalist (her objectivism), but no brand of rationalism has ever supported an individual power so extreme that it excludes most of human kind from the human equation and raises up the "talented" individual to a kind of sacred totalitarian superiority over the rabble. It's one thing to exclude god and declare the individual to be the measure of all things; it's quite another to raise up a rare, few super men and women over all others and to say, grandly, that they are the complete masters of nature and the real world as well. Even ordinary egomaniacs have a few doubts about their power and superiority. Not Ayn Rand or her followers.

Ayn Rand's followers fiercely embraced her belief system, but, when one of them runs for political office, that philosophy gets watered down in a hurry. Nevertheless, what remains is still powerful enough to seriously damage the American democratic system and it is doing so right now (2010) in a big way. It is also hypocritical in the extreme. For example, Ron Paul (and his son Rand Paul), darlings of the libertarians, express their contempt for civil rights, claim that secularists "hate" the Paul's Baptist religion, and want government to control the religious as well as the sex and reproductive lives of citizens. Paul Ryan also says he is a great believer in the libertarian beliefs of Ayn Rand and yet he is a devoted medieval-style Catholic with religious beliefs very much the opposite of hers. But then, they were all very much in favor of the cold war too—despite their claims to be against wars and interventions—considering it a defense of noble corporatism against evil socialism. Thus, in the hands of the tea party boys and girls (fascists all), this fake libertarianism is corrupting this country's electoral process and spreading fantastic lies and distortions in every direction.

Its Nature

Libertarians don't believe in liberty. Their claims are fraudulent. When they use the word "liberty," they mean the liberty of large property owners to use "their" property in absolutely any way they choose without any consideration whatever for the rights or the welfare of others. Libertarians believe that property is sacred but they are not really talking about the personal possessions (a car, a house, clothes, etc.) of ordinary citizens. They are talking about commercial property, especially property in the large, that is, corporate property. Libertarians—in fact, all Republicans these days—want absolutely everything except military and police power privatized (but in their Iraq war, they began to massively privatize even the military itself); and they don't want any taxation or regulation at all of that private property. In other words, they want to do away with democratic government altogether. What they believe in is an aristocracy based on money and property. Thus, according to them, the owners are supposed to rule everything and everyone under the protection and with the force of military and police authority.

Recently (2010), Rand Paul (named after Ayn Rand), running for congress as a libertarian Republican, came out foursquare against civil rights. He claimed that personally he believes in treating all people as equals but that no business must ever be required to treat others as equals. He said that businessmen have an absolute right to discriminate against anyone they dislike and for whatever reason. He said that this is what liberty and free markets mean. This is the libertarian philosophy spelled out in discriminatory letters.

I think the libertarian movement has redefined the conservative movement and the Republican Party. Although the libertarian movement takes its claimed belief in civil liberties and its opposition to unlimited military and police power from liberalism, it departs from liberalism in its hatred of democratic government and its fevered belief in the sacredness of private property. This love of property manifests itself as a predatory capitalism unregulated in any way by the instruments of democratic governance. Without the influence of democratic liberalism, theoretical libertarianism would be easy to see as conservatism and even straight-up fascism.

Some non-religious liberals and almost all libertarians agree that religion is an instrument of social control. They say its purpose is to keep the people docile and obedient. In fact, the Christian religious system parallels and supports the economic system and it seeks, and has, massive amounts of property and privilege. The religious system is even more rigidly hierarchical and at least as predatory as the money system though it professes to be about morals rather than about material gain. It seeks to supervise the private lives of the people and to tell them what they may and may not believe about the nature of the world and the story of its beginning and its ultimate ending. Thus, religion roots out a wide space for itself in the niches of the economic system and helps that system keep the people under control and servile.

In theory, libertarianism is based on individual liberty and owning property is considered a necessary part of that liberty. Thus, each person is considered to be the absolute owner of his life and property. Despite their differences, libertarianism is allied with conservatism. Some libertarian theoreticians like Ludwig von Mises, Fredrick von Hayek, Milton Friedman, and James Buchanan claimed that liberty is tied to economic efficiency and that, therefore, they can tolerate a very limited political democracy as long as it is used to promote the interests of commerce and so-called free markets.

Libertarians say that there must be no infringement on the rights of business owners. They say that everyone must be left free to discriminate against others in all personal and business dealings. They say that everyone must be allowed to take risks even to the point of harm, injury, or death for themselves and others. They say there must be no ban on any medical treatment or any drug or other substance. They say there must be no ban on and absolutely no regulation of gun ownership no matter how many people are killed by gunfire. They say that government must not ban or require a license for any product or service whatever and must not prevent or regulate any kind of commercial advertising whether false or true. Libertarians justify economic inequality and overt racism as outcomes of people's freedom to choose their own actions. They consider all government ownership and regulation as forms of mass compulsion. For these reasons, libertarians oppose liberal democracy. Without any evidence, they claim that Thomas Jefferson was a libertarian. This seemingly romantic individualism appeals to many people but it is secretly antidemocratic and, finally, despotic.

Contradiction

There is a fundamental contradiction in the libertarian philosophy. When people live together, they have to establish some level of order and predictability in their shared communities and in their personal lives and relationships. It's up to them to decide collectively just what rules and standards their shared community can and should have. The only way this can be decided with any degree of fairness and with any hope of stability is through a system of voting or some other means of mutual agreement. This is known as democratic or at least representative government. Libertarians don't like democratic government. They call it "collectivism." At best, they consider it a necessary evil. At worst, they consider it automatically tyrannical and somehow socialist or even "communistic." They greatly fear majoritarian tyranny and want a special niche for themselves at the top of the pyramid. They don't admit that aristocracy at the top means subservience below.

The American and French revolutions took up these concerns and the revolutionaries decided that a declaration of individual and personal rights was necessary. Thus, the Americans adopted a Bill of Rights to protect individuals against majoritarian tyranny in certain private and personal areas. Later, the French adopted a Declaration of the Rights of Man and the Citizen. They went even further than the Americans in affirming the rights of their citizens. Ever since, the whole world has been phasing out divine kings and the aristocracies that helped them control the common people forced for so long to live under their dominance.

Libertarians do not want to compromise with their neighbors or live under any community or state rules and standards. They believe that they should have the unlimited right to use their personal force and their property to exploit others. What they want for themselves is aristocracy, not democracy. They know that they can live the privileged lives of extreme individualism and what they falsely call "liberty" only if they can find or create a system that allows them to rise above other people. Their chosen system is unregulated capitalism, also known as competitive "free enterprise."

Rand Paul, the fervent libertarian Senator from Kentucky, says he personally believes in civil rights but that commercial property is so inviolate and so sacred that no government has a right to tell a property owner, through civil rights enactments or anything else, what he can and cannot do with his property. He describes this unchecked use of property as "libertarian," that is, as freedom incarnate. Indeed, if commercial property is owned and used strictly in private and for no public purpose whatever, then such behavior might be somewhat rational, maybe even permissible, though a product of discriminatory hatred. However, if any property has a public use and/or purpose, then its use becomes a community matter and not just a personal and individual matter. Intruding private property into public space or air and using it for public purposes makes it public just as the violence of police and military acts are public functions governable by democratically elected officials and not by private individuals serving their own personal interests alone. No foreign power would be allowed to push its property, its people, or its functions into public space inside our country while pretending it was exercising a private right of property not subject to anyone else's control or regulation. Alien bodies and interests do not have privileged protections under a democratic society or any other.

It Is Undemocratic

It really ought to be clear to anyone that the very purpose of democracy is to establish a public sphere under the control and management of the people through their elected representatives. In other words, democracy establishes a common ground (call it a "marketplace" of ideas and activities if you like) on which we can all stand and act as equals, as citizens with full rights and full access to public goods and activities. Democracy does not abolish or appropriate private property or seek to tyrannize private behavior but it does insist that the private stay within its own bounds and not intrude on the public domain just as it insists that other foreign or alien bodies respect its sovereignty. Nevertheless, democracy does have a stern duty to regulate the often-aggressive encroachments of private power, especially the encroachments of religion and commerce. If everything is privatized, as libertarians wish, and, if nothing private is ever regulated by democratic enactments, then there can be no democracy and no liberty. The idea of a dominant private force immune from any and all democratic controls is totalitarian. Thus, the libertarians are not libertarian at all; instead they are or want to be elitist rulers practicing an especially aggressive form of extreme individualism. Libertarianism is a system of aristocratic privilege for the few, not a handmaiden of freedom as its supporters pretend.

To square the circle, libertarians claim that they are devoted to a vague "non-aggression principle." Presumably, this means that they will not allow themselves to exploit, injure, or kill their neighbors. Obviously, this principle can only apply to direct aggression but not to the indirect aggressions that are an inevitable part of owner-worker and owner-consumer arrangements. Libertarians say that all such arrangements are entirely voluntary and never hurtful or demeaning. In any case, they say, competition results in the rise of the fit and the proper positioning of the unfit at the bottom of the pyramid (social Darwinism). The rich deserve to be rich, they say. The poor deserve to be poor. No government has any right to "level" the reward system or even the playing field. Some are inherently superior to others, they say. This is natural selection, they say, a matter of biology. Competition is the way nature (or God) determines the right levels of existence for us all. Efforts by government to create any degree of "artificial" equality are tyrannical and unnatural.

Conservatives and libertarians share a common contempt for democratic government and an intense desire to privatize everything in existence so it can all be made profitable. In fact, they not only want everything privatized, they also want to do away with democratic regulation altogether. This two-pronged policy seeks to turn all public property into private property and then seeks to prevent the public from regulating any of it. This is a clever way of canceling democracy entirely and it is a formula for aristocratic totalitarianism. Of course, they do make some exceptions for the military and police power they know they need to protect their property and to keep down the resentful masses. That's why Republicans turn every election into a patriotic guise in praise of "our boys over there." They also virulently attack their electoral opponents as "soft" on communism and terrorism, or they use some other "security" issue to demean them; indeed their attacks are so extreme that they invariably call their opponents "traitors."

Libertarians don't want to live in a community of cooperating citizens. When they are forced to do so, they refuse nearly all shared responsibilities. They don't see that they have any duty to others as a condition of citizenship. They want to be totally free to discriminate against others, to use their money and property with no strings attached and with no care about what their "liberty" is certain to do to others. They don't think that government should tax them at all or require anything of them, no matter how much their behavior impinges on the lives of other people. In other words, libertarians believe that their property is sacred and that the people in their communities or businesses and on or near their property have no right to regulate, restrain, tax, or punish them no matter what they do.

Like conservatives, libertarians oppose everything public including free milk for children, vaccinations, free mail delivery, speed limits, traffic laws, gun controls, public parks, national forests, public roads, canals and harbors, public education, libraries, racial integration, the minimum wage, usury laws, unions, food for the hungry, public shelters, free burial even for veterans, all public health and sanitation programs, public radio and television, Social Security, environmental laws and regulations, and on and on endlessly.

No one should mistake Thomas Jefferson for a libertarian. He thought that the rising Hamiltonian commercialism he saw around him was tyrannical. Unlike Jefferson, libertarians claim that property is sacred; their greatest icon is commercial property, not so much ordinary personal property. They like property in the large and want it to be used for gain and exploitation. Their stock terms for their version of liberty are "free enterprise" and "free markets." They idolize "competition" and regard it as the motor of commercialism and the corporatism they so dearly love. They extol businessmen as heroic creators of wealth and condemn working people as business fodder, forever rebellious, disobedient, and completely unfit for anything better than everyday toil. The loyalty of libertarians is reserved for businessmen, entrepreneurs, and Republican politicians who want to privatize everything public and "free" it all from any democratic regulation whatever.

Conservatives and libertarians are very much alike but, unlike conservatives, libertarians do believe somewhat in civil liberties and oppose foreign wars and interventions most of the time (not during the cold war, however). They each hate democratic government and love private commercial power and they each hate liberalism and all public enterprise. They both want to privatize everything public (nowadays even the military and police forces) and they both want to wipe out all forms of regulation and oversight over business activities. Unlike conservatives, most libertarians are not religious or theocratic. Indeed, most are atheists as was Ayn Rand, their goddess. Also unlike the conservatives, they say (falsely in the case of the two Pauls and others) that they are not in favor of using government power to oversee and dictate the sex and reproductive lives of citizens, and they usually disapprove of government spying and wiretapping (unless it is directed against alleged communists, terrorists, and sometimes liberals). On the other hand, conservatives sometimes approve of social services and welfare measures. Libertarians never do.

It Contradicts Itself

Libertarians are people who pretend to believe in liberty above all else. So, did anyone ever hear of a libertarian who was a member of the Democratic Party? Did anyone ever see a libertarian marching with Martin Luther King or supporting integration or affirmative action? Were there any libertarians in the streets opposing the unjustified American attacks on Vietnam or Iraq or even its attacks against Guatemala, Nicaragua, El Salvador, Cuba, Grenada, or Panama? Do any libertarians agree with Michael Moore, Cindy Sheehan, Ralph Nader, Noam Chomsky, Amy Goodman, or Howard Zinn about anything at all?

Are libertarians secularist in any sense whatever? Many libertarians claim to be Ayn Rand atheists but do any of them ever join liberals and democrats in efforts to protect children against forced school prayer or to protect government property and public discourse against the strictures and assaults of fanatical Christians out to force their religion and their rituals on everyone else? Do any of them belong to Americans United for Separation of Church and State?

What liberty do libertarians support then? Well, they support the "liberty" of rich people with large amounts of property. In fact, they regard private property as sacred and worship predatory capitalism, which they regard as the one and only true depository of liberty. They think that the wealthy have a right to rule working people and consumers, because the successful and prominent have made it on their own, or through "just" inheritances of unearned income untaxed by any "death tax;" and they think that this makes them superior to the unfit middle and lower classes. Libertarians are social Darwinists and reverse Marxists. They have no use at all for civil rights, human rights, or the rights of working people. They are fervently antidemocratic because democracy is the great leveler and the great regulator of private power. Anyway, they say, government is always incompetent and always wrong because it is insufficiently obedient to the property owners.

Even their dead beloved, Ronald Reagan, did not go far enough in his assaults on the evil democratic government of the United States and in his efforts to cancel out such abominations as civil rights, human rights, environmentalism, regulation, and all government interference with the privileges of the wealthy property owners. Although his lust for a vast privatization of everything except military and police power accompanied by the rise of a dominant Christian religion was noble, it did not go far enough and needed an even more fanatical Republican, George W. Bush, to complete the job and save America from the liberals and the so-called "communists"/"terrorists."

Of course, a few of the libertarians were slightly disturbed by the Reagan/Bush support for unbridled religion but they were always loyal and never said so out loud and in public. After all, they knew, or thought they knew, that their religion of unregulated capitalism was more powerful than that of the mumbling evangelicals. Better yet, many of the evangelicals have been converted and now describe themselves as "free-enterprise Christians."

Mises, Hayek, and Friedman

Ludwig von Mises, Friedrich August von Hayek, and Milton "von" Friedman were responsible for the preposterous claim that socialism is a system of centralized economic planning that leads inevitably to tyranny. In fact, like it or not, socialism is the ultimate decentralization, a means by which the worker, singly or in voluntary association with other workers, exercises control over his own work and the product of that work. It is capitalism that centralizes all authority, planning, and profit in the hands of a central owner (often a single owner) who exploits the work of others for his own profit and privilege. Centralized planning and control are the very essence of capitalism but the conservative and libertarian ideologues pretend that capitalism is, somehow, a system of rugged individualism that is the true expression of democracy.

One definition of tyranny is the arbitrary control of the many by one or a small number of authoritative figures. A factory owner or other business owner is such a figure. Has anyone ever heard of a factory owner being elected by the workers in the factory or even by the general population? Has anyone ever heard of a factory owner conducting a referendum on his policies and business practices or on anything at all? If language means anything, then quite obviously it is the owner in whom all the authority and power is centralized and it is the owner who is the tyrant, not workers controlling their own work and acting in voluntary association with other workers in their own interests. Socialism is obviously democratic by definition and capitalism is obviously anti-democratic. It is impossible for any rational person to draw any other conclusion.

The smartest of the conservative and libertarian lot don't quite say that capitalism is democracy because they know it's an absurd claim. Instead, they say, "Capitalism is a necessary condition for democracy." In other words, the only way to have political democracy is by having economic tyranny. They pretend they don't understand that the absolute dominance of corporate or lesser bosses over all working people and all consumers restricts political democracy and corrupts it. Instead, they claim to believe that democratically elected government is tyrannical when it regulates, restricts, or taxes business owners in the interests of workers, consumers, the poor, the unemployed, and the down and out.

To be very generous, the two vons—Mises and Hayek—and Milton Friedman were certainly oddballs. That they were incredibly irrational and dead wrong is obvious. To be less generous, they were totalitarian capitalists, that is to say, fascists.

Love of Private Power

You will never hear a conservative or a so-called libertarian criticize private power. The only power they hate is the power of the federal government. However, it is not the coercive power of the feds that they hate. Rather, they hate the power of the government to regulate and diminish the coercive abuses of their private force. Conservatives and libertarians love private power, that is to say, the economic and religious power of their clients, the corporatists and, for the conservatives, the Christian zealots as well. The government power that they hate is the democratic power that seeks to limit and regulate local and private tyranny.

They argue that the constitution protects the people against the power of democratic government but not against the tyranny of local and private power. They have always made such arguments. They have always believed that the democratic government of the United States has no power over the actions of business and religious interests. In other words, they believe that business and religious groups have a perfect right to oppress the people in any way they choose and that the government has no right to intervene.

Of course, this is a preposterous argument. To argue that laws and prohibitions are tyrannical when applied by democratic government but wonderful, free, and noble when applied by local authorities and private companies and religions is insane. It is only a way of devolving tyranny. They argue that even the Bill of Rights doesn't protect individual citizens from abuse of their rights unless the federal government is the abuser. Such a view not only devalues but utterly destroys the rights specified in the Bill of Rights, the "freedom amendments," and everywhere else in the constitution.

Can there be any doubt that what conservatives and libertarians really want is the total destruction of democratic government and the establishment of an absolute tyranny over the people by local authorities and by private economic and religious powers? Can there be any doubt that they hate democracy with a venomous force never equaled by any foreign enemy?

John Dewey

We have in this country a number of people who call themselves liberals but who believe—with Republican conservatives, neoconservatives, and libertarians—that the system we have is "democratic capitalism." It really ought to be obvious to anyone capable of reason that capitalism cannot be democratic. It is this false belief that has led the United States to exploit its own people and to conduct an endless collection of wars and other aggressions against most of the rest of the world. The Vietnam War and the numerous wars and other aggressions so viciously and so indiscriminately waged against the innocent people of Iraq are the two most recent wars we have carried out in the name of "democratic capitalism."

In an essay called "Freedom," John Dewey wrote the following words about the growth of corporate tyranny and the part war has played in undermining freedom:

> But the situation...changed radically. Free land practically disappeared.... [H]abits...changed from those suited to agrarian conditions to those demanded by mechanized industry.... Industry...

became more and more centralized and...came more and more under the control of concentrated finance....

Success came to be popularly measured by the acquisition of property, enlargement of income, and increase of size and quantity generally.... The result...was identification of liberty with laissez-faire individualism.... privileged classes (embraced)...ideas (that) exercised...a supreme influence upon courts of law and... moral beliefs.... Exclusive identification of freedom with political freedom means...loss of even political freedom....

(There are) dangers from regimentation (caused by) undue political centralization. But...immense...regimentation...proceeds from individual and financial centralization. Jefferson extolled... small independent producers and shopkeepers, and...prophesied the evils (of)... industrialization. Under...centralized finance and industry... subordinates tend to become cogs in a vast machine whose workings they do not understand and in whose management they have no part or lot. If universal freedom is to become...a reality, methods must be found by which the mass of individuals will have a much larger share in directing industrial processes....

No other...force [is] so completely destructive of personal freedom as is modern war.... [W]ar is a...wholesale moral enslavement of entire populations. Peace is a necessary and urgent condition...of the goal of freedom.

There you have it. Dewey understood in 1937 that the greatest future threat to liberty would come from "industrial and financial centralization" and from "representatives of privileged classes." And so it has. The greatest danger is here at home, but the obsessions of our leaders with false wars waged fanatically and uncritically against exaggerated and abstract enemies like "communism" and "terrorism" are distortions of truth and freedom. They are as well greedy grabs for resources and for power overseas and among aroused and deceived partisans here at home. The Republican Party has engineered these wars even when Democrats, smeared as weaklings and cowards in cahoots with communists and terrorists, have at times waged them. The Republican Party cannot win elections without its wars and lies. Consequently, the people of this country have been kept in a continuous state of fear and hatred for many years but especially so since the rise of McCarthyism, Nixonism, Reaganism, and Bushism.

McCarthyism and Judicial Fascism

McCarthyism was the attack mode of the Republican Party and it has continued without stint to this very day. Indeed, it has been intensified and broadened by corrupt politicians, by wealthy schemers behind the scene, and by a burgeoning right-wing media dedicated to the evisceration of democratic government and the utter vilification of liberals and members of the Democratic Party.

Both political democracy and economic democracy have been wiped out. Democracy is in the ash can along with real freedom of speech and any degree of equality for working people and dissenters. And the people do not even know that their democracy has been converted into a predatory commercial dictatorship propped up by lies, distortions, and false wars.

Chapter 2. Early Times

Our Supervisors

The history of humankind has been a history of kings over subjects, of masters over slaves, of bosses over workers. In early times, the lust of some men and women for power over others led to tribalisms, regionalisms, and then nationalisms. Nation states emerged. The larger collectives began to gobble up the smaller ones and began to impose religious, social, political, and economic dogmas and beliefs on them by force of arms and brute pressures. The collective idea gained force and the communitarian and tribal arrangements became generalized and dispersed. Revolts of all kinds were common. Even today, national governments still struggle to hold together their peoples and territories. But there are frequent secessions and displacements. The world map is always changing. Some would like to see world government, one central power over all. Others would like to see massive scatterings and local independence right down to the level of the ancient tribes and villages. Some even want an individualism so radical that no man may govern any other or collaborate with him in any undertaking—a kind of caveman isolationism or hermiting away in single-family units or even away from the family unit altogether in lonely pairings. Some even abandon organized society altogether but compromise enough to sit in the streets with their begging bowls while they contemplate their navels and dream of a painless, sexless nirvana beyond humanity and all joinings and pairings.

Is it any wonder that some huddle together in self-protective units, large and small, or that others seek escape and independence from the common herd? Given a deep human desire to supervise others, is it any wonder that entrepreneurs and other warriors set out to conquer and control everything they can grab, and everyone? This drive to conquer and use others is not universal, however. Most people only want to live their lives without onerous supervision or minute surveillance. But the entrepreneurs will not leave them be. Conquest is their game. Thus, the world is divided into two parts, the supervised and the rest of us. The organizing principle of civilization seems to be supervision. To get things done, the supervisors say, we must have ardent and massive oversight. To get enough food, water, land, and other things of value, we must let them herd us all together and command us toward their purposes. Then, we will all have improved lives, they say, but they also say they must take the largest proportion of the gain and none of the loss, or they will lose their incentive and abandon us to our own individual devices. They think we will starve without them. We need them, they don't need us, they say. All too often we believe their propaganda.

Work and Religion

Work and religion are the two most dominant organized forces in human history. The simple definition of work is "effort." The simple definition of religion is "belief."

These polarities have knocked against one another for a big portion of civilized history. They have been used as instruments of control by the rulers of tribes, villages, cities, and states throughout the ever-more complex gathering together of populations in political, economic, and religious units. Human beings have not always fitted neatly into the categories created for them by their masters. Often, the result has been strife, antagonism, civil revolt, and war.

Using dictionary definitions, these simplifications can be expanded. Work is physical or mental activity directed toward the production or accomplishment of something. Religion is belief in and reverence for a supernatural power or powers regarded as creator and governor of the universe; and further, a personal or institutionalized system grounded in such belief and worship; and still further, a set of beliefs, values, and practices based on the teachings of a spiritual leader; and at last, a cause, a principle, or an activity pursued with zeal and conscientious devotion.

This definition of work is still quite simple and practical. The definition of religion is considerably more expansive, abstract, vague, and otherworldly. Indeed, the definitions of religion can be applied equally well to the way people promote ideologies such as "communism" and "capitalism." As a matter of fact, I myself consider both of these economic and political ideologies to be religions because of the zeal and frequent irrationalities (fanatical belief rather than reason based on evidence) that go with them. This topic will be explored further in Part Two.

I write about work and religion together in the same book because they so often clash or meld and because their power structures mirror one another. This comes, I think, from the early rise of tribal leaders who took or had thrust upon them both political and religious power. At times, one leader had both powers but, I think, most often there were two leaders, a chieftain and a shaman or priest. It seems to me that there is a natural separation of church and state: work and practical matters on the one hand, worship, meditation, and talking to and bribing the gods on the other.

Let me say a little more here about the definitions of work and religion. Work is for the people, not for owners and bosses. Religion ought also to be for the people and not for priests and preachers and not for popes and mullahs either. Thanks to the Enlightenment and the American and French revolutions, the rule of most divine kings and their royal aristocracies have been overthrown and more-or-less democratic governments have replaced them. Though there has been much backsliding, especially by the United States, many somewhat-democratic governments continue to function. But when are churches and corporations going to be democratized?

Work is an important part of a nation's way of managing relationships among its citizens. Work arrangements as well as methods of property control and exchange are defined by the type of government a nation has. Political and economic systems are intertwined to one degree or another in every country, and religion often plays a part as well. In some countries, political and economic power centers are more or less separate; in other countries, they are closely integrated. The following chapter sets forth a view of ways the political and economic systems in the United States work together and against one another, quite often with considerable hostility for the general population.

CHAPTER 3. POLITICAL DEMOCRACY AND ECONOMIC TYRANNY

False Definition of Corporate Capitalism

This chapter is mostly about the false definition of corporate capitalism as "democratic capitalism." The separate essays herein explore the different facets of the American economic and political systems and describe the damage done to democratic government by those who embrace that false definition and use it to subvert democracy.

Though I embellish them, these ideas are not entirely original. They come most directly from Noam Chomsky, the greatest of the American critics of this country's economic system and its unbridled military aggressions against other countries and peoples. Many of the associated ideas in this book are my own but they too are conditioned by Chomsky's contempt for the irresponsible and irrational behavior of the corporate capitalists and by his dedication to the facts of human history.

There's quite a bit of differently angled repetition in this chapter but the tyranny all around us, in our economy especially, is pervasive. I seek to explore the deeply false ideas that circulate around the claim that capitalism is democratic and everything else is the enemy of liberty and the enemy of America's God-driven exceptionalism.

In a September 2014 essay in *Harpers Magazine*, Joseph Stiglitz praised Thomas Piketty's book, *Capital in the Twenty-First Century*, for providing extensive evidence for the increase in economic inequality and inherited wealth that has been the cause of a "new plutocracy." However, Stiglitz complained about Piketty's argument that "inequality is the natural outcome of capitalism." Stiglitz said that there is no such thing as "pure capitalism" and went on to defend the "mixed economy" he says we have here in the United States.

Thus, Stiglitz is defending the right kind of capitalism ("a truly competitive economy") rather than "ersatz capitalism." I think that Piketty is right in saying that "inequality is the natural outcome of capitalism." This chapter shows that capitalism is not and cannot be democratic and hence not egalitarian either. All of the essays in this chapter discuss the inherent inequality of capitalism and argue for a more democratic form of work management than that provided by capitalism, whether pure, mixed, or ersatz. I argue that the democratic control of one's own work is more important to human beings and society than great profit and productivity for the benefit of the few.

I think that, without economic democracy, inequality is certain. I also think that some considerable degree of approximate economic equality and participatory democracy are public goods. I think that all citizens have a fundamental right to manage their own work and its uses, including both its gains and its losses. Thus, I believe that every economic unit should be democratically owned and directed, whether or not it is successful in terms of profits and losses; I also believe that even decisions about an economic unit's continuance, alteration, or termination should be democratically decided.

I do not think it is a good idea to create tiered systems of work and wealth with only the "fit" and "successful" at the top and everyone else beneath them as servants, wage slaves, or even chattel slaves.

Liberal Rebellion

The American Revolution was the first great rebellion by liberal democrats against the divine rule of kings and against the royal and conservative aristocracies that enforced their tyrannical systems for them. Since then, gradually, more and more kings and other such dictators have been overthrown. At times, their systems have been replaced by democracies but, in some cases, new forms of authoritarianism have arisen. One of those called itself "communism." Another called itself "fascism." Both such systems consisted of one-man and one-party rule. Though they claimed to be opponents and based their systems on different purposes and ideologies, they were both undemocratic. As for "fascism," Benito Mussolini was the man who first used that term to describe his form of one-man rule. His immediate imitators were Adolf Hitler, Francisco Franco, and Antonio Salazar, but there have been many others. I think that all of them have been mere replacements for the old "divine" kings. On the other side, Lenin and Stalin, as leaders of the revolution (the revolt against the exploitation of working people by capitalists), resorted to the same means of rule by the "avant-garde," that is, rule by the leaders. In conclusion, both of them, communism and fascism, were rule by the "leaders" as opposed to popular democracy.

It is certainly clear to me that capitalists do indeed exploit working people. Nevertheless, I do not think that so-called "communism" ever was a cure-all for society's woes. After all, both the capitalists and the communists ruled absolutely from the top. This observation, I know, leads to a tangle of confusion, among Americans especially, about the definitions and characteristics of the different ruling systems I have named.

This is especially true of the system of capitalism that, in my opinion, has been vastly misrepresented by its supporters, especially in the United States. Those supporters use terms like "democratic capitalism," "competitive free enterprise," "free markets," and the like to conceal the true nature of capitalism. Capitalism is not and cannot be either democratic or free. It is a hierarchic and authoritarian system based on top down and absolute rule by one or a few owners. In other words, corporations are smaller versions of the old nation states but with the same kind of ruling figure at the top of each corporation.

I call these corporate owners "money kings." Often they have vast property that spreads across the world and exceeds the national wealth of many entire countries. Corporations are not democratic or freedom loving. In fact, they are a long step toward a one-world economic monolith completely oblivious of the rights and needs of working people and consumers.

From this perspective, words like capitalism, corporatism, communism, and fascism describe the same alignments of the upper ruling the lower. Naturally, there are overlaps and contradictions in the applications of these ruling structures but the essential nature of these systems of rule are the same.

Every Economy

Every economy requires the existence of two mutually supportive groups of people: workers and consumers. Workers are people who make things or provide services. Consumers are people who obtain products or services from such workers. What connects these two groups is called "trade." Trade can be defined as buying and selling. Naturally, there are overlaps among the activities of workers producing things and consumers obtaining those things.

The method of exchange itself (trade) can be vastly complicated. It can and did result in the creation of an entire network of what might be called middlemen or trade enablers. This in-between group is not really needed at all. Unfortunately, it seems always to get on top and to take control of both the workers' work and the consumers' consumption.

Trade is the original link between workers and consumers. But when economic transactions stopped being a direct exchange between workers and consumers, a collection of greedy manipulators stepped in and grabbed control over the machinery of trade so they could enrich themselves by turning working people into their servants and consumers into the victims of their salesman propaganda. The entire system of trade thus became the linchpin for economic tyranny.

When workers stopped selling or bartering their products and services directly to consumers, they became the obedient underlings of leeches and parasites. Their independence was wiped away and they sank into a degrading form of obedience that took away their ability to control their own products and services. Instead of working for themselves, they had to bow down to a hoard of master overseers who thereafter would make all the policy decisions involving trade and would completely dominate all business operations.

Instead of being independent agents, the workers became mere employees, another name for servants. They no longer owned their own jobs. Thereafter, they could be exploited, underpaid, endangered, moved about, and fired at the will of the business owner, a tyrant who took what he wanted out of their labor and extracted massive profits from unsuspecting consumers blinded by the lies of ideological salesmanship.

People in this group called their controlling activities "businesses." Today, if they can get a license from their government, especially here in the United States (a thing easy to do), they can call their concoctions "corporations." The Supreme Court of the United States has ruled that this intangible, abstract, invisible and imaginary system of rule over workers and consumers is in itself—in its corporate body—a living "person" with all of the rights of any citizen. Indeed, those corporate persons have infinitely more rights and privileges than any citizen or any group of citizens can ever hope to have since they and their fellow corporate "persons" own absolute and total control over the working and consuming lives of all mere citizens.

To seal up this corporate grant of immortal life and economic dominance, the Supreme Court added, in its decision, the claim that the expenditure of corporate money is actual freedom of speech and thus forever free from any restraint or control by democratic regulation by the citizens themselves through their elected governments. This means that the corporations can freely spend, in secret, any amounts they think necessary to dominate the political process by destroying the reputations of political candidates they dislike and can give any amounts they like to their very own special candidates. In other words, they not only control the economic world; now, they also control the political world.

Thus, it is not workers who control their own work or consumers who control their own consumption. Corporations are dictatorships. They are ruled from the top down. They are entirely hierarchic. The ladder of supervision runs from the big boss at the top down through receding layers of authority to the bottom where powerless workers dwell. They have no power at all. They do not even own their own jobs. They can be fired at any time and for any reason. They do not own or control any part of the corporation. They can only surrender and obey. They are ciphers to their bosses and to the Supreme Court.

These self-imposed intermediaries have seized all of the power for themselves. They are answerable to no one, least of all to the puny workers and the hungry consumers. When the workers have tried to organize or unionize against the abusive power of the owners and bosses, they have been assaulted by the organized military and police power of the corporatists aided and abetted at every point by the Republican Party and sometimes also by the Democratic Party, a party that claims to represent them but always abandons them when the corporate bosses turn up the heat by depriving them of money and corporate support in political campaigns. Naturally, the military generals and the police chiefs are owned by the corporatists and the politicians they control.

As I said early in this essay, the corporatists are not needed at all. Those of us who only work and consume and do not have any part in their supervisory construction could actually take over the system that dominates us all. Maybe it could even be done without violence. Violence has a way of enabling a new set of dictators. It can be done better by incremental actions. One key is a democratic instrument called a "co-operative."

Co-operatives are businesses owned and controlled by the people who do the work. Quite a few already exist in the United States and in many other places. In Norway and Denmark, employees participate in software design; in Germany, there are labor-management partnerships; in the Basque area of Spain, the Mondragon cooperatives have operated successfully for many years. There are as well cooperative arrangements such as the John Lewis Partnership in the UK and the Lincoln Electric cooperative arrangement in the United States. So, there are plenty of models to study and copy. There will be much resistance, of course, by the corporatists and their allies. And it will take a long time for the workers and consumers to gain substantial control over their own lives, their work, and their consumption.

But keep in mind always that workers and consumers are the only necessary parts of a natural economic system. The corporations are an artificial and tyrannical imposition based on greed and dominance. We need to defeat them. They cannot enslave us any more than they have already done and they cannot kill us all. Who would do the work, make the products, and provide the services needed to enrich them and serve their every personal whim?

All of the economic systems we have on earth today are tyrannical. They all consist of ruler owners and bosses at the top and workers on the bottom. All power, property, privilege, and money are distributed according to rank and positioning. Those at the top are rich and those at the bottom are poor. There are many, many more poor people than rich ones. Why should the many tolerate the oppression of the few? The American corporate system is richer and more stable than most other systems. However, it is also substantially less equal, less fair, and more brutal than the social democracies of Western Europe and England and probably also the one in Japan and in a few other places. American corporate power is not based on morality, equality, or any human decency but instead on immorality, greed, force, and vast threatening and killing power.

The American Revolution closely followed by the French Revolution began the overthrow of divine kings and their royal aristocracies. The Industrial Revolution then resulted in the rise of a new set of rulers—the money kings—who thrust aside but did not really replace the old kings and lords. In fact, the two groups merged but most of the old titles, rites, rituals, and lordly positioning diminished. The Americans substituted celebrity for royal standing and came to worship their rich people, politicians, movie stars, athletic heroes, and musicians. Much of the world imitated the Americans in style if not in vulgarity and also in a new kind of anti-democratic elitism.

Unfortunately for the world, the Americans soon abandoned the democratic rights they had won for themselves in their revolt against divine authority; and then they began to ally themselves with the world's kings, oligarchs, plutocrats, and military dictators provided they promised not to set a bad example by redistributing any property and agreed to hand over their country's property and resources to American corporations, churches, and the military.

The United States is firmly fascistic especially when the Republican Party is in control of the government. The Republican Party has aligned itself so closely and so fanatically with the corporate complex that the entire country must be seen as fascist right to the core when that merger is in place. The Democrats are problematic and partial fascists. They try to represent a few of the rights of working people and try to prevent the corporatist juggernaut from raping the common people entirely.

There is a corporate complex in the United States. Without much abusing the word, it can be accurately described as a "conspiracy" or a class war being waged against working people and consumers by the united corporations, the Republicans, and, lately, the Supreme Court. An organization called ALEC is the coordinator of this class war. It writes the laws of the nation, trains politicians at every level of government to maneuver them into place where they are forced on the population in disguised form. The resulting despotism is hailed by them as a way to increase efficiency, reduce taxes, and disempower the evil power of democracy. Too many Americans regularly support and vote for the Republican Party and aid it in its systematic efforts to destroy democratic government and wipe away the freedom and prosperity of workers and consumers.

Nature of Capitalism

How can anyone look at the organizational structure of a corporation and draw any conclusion other than that it is authoritarian. To call capitalist (corporate) systems "democratic" is absurd. The whole corporate system is based on handing down orders from the top of a pyramidal arrangement to lower levels of decreasing authority until—at the bottom, the worker level—there is no authority at all. Whether such arrangements are literal slavery or mere servanthood is just a matter of degree,

Slavery is outright ownership of a person in the interest of using him or her in any way chosen by the master, usually to do profitable work. Servanthood is not total bodily ownership but it does consist of partial ownership for the purpose of extracting work. One of these supervisory systems is called "chattel slavery," the other "wage slavery." In each case, there is a master and a subject. Such arrangements cannot be called "democratic capitalism." No version of capitalism can be called "democratic." Such systems are authoritarian and, depending on degree, even totalitarian.

Here is what Abraham Lincoln said about capitalism: "Labor is prior to, and independent of, capital. Capital is only the fruit of labor, and could never have existed if labor had not first existed. Labor is the superior of capital, and deserves much the higher consideration."

Benefits of Capitalism

If your purpose is to turn human beings into worker ants so you can produce ever larger and more profitable amounts of something, then capitalism is your system. But if your purpose is to help most people live better lives though not necessarily more productive ones, then capitalism won't work.

If you want the few to be very rich and the many to be much poorer, then capitalism is your system. This is why conservatives hate equality so much and babble such nonsense about "liberty" as if liberty were itself a commodity and human beings mere machines in service to property owners and other profit mongers.

Liberty depends on some reasonable level of equality and also on the existence of a truly democratic government or at least on a government representative of the wants and needs of most citizens.

Corporate Collectives

If the word "trade" is used merely to describe an actual system of exchange, then there is no particular reason to object to it. Obviously, every economy must be based on some organized system of trade. However, capitalism has come to mean something far more complex, more aggressively brutal, and more deeply anti-democratic than that simple idea. I see today's capitalism as a system of totalitarian corporatism and, in its global form, it is contemptuous of the sovereignty of mere states and even more contemptuous of the rights of working people and consumers all over the world.

When today's capitalists describe their system as a "free market," system and claim that they believe in an individualist system of "competitive free enterprise," I think they are massaging the truth to make it seem that they are believers in a true freedom of effort and an untrammeled individual self-reliance. I don't think that their system is free at all. To the contrary, I believe it is a system based on servanthood and wage slavery. It should be clear to anybody that such a capitalism is hierarchic; it puts the few above the many and all the orders come from the top and are devoted to wealth and privilege.

Though it may seem overbroad to include unincorporated companies in this mix, I believe that all the controlling interests are corporatist in essence. Small businesses, described as family owned and operated businesses or businesses with one or a few employees, do not stand with corporations; they are the prey of the corporations almost as much as are common working people. I see small businesses as virtual co-operatives. It is difficult for them to compete with the big boys. I think that corporations are collective enterprises consisting of a dictatorship at the top and a herd of workers— mere powerless servants—beneath them. Small businesses and farms are not like this.

Farmers markets are the best expression of democratic commerce in America. The people who sell the product are, for the most part, the people who grow it, transport it, display it, and deal directly and humanly with their customers. These farmers are workers as much and perhaps even more than they are business people. They have not separated themselves from the earth, from every day work, and from human contact as the soulless graspers of commerce so often do. The things that are commendable about these small farmers are their independence, their directness and honesty, their modesty, their lack of greed, and their connection to what they sell and the people they sell it to. Most small farmers and many other small "business men" do not much resemble the usual commercial hucksters who rule American life and corrupt its politics.

These small marketers do their own work with the help of their families and perhaps a very few hired hands. They are bosses in only the most limited sense and their personal involvement in the work and with the production of the food gives them dignity and humanity. Sad to say, many of them are political conservatives. It's hard to see why. The political conservatives are the enemy of everything they love and do with their lives. What they do is more socialist then capitalist. In fact, it isn't capitalist at all. The bottom-line definition of capitalism includes the exploitation of the work of others for one's own leisure and profit.

Those who work their own businesses belong with the liberals and the democrats (not necessarily with the Democrats). All too many of them have allowed themselves to be deceived about the so-called evils of big government and the nobility of all commerce, especially the big business versions thereof. Big business invariably undermines and often wipes out the small worker-seller. They have no greater enemy.

Political conservatives say that "collectivism" is a word that applies to communism or socialism and not to capitalism, a weird corruption of language. Indeed, many conservatives claim that the United States wasn't supposed to be a democracy; instead, the founders were establishing a "constitutional republic," they say. This claim came from the John Birch Society and is routinely used by the Republicans to attack the democratic government of the United States as somehow illegitimate. When Ronald Reagan said, "Government isn't the solution, it's the problem," he meant that democracy isn't the solution, it's the problem. He said this over and over again while he was president and in charge of the very government he hated. He meant he hated real democracy itself; he did not mean he opposed some fake democracy somewhere. And his foreign policy was similarly devoted to destroying democratic movements in favor of plutocrats and oligarchs all around the world; the government we have is the only democracy there is, or *was* before the Republicans and Reagan destroyed it. No one sane thinks that corporations are democratic or that plutocrats are freedom lovers.

It is true that democracy is collectivist; after all, it is based on majority vote and, in that sense, it is indeed collectivist. But, since our political system is democratic, it cannot be tyrannical except when a majority sometimes and in some ways imposes its will on a minority. That is why the American founders and their successors set aside certain minority rights in a Bill of Rights and later in the Freedom Amendments that followed the Civil War as well as in the nineteenth amendment which provided voting rights for women.

Corporations are collective in a different way. All the power and all of the privilege is at the top in a corporation and the corporate collective consists of servant workers who have no power and no rights. The founders did not mean they were protecting rich owners when they wrote the Bill of rights so as to protect minority rights against the possible abuses of a majority. They most certainly were not trying to protect owners and bosses from workers and their unions.

A co-operative enterprise is the opposite of a corporate enterprise. In a co-operative, the workers own the business and decide the policies and the operational processes of the enterprise. Co-operatives are democratic. Anyone who thinks that unionism or the use of co-operative enterprises are descriptions of communism as practiced in Stalinist Russia or Maoist China is out of touch with reality. The word "socialist" has been badly mangled and falsified by both the so-called communists themselves and by the anti-communist corporatists who rage against social democracy while pretending it is communistic and that they themselves are true democrats.

Is this Socialism?

Ultimately, all so-called "free enterprise" systems have to be based on greed, coercion, forced inequality, and exploitation. There is nothing "free" about taking from others to enrich yourself. Competitive free enterprise is neither fairly competitive nor free. Using the word "free" to falsely label a collection of non-free enterprises and activities is just a corporatist ploy designed to conceal the true nature of economic tyranny.

It cannot be said too often: corporations are dictatorships. They are top-down hierarchies with absolutely all the power at the top and absolutely no power at the bottom, that is, in the hands of actual working people. If you can't see that work and those who do it are at the center of all production and that those who pretend to create the work enterprise are peripheral and not essential, then you aren't thinking straight. Glorifying owners and bosses doesn't make them indispensable. They can be cut loose (fired) and all work can be placed under the cooperative control of working people and consumers, that is, under the democratic control of the people who do the work and use the products and services. Only workers and consumers are essential to an economic system; they do not have to be under owner/boss control.

Is this socialism? Of course, it is. So what? Don't be fooled by the silly pretense that Lenin, Stalin, and Mao were socialists. They were "state capitalists" and they established and ran one-party, one-corporation states. All means of production were public property, property of the state in the name of the citizens of the country. Any profit reverted to the society and was used for re-investment. This was done under the control of the Communist Party, their own-everything corporate monolith. Anyone who thinks that the Soviet Union and China were socialist or worker states practicing democratic decision making is out of touch with the historical reality.

Supporters of the Soviet system say that we should not confuse centralized decision making with the concentration of personal wealth and the income inequality characteristic of the corporatist systems. Yes, the Soviet Union and China were both totalitarian, and authoritarian, but the Soviet system fundamentally served the national interests and the interests of the working "masses"—against the oligopoly—and did not serve an oligopoly. Stalin didn't own anything and his offspring didn't inherit anything, and all of his entourage were just temporary functionaries of the state; while the fascist systems served the interests of the oligarchy, corporate "barons" such as Krupp, Farber Industries, Deutsche Bank, etc., and their oligarchic owners—a fundamental difference.

When people like Friedrich Hayek rage against social democratic or welfare states for being "collectivist," they're talking nonsense. It is corporations that are massively collectivist and yet are always under single or limited ownership and control right at the top. Democratic control is dispersed control by definition. Corporate control is narrow control based on wealth and exclusivity.

When Hayek attacked "central planning" by democratic governments, he completely ignored the fact that all corporations plan and plan and plan. The closest model for state planning in the Soviet Union, for example, was corporate planning in large American corporations. In fact, Lenin and then Stalin were imitating Western corporations when they were issuing their various five-year plans. Communism was a form of intense capitalism and its leaders got their ideas about rapid industrialization mostly from England and the United States.

The principal difference between the Soviet corporate system and Western ones was that Western states have seemingly multiple political parties and, in appearance at least, multiple corporations nevertheless operating in tight collaboration with one another. It's better to have multiple political parties and multiple corporations, as in the West (no matter how collaborative), not just one as in the Soviet Union where the Communist Party was the only political party as well as the only corporation.

Sad to say, American corporations are so rigidly welded to one another, to the Republican Party, and to the conservative and libertarian movements that they might as well call themselves Soviets. These kinds of collective corporations, whether in the Soviet Union or in the United States, are in fact fascist. Corporatism, by definition, is fascism and American corporations are no less fascist than was the Communist Party in the Soviet Union. For all practical purposes, the Republican Party is the American Fascist Party.

American Socialism!

Environmentalism is socialist in that it treats the land, the air, and the water as public possessions, not private ones. Public parks and national forests are socialist lands. Rural electrification was socialist. All things that serve public interests rather than private ones are socialist.

Consumerism is socialism. Unionism is socialism. The social security system is socialist. So are Medicare, Medicaid, and the food stamp program as are child labor laws, the minimum wage, the eight-hour workday, industrial safety, public roads, public radio, and public television. Democratic movements like workers' unionism and citizens' consumerism are direct forms of socialism. Socialism is economic democracy and public control of all the things that directly affect the great majority of citizens. Public control is democratic control and it stands squarely in opposition to private and autocratic control over the lives of citizens. Thus, socialism is anti-hierarchical and anti-authoritarian.

Capitalism is economic authoritarianism by definition. What it seeks is private and tyrannical control over the work of others. Capitalism is the use of property to control others, not merely the ownership of property. Acquiring property alone does not make anyone a capitalist. Using it to control others for a profit does.

There have always been arguments about the definition of socialism. To make any kind of historical or political sense, I think it must be defined as economic democracy, not economic equality. At the root of socialism is the idea of cooperation, of collective action for the common good. Obviously, democracy cannot be anti-cooperative or anti-collective and remain democratic. For the most part, democracy is a political process, socialism an economic one; but the two overlap and reinforce one another.

We need to redefine the terms we use to describe the economic and political world we live in. Capitalism is the means by which the few use the work of the many to enrich and empower themselves. Capitalism is not primarily about the ownership of property; it's about the control of work. Socialism is economic democracy, not economic equality. The notion of an absolutely rigid economic equality imposed by the state has always been totalitarian as well as ridiculous. It's bossism that has to be eliminated or at least reduced, not differential rewards fairly and proportionately based on differences in effort and output. Of course, there needs to be a much greater equality than that provided by capitalism but that will be the natural result of economic democracy.

The central insight of socialism was that, under capitalism, the worker has no control over his work and, therefore, little general control over his own life and his environment. When you work eight or more hours a day, sleep another eight so you can rest enough to go on working, and use the remaining eight to prepare for work, travel to and from work, and feed, clothe, and nourish your body so it is able to keep on working, there isn't much time left for any other purpose. And when all of this is more or less dictated by business owners and bosses, then life loses its autonomy and the worker is forever locked into a closed system from which he cannot escape, since he has no power and no independence of his own. Under these circumstances, even relatively good pay and an abundance of consumer goods are not tremendously satisfying.

All wealth comes from the collective condition of those in a given political unit, not from isolated, individual accomplishment. People succeed only because many others allow them and help them to succeed. All success comes at the expense and rests on the shoulders of other people. It is the poor and the lower orders that make the rich rich. No one becomes rich or even moderately well off in an economic, social, and political vacuum. The systems of money and commercial exchange are common creations of society as a whole. Some few succeed because their fellow citizens and their ancestors created and maintain a system that permits them to do so. Wealth is never earned alone. It is never entirely individual and it is never entirely deserved by those to whom it migrates.

Even under the best conditions, working for someone else's benefit is oppressive. However, the best conditions have rarely ever existed in the history of work. Rather, working people have almost always been brutally exploited, worn out, injured, and often killed by their work or, more directly, by their bosses. Bossism is by far the most murderous force ever to exist on the face of the earth. Work has injured and killed many, many more people than war. Millions have suffered and died so that a few could live rich lives.

If any system of socialism is ever established on earth, it will not resolve all problems or be free of error and failure any more than capitalism is. It will not be perfect or utopian. Unlike capitalism, however, it will not claim that there is magic in the economic machine or that the system is self-correcting and ordained by the gods. If such a system is ever established, rather, it will be democratic by definition and it will put power in the hands of working people and their families. It will take power out of the hands of owners, bosses, and politicians and it will result in much greater equality and stability than now exists. And most important of all, it will serve the everyday interests of human beings rather than those of the beneficiaries of bottom lines, production numbers, and profit margins. Life will be better simply because people will all be free of the fanatical obsessions, aggressions, and compulsions of capitalist greed and of the irrational competitiveness that drives the industrial enterprise.

Marxist Utopianism!

I accept the Karl Marx observation that capitalism is an authoritarian system under which masters (owners) exploit and abuse servants or even slaves (workers) for a profit. However, even before Marx, lots of people understood this fact and wanted vaguely to change it to something more democratic and egalitarian. Marx did not hate capitalism as the anti-communists believed but admired it for its productive capacity. He thought he was doing history when he predicted its end, but he underestimated its survivability.

Marx's utopianism was another matter. I think it was off. He spoke of a "dictatorship of the proletariat," understood by the Russian and Chinese communists to mean an actual dictatorship, a one-man and one-party tyranny. This understanding, or misunderstanding, gave the Communist revolutionaries a chance to seize absolute power and to destroy any possibility of democratic reform. Less literal-minded Marxists thought it meant the rule, through democratic means, of all working people together rather than the rule of a narrow group of czarist or capitalist dictators. What the Soviet and Chinese Communists made of this interpretation enabled them to force "equality" (a false equality) on the entire population from above and through viciously undemocratic and murderous means.

Ignoring the fact that this was a two-class system with the dictators of the Communist Party in the top class and everyone else in the bottom class, the communist dictators set out to force an intense industrialization on their populations through state fiat. This undertaking was supposed to eventually produce "new men and women" who would be magically transformed into creatures without greed in their hearts or any drive for economic dominance over others.

This was crazy stuff, of course. A corollary was that this magical equality would result in the "withering" of the state. Today, Republicans who want to "drown" the democratic government of the United States in a bathtub seek this same end. They cry always that they believe in limited government, in truth in no government at all. Instead, they want to privatize everything public which can only mean turning everything over to their beloved private corporations and then preventing the shards of government, if there are any left, from taxing or regulating the corporations in any way at all. This would certainly "wither" the state. It would also establish a dictatorship of the corporations every bit as dominant as the communist dictatorship of the proletariat.

This is a striking comparison. The corporations are stand-ins for the withered communist state and both groups are supposed to rule without government interference. Both ambitions seek the triumph of their particular class: transformed men and women in the one case, corporate owners in the other. These are the paradisal and extreme daydreams of those old opponents: owners and workers. Both sides want to use the state in this telling so they can achieve their ideal system of dominance. Both systems fail to take into account the historical and social complexities.

Economic Equality

One of the oddities of the free market idea is that its adherents assume that the superior people at the top have to be endlessly rewarded to keep up their initiative and drive. Unless we give them immense tax breaks and don't harass them with onerous regulations, the whole system will collapse and ruination will follow for us all, they say. What's truly odd about this is the idea that all the variables are in the hands of the top dogs, and we mustn't thwart them or they won't trickle anything down for the rest of us. They think they are the fount, the creators, and the controllers of all economic benefits and that poor people and the government are the cause of all problems and inequalities.

I think the opposite is true. Economic equality of some considerable degree is the force that creates and sustains the stability and the success of every economy. The best way to get a stalled economy moving again is to put money in the hands of the poorest people in the economy. They are the ones who must spend in order to survive. This means government spending to create jobs and do needed work. It does not mean waste though even outright waste benefitting the lower levels is better than senseless balanced budgets forced into place by nutcase Republicans hung up on their vast hatred of democratic government and all of its programs however obviously beneficial they may be.

Doing needed work is an investment, not an outrageous waste of the taxpayers' money as Republicans pretend. Infrastructure improvements are investments. So are social services that improve the living conditions of ordinary citizens so they can function as contributing members of the economy, both as workers and consumers. One of the purposes of any economy must be to raise the level of those at the bottom even if it means lowering the level at or near the top. This was what Jefferson, Madison, and Franklin believed.

The conservatives claim that the Virginians, led by Jefferson, believed that proper economic policy was simply getting out of the way. I don't think that Jefferson saw it that way at all. He wanted to suppress the overweening power of banks, industry, and religion. He didn't want despotic private power any more than he wanted despotic government power. Shocked by the poverty he saw in France, he said, "Legislators cannot invent too many devices to subdivide property. We cannot let this happen in America." He also said, "Another means of silently lessening the inequality of property is to exempt all from taxation below a certain point, and to tax the higher portions of property in geometrical progression as they rise." James Madison, a Jeffersonian to the core, said he supported "laws which would, without violating the rights of property, reduce extreme wealth to a state of mediocrity, and raise extreme indigence toward a state of comfort." In the same spirit, Benjamin Franklin submitted a provision for inclusion in the Pennsylvania constitution which said: "That an enormous Proportion of Property vested in a few individuals is dangerous to the Rights, and destructive of the Common Happiness, of Mankind; and therefore every free state hath a Right by its Laws to discourage the Possession of such property." The wealthy property owners in Pennsylvania voted this provision down.

Property as a Sacred Object

It's one thing to use a business to gain a decent level of life for yourself and your family. It's quite another to turn property and money into sacred objects the pursuit of which becomes an all-consuming passion, a full-out dedication to personal acquisition so extreme that it harms others and corrupts the basic functions of life and endeavor. In the United States, terms like "free markets,'" "free competitive enterprise," and "democratic capitalism" have become dominant dogmas that engulf everything and suppress democracy and human freedom.

Greed is not good. Trampling other people in order to get rich and richer is not moral. It isn't even satisfying. The greedy can never get enough. There is no stopping place for them. They can't help themselves. They get pleasure and meaning out of taking advantage of others, out of defeating them and rising above them. They are waging war and they are fanatically determined to win no matter what.

In the end, the greed heads aren't just trying to acquire massive amounts of money and property. They want total dominance over others and they want their philosophy of competitive victory to rise up over all else and they want it to smash, decimate, obliterate, and wipe out any opposing idea or philosophy. They regard negative consequences for other people as mere guideposts on the way to capitalist/corporatist victory. They are unyielding would-be world conquers, not just business people out to support their families. Commerce in the United States isn't just about property. It's about massively swollen egos and insatiable hunger and lust.

Taxing Unearned Income

Rich people hate paying tax on any kind of unearned income including interest, dividends, or inheritances. They not only want to grow their wealth without doing any work at all; they also want to hand it down to their relatives or other beneficiaries without their doing any work at all. Being in the line of succession is enough. Keep in mind that these are people who pretend that they themselves are wonderful job creators and self-reliant Randian heroes. Nevertheless, they want everyone else, specifically ordinary working people and the poor, to earn what they get by working for it. They want no "handouts" even for the hungry, the sick, the homeless, the unemployed, or for those born abjectly poor and without any way to acquire wealth without wearing their bodies out for it. They claim that hard work is good for the poor but not good for themselves and their children.

Obviously, investors are people who already have money, people who are more or less rich or who at least have disposable income. Why should rich people be rewarded for just owning money and for handing it over to a money handler to invest for them while they sit on their asses and do no work at all or for that matter no informed thinking at all about their investment? The fruits that come to a person from being born into a rich family are enough and should not make them eligible for special tax treatment. Mere existence and the accident of birth should not qualify anyone for special privileges.

The rich are so utterly hostile to any taxing of their inheritors, usually their sons and daughters, that they have invented a fanciful way to attack the possibility of any such tax by inventing a sneering term for it, a "death tax." In other words they are saying the government is so evil that it even taxes death. What an outrage! Sad to say, a lot of gullible working people join them in their hatred of "the government" for doing such a terrible thing.

Inheriting money and property is itself an institutional habit passed down from the reign of divine kings and the privileged aristocracy that made up the kings family and members of his court. This was merely a way of perpetuating aristocracy and of keeping all of the power and all of the wealth in the hands of the royal class. If the upper classes of today truly believed in self-reliance as they pretend, they would not go to such extreme ends to protect unearned income for themselves and their families and their other inheritors. The overthrow of kings and their aristocracies was supposed to eliminate economic injustice and create a new system that would require citizens to actually earn their wealth and property by working rather than by having the state invent laws and arrangements to favor the rich and their children.

No democratic society should give special privileges to the rich through a permissive tax system that favors the rich and gives them special title to live off of unearned income while ordinary people are required to work at often demeaning and trivial jobs just to stay alive and provide for the needs of their families. Each citizen should be expected to earn his and her way through life by his and her own efforts and contributions and not by being given special treatment simply because of the accident of birth. It's quite incredible that Republicans uniformly attack working people and the poor by opposing every effort to establish a fair economy that treats all citizens as equals at least with respect to unearned income and royal privileges for the already rich.

Lies About Debt

The American economic system is based on debt, not so much government debt but instead private debt. Every corporation and every business of any significant size was started and grew through borrowing and debt. Every purchase of a stock or a bond by a private citizen is immediately or eventually turned into a loan to a businessman. All large and medium size businesses are continuously in debt. The entire money system is designed to put money in the hands of businessmen and take money out of the hands of ordinary people.

Every kind of investment is a loan and every businessman is forever in debt. Borrowing OPM (other people's money) is precisely how entrepreneurs get their businesses started and how existing businesses and corporations grow and expand. Corporate and company leaders don't use their private money to start or run a business; they borrow from banks, Savings and Loan companies, and from other financial institutions all of which get the money they are lending from the general public. It is the American investors and savers (common people) who provide all of the capital through bank deposits, stock purchases, bonds, and through their participation in endless other financial schemes and rackets invented by Wall Street and other experts. The manipulation of housing purchases, the rental of property, and many other instruments, futures, derivatives, credit default swaps, stock options, and economic artifacts are other ways the exploiters gather money from uninformed and unsuspecting citizens. Owners and bosses don't "create" wealth and they "create" jobs only by borrowing money that they then use for a start up, an expansion, or just for everyday operations. Rich people get rich and stay rich only because the general public—working people and consumers—supply all of the resources and labor that enrich them.

I think that economic excess is evil, especially when it comes to trade and lending. The good purpose of trade is to put goods and services in the hands of citizens for their useful application. This good purpose requires a simple method of exchange, one needed or desirable thing swapped for another needed or desirable thing.

The use of money or some other intermediate token that represents value seems like a good way to facilitate exchanges of goods and services. The trouble with using artificial tokens (money) to represent value is that tokens themselves soon become desirable products in themselves. Such tokens are not inherently useful or valuable. They are artificial and they can disguise, divert, and corrupt the real acts of trade that those tokens represent.

Thus, very few people understand or even bother to read the business papers that enable trade transactions to the great legal advantage of the manipulators. The law itself is designed to serve the seller and disadvantage or even cheat the customer. Ordinary people are always the prey of business people and their agents. The financial manipulators become obsessed with the acquisition of artificial tokens (money) and hoard a large number of tokens rather than directly selling actual goods and services.

Money is used to make more money. This is called "usury." Lending or renting money for promises of future paybacks augmented by "interest" and late penalties are the result. In Europe in the middle ages, usury was considered immoral and was outlawed. The idea was to stop people from buying and selling the artificial tokens of trade themselves. Doing so led to the inherent confusion and misplaced valuing of something artificial (money) rather than something real (products and services). This distancing between artificial value and real value opens up endless opportunities for dishonest money manipulators to disguise their purposes and to trick their victims. Wall Street has long been the name of a center of trade based on convenient but hugely secretive, tricky, and complex manipulations. The "instruments" invented and used by Wall Street operatives are so bizarre, so deliberately misleading, and so twisted that no one understands them very well. Nevertheless, they offer and deliver immense and immediate wealth to the most guileful and agile of the operatives.

When Republicans and their fellow manipulators use terms like "free markets," "competitive free enterprise,' and "democratic capitalism" they are merely praising their own manipulations and disguising them. There is nothing "free' about their encomiums. The very word "market" no longer makes any sense at all. It doesn't refer to real markets, only to Wall Street and other centers of money manipulation including especially banks, insurance companies, and S&Ls. The money system is so overdeveloped, so artificial, and so confusing to everyday people that just about everyone is a potential victim of the money managers in just about every transaction required to live a normal life and earn an honest living. All contracts are jungles of confusion full of escape clauses, hidden profits, and self-promotion for the commercial interests involved. They are so long and so blindingly confusing that ordinary people rarely understand them.

Job Destroyers

The Republicans at Fox News are mistaken. The corporatists aren't job creators; they are job destroyers. Right now, their drive toward massive automation is destroying the basis of capitalism. Within a century, or perhaps half a century, almost everything will be automated and there will be very few jobs of any kind left. Without jobs, capitalism cannot exist. A dictator capitalist might seize control of the means of production—the literal machines themselves—but where will he get his consumers? Without wages, how can anyone buy anything?

No economy can exist without consumers and workers (perhaps robots instead of people as workers). However, an economy can exist without corporations or owners or bosses. The last alternative, of course, is some kind of socialism, the common ownership of the machines by the few remaining workers and the consumers themselves. The rules will have to be made in some democratic fashion by these common owners. Having a job will be a privilege. Most people will not work except by individual choice, presumably by producing something artistic or uniquely human in ways not machine driven. The very nature of life will change massively. There will be a huge leisure class. Will it be worldwide? That is a big question. Young readers, are you ready for the end of capitalism?

Co-operatives

Even truly democratic structures need some kind of supervisory arrangement but it need not be absolute, autocratic, or permanent. People who perform work should have some say about their work and its uses. Voting and participating are two legitimate ways in which democratic structures can function. Supervisors should be appointed and removable by those under their supervision; bosses should be answerable to those they control. This means there should be some kind of cooperative arrangement rather than a corporate one. Corporations are based on top down rule. Co-operatives are egalitarian; those who do the work should have shared control over the work, its direction, its gains, and its losses.

Corporatists often tell us that democratic cooperation doesn't work. They point to communism to prove their point, ignoring the fact that the communist countries were not socialist, democratic, or cooperative. Indeed, they were corporatist, that is, state capitalist. Nevertheless, it might be true that tightly organized corporatist structures can be more efficient and more productive than loosely organized co-operatives. But is the fundamental purpose of work and life maximum production? If so, then dictatorship—whether communist or capitalist—is preferable to democratic co-operative systems based on more humane environments.

The argument then is between economic democracy and economic tyranny. Is it better to maximize production rather than something less destructive of human needs and democratic principles?

People who live their lives strictly for business and career gains are not happy people or fulfilled ones. Gaining huge amounts of money, property, and power are not decent or satisfying aims but, for some reason, acquirers can never get enough. Striving all the time can only harden personal character and warp the very nature of human interactions and the social systems in which they occur. It's better to be a moderately prosperous democrat than an all-out competitive free enterpriser, however rich.

*

Democracy

I've written a good deal about the falsity contained in the expression "democratic capitalism" and of how capitalism is not and cannot be democratic. So, what is democracy? I think the basic definition of democracy has to be majority rule based on free and universal voting, including a Bill of Rights to protect certain basic individual rights against the abuses of the majority. Except on a limited number of issues, it isn't possible for a large or even a medium sized country to determine what a majority wants in particular instances. Thus, some representative form of government is needed. That means the election of a group of people to represent the populace by voting on issues of common concern. This is not greatly different from the system put in place by the American Revolution but that system has been corrupted.

A big problem with majority rule is that the basic rights of minorities can be easily overwhelmed by majority preferences. The founding fathers of this country worried about the oppression of minorities by the majority. Therefore, a Bill of Rights was written and attached to the new constitution in the form of amendments. There were ten such amendments added to the original constitution. Since then, there have been additional amendments periodically added to resolve problems; a good many have increased the rights of minorities and individuals. That means the constitution has grown and the rights of citizens have grown beyond what the founders specified.

What I speak of here is political democracy. However, some of the provisions of the constitution have had vast implications for this country's economic system. Supreme Court interpretations have often expanded the "rights of corporations" as if such bodies were "persons" entitled to the same rights, and even greater rights, than those accorded actual citizens. Indeed, I think that this country's economic system is not at all democratic and that various Supreme Courts have expanded the powers of corporations to the detriment of democracy and the citizenry. One of the reasons for these foolish decisions by judges is the pretense that there is such a thing as "democratic capitalism." Such a presumption must lead directly to economic tyranny. Capitalist corporations are not democratic bodies and their sole purpose is to exploit ordinary citizens—workers and consumers—for the corporation's own profit and privilege. Until the Supreme Court accepts the idea that corporations are authoritarian and not democratic bodies, they will continue to despoil democracy and to help the economic plutocrats in their assault on the people who work for them and buy "their" products and services. Only rarely have Supreme Courts advanced the rights and the freedoms of ordinary citizens; instead, they have aligned themselves with the power and the privileges of the corporations and their instruments of material dominance.

Government Branches

At best, the United States has a greatly compromised system of political democracy. It has regular elections and pretends that they are free and representative. It has three branches of government that are supposed to act as checks against the concentration of too much power in any one of the branches. The trouble is that all three branches are regularly and routinely corrupted by corporatism or concentrated wealth. Narrow and extreme wealth always compromises every principle of egalitarian and representative government. After all, rich people are always determined to protect their property and privilege against any threat of equality, taxation, or regulation. They want to stay rich and get richer and they fear any democratic threat from below. They don't like democracy or trust it at all.

Money decides most elections and the results of those elections determine the make-up of top leaders in all three branches of government. Few people can even contend for the presidency or a legislative seat in the congress without scads of money. Presidents fill judicial seats with the consent of

Congress. Nearly all such judges come from the ranks of an upper class elite, one might say from the oligarchy. Very rarely do they represent dissidents or truly populous segments of the population. Thus, the three branches of government are not especially representative nor are they very often out of step with the moneyed interests, that is, the plutocracy.

Two other forces (religion and the media) also hugely influence public policy and bend it usually in directions that are neither progressive nor democratic. These special interest groups are moved often by superstition and celebrity and, as always, by money. Nevertheless, they are, in a pell-mell fashion, somewhat responsive to popular sweeps of emotion, often aroused by rich demagogues such as the Koch brothers, accusatory McCarthyites, and other false patriots. Money plays a very big role in arousing and directing these non-government groups in directions favored by the money kings. This mélange creates confusion and poisons dialogue to the advantage, I think, of the haters of democratic government and its helping purposes.

Capturing America

The conservatives are determined to capture the citizens of this country by imposing commercial and religious dogmas on them. The deceptions being used to accomplish this consist of the manipulation of property and belief to establish connections between would-be bosses and masses of shortsighted people willing to accept the claims of their bosses that the democratic government of the United States is their enemy and that the corporations are their friends and enablers. This model came mostly from European ruling systems under divine kings and the lords and priests placed over the masses by old systems of authority, fearful belief, ignorance, blind obedience, and human gullibility.

Humans are pack animals and they are accustomed to following leaders stronger than they are. The strength involved early on was physical strength but other elements of "leadership" such as determination, greed, social manipulation, and the ability to deceive others for advantage came into play as time passed and systems of control hardened into routines based on habit and dedicated belief. As animals became more human, consciousness and intelligence improved and the old systems of pack instinct advanced to more orderly and broadly organized systems of belief and authority. Tribal leaders ruled over small groups of wandering hunters and gatherers. They wandered because their food supply wandered. Migrating animals and seasonal flowerings and dyings caused the early hominids to move so they could eat and drink. They became hunters and eventually farmers when they discovered that they could sow and reap grains and other plants by inserting seeds in rich ground, by watering the rising sprouts, and by tending them until they grew to useful maturity. With the invention or discovery of agriculture, they could then settle in one place and stay there to raise their crops under the periodic arrival of beneficent rain or snow or the flooding of rivers. It was hardly surprising that they should have come to worship the sky and earth, the rivers and clouds, the very plants and animals that kept them alive and shaped their improving ways of life.

Under these new conditions, the old pack instincts led to new forms of authority and tyranny. The new forms were often oppressive and cruel but also useful as producers of common rules and predictable patterns of behavior and collective purpose. Pack leaders became tribal chiefs and/or priests and then city rulers and at last regional lords and national kings. Political, social, and religious hierarchies evolved and some men and women began to rule over others as supervisors; thus, as of old, there were "pecking orders" in every gathering and there was an alpha leader at the top. Whole ladders of supervision and authority were cemented into place by ambitious rulers out to promote themselves, their families, their fellow lords and priests, and their friends to greater and greater levels of privilege and wealth.

Naturally, the most powerful of these rulers wanted to make their rule permanent and unchallengeable. Divine rule was invented so that kings could establish themselves and their progeny as permanent and absolute rulers for all time. These divine kings claimed that god himself had put a special, superior blood in their royal veins and that kings were god's true representatives on earth. This sweet lie lasted for thousands of years and multitudes of followers believed in and supported it as a matter of religious faith and deep patriotism. It thus became unthinkable "to kill a king!" or bring him down. Remnants of this sacred belief still shoot through today's conservative belief system though in somewhat altered form.

In the United States, many Republican conservatives and libertarians treated Ronald Reagan and George W. Bush as if they were "god touched" and as if they were placed in power by god himself. Reagan especially is treated as a sacred figure and a beloved totem of greatness, to be worshipped and imitated by the entire membership of the Republican Party. Reagan said that the Democrats were deliberately on the side of the communists and wanted to send this country into a thousand years of darkness. In fact, he himself hated this country's democratic system and raged against it even when he was in charge of its government. He was a fervent anti-democrat and a lover of foreign military dictators and their death squads as well as at-home and overseas oligarchs and plutocrats, all in the name of liberty. Republicans do not extend the same worship to any members of the opposite party, however. Indeed, they consider Barack Obama to be wholly illegitimate, a communist, a secret Muslim, a terrorist, the coming of the antichrist.

A Military Garrison and a Police State

The United States today looks more like Hitler's Germany than it does any other country in modern history. The US today is a military garrison and a police state. It is not a democracy anymore. It has more economic, military, and police power than anyone else has ever had. It imprisons more of its own citizen than does any other country. It has nearly a thousand military bases on its own soil and more than eight hundred additional ones around the globe in something like one hundred and fifty other countries, that is, almost everywhere.

Our own population is under supervision almost all of the time either by its police, its security and spy forces, its schools, its corporations, or its political parties and their informants. Add the corporate media and the ever-burgeoning prison and probation systems and you have as complete a control complex as has ever existed before anywhere. Let me repeat, this is not a democratic country anymore. It is a thoroughly totalitarian country.

Organized Work

Organized work began with the first tribes or even with pack animals. There were chiefs, priests, and alpha males at first (any alpha females?) and, of course, there was supervision or at least "pecking orders." Some placed themselves above others because they were physically stronger. However, in time, the many began to revolt against the few because they disliked being dominated and abused. This was the start of a democratic impulse in human beings. It took a long time for the many to free themselves enough to force more representative and more egalitarian systems of supervision on their societies. Most animals never advanced toward a greater freedom. Humans traveled through many phases including even "divine" rule by false prophets and royal kings. We have still not freed ourselves from the absolutist rule of priests and kings, including, in current times, the rule of money kings.

Under the money kings who rule us today, their "big" property is considered "sacred" and "inviolable," and those under the supervision of money kings are considered unfit to belong to the owner/management class or to be anything other than mere powerless employees, that is, servants or even slaves to the ruling elite. Conservative and libertarian ideologues support this ruling system but stupidly pretend it is a system of "liberty." They believe that success under the corporate system is the only true and "free" way to measure fitness to rule.

They use terms like "unfit," "unsuccessful," "takers," "users," "dead beats," "welfare queens," "shiftless bums," "free riders," "lazy lay-abouts," and the like to show their contempt for the working rabble.

It was not so much Karl Marx as it was the kings, the priests, the plutocrats, and the oligarchs themselves who cemented into place the idea of classes, elites, overseers, job creators, servants, employees, low lifers, and underlings. These "fit" people think of working people as mules or beasts of burden and think of consumers as garbage disposals. The contempt of the ruling class for working people, consumers, and the poor is massive.

Our Corporatist Supreme Court

The Supreme Court's *Citizen United* decision was the most thoroughly fascist (read "corporatist") decision in the entire history of jurisprudence. Inventing "personhood" for abstract and intangible elites like corporations is utterly bizarre and is opposite to the beliefs of this country's founders. Even Hitler and Stalin did not ask their judges to declare that their Nazi and communist parties were actual human beings.

This absurd decision was based on the preposterous pretense that this country operates under a system called "democratic capitalism." Capitalism is not and cannot be democratic. Owners and bosses are not voted into their roles nor do working people or consumers have any vote on corporate policies or operations. Stockholders are not democratic voters and corporations are not seriously answerable to anyone, especially not to holders of small shares of stock, or to corporate employees. The Supreme Court tried to invent a new reality made up of nonsensical abstractions and imaginings in order to give corporations partisan control over the political system to go with their already near-total control over the economic system. This decision was a partisan attack against democracy.

The spending of money certainly does translate to electoral victories and, when it is done in secret, it deprives ordinary citizens of any effective opposition to the rule of the money lords. There is no greater threat to democratic governance than this.

Several of the justices compared the unlimited spending of political money to the operating costs of newspapers and magazines. First of all, newspapers and magazines are almost always owned by those same secret controllers. This further enhances the control of the rich over the electoral system. However, newspapers and magazines do not operate in total secrecy and usually make some small effort to give readers a slight chance to have their say in a letters to the editor column.

In and of itself, money is not speech nor does "freedom" consist of an immense difference in "voice," one that allows the rich to drown out and squelch the opinions and suppress the votes of ordinary citizens. Literally equating the spending of money with freedom can only put overriding power in the hands of a narrow segment of the population, the plutocracy.

This decision is just one more attack against democracy by an extremist and corporatist Supreme Court.

H.L. Hunt had a belief in what he called "Cashocracy—the more money you have, the more votes you should get." The Supreme Court, in effect, implemented Hunt's plutocratic daydream. That formulation was fascist then and it is fascist now.

Here's what Tom Perkins, a man worth $8 billion dollars, recently said, "The Tom Perkins system is: You don't get to vote unless you pay a dollar in taxes. But what I really think is, it should be like a corporation. You pay a million dollars in taxes you get a million votes. How's that?" Perkins also insists there is a war on rich people and he compared hostility against the rich to the treatment of Jews in Nazi Germany. In fact, when Otto Strasser, one of Hitler's aides, challenged the loyalty of the capitalists, Hitler said, "Do you think I would be so crazy as to destroy German industry? They are an elite. They have a right to rule." How's that, Mr. Perkins?

Flaneurs

All rich people are "flaneurs," a useful French word that means loafers, lazy idlers, loungers, street prancers. With few exceptions, rich people live off of unearned income; they sit back in comfort and ease and let their money and property work for them. They sweat not and neither do they toil or bleed. They live off of interest, dividends, and the incomes derived from the corporations they own but do not themselves manage; instead, they hire CEOs and other pirates and slave drivers to extract money and value from their inherited or falsely acquired properties and from the workers and consumers who are used to dishonestly to support it all.

Even more incredibly, they demand that the government must tax their "earnings" at very low rates or not at all. Indeed, they claim that the money will not trickle down and the economy will not function if their wishes and privileges are thwarted and they are required to pay taxes at the same rates as those who actually work to earn what they get.

They also demand that their businesses and properties must not be regulated in any way at all lest they and their hired pirate managers lose their initiative and stop creating jobs out of spite and a personal need for endless reward. At the same time, they demand that the government crush labor unions, the only democratic instruments workers have to help them increase their meager wages and to assure their safety on the job as well as to guarantee their ultimate welfare as human beings.

The rich insist that working people have and should have no rights at all. Those who say that working people have rights are communists, they say. They also claim that Barack Obama proved he was a communist when he told John McCain's agent, Joe the plumber, he wanted to "spread the money around a little." The rich also believe that consumers and environmentalists are criminals and communists for interfering with their property and with their exploitations of the natural world for a profit and for their own enrichment.

Democracy has been stifled at every turn by the Republican Party and all of its offshoots including the conservatives, the neoconservatives, the libertarians, the military generals, the police chiefs, the CEOs, and, of course, the Supreme Court justices and their bizarre decisions.

Yet, the plutocrats and their spawn call themselves "democrats" even as they snarl at and attack the democratic government of the United States on the fantastic charge that it is communistic because it dares to tax and regulate them. They regard their rule as a gift from god and themselves as noble patriots protecting "liberty" from the evil liberal democrats.

Governments

One can think of governing systems as either political or economic. Often a third governing system is also present: religion. These systems are all devoted to the supervision of people sometimes for divergent and sometimes for common ends. In truly democratic systems, the best arrangements separate church and state. Political and economic arrangements are not as easy to separate largely because money and property (the prime elements of economics) so often trump government and corrupt its purposes.

Unless the government (politics) is the strongest of the three, there are bound to be abuses and imbalances. When the economic system merges with and commands the political system, the result is corporatism, that is, fascism. Corporatism (fascism) is just another name for predatory capitalism. The government has and must have taxing and regulating power over the corporate system. Narrowly concentrated wealth must not be allowed to dominate the economic lives of citizens. The great danger here is that concentrated wealth has the means to dominate everything and everyone unless it is restrained. When wealth is broadly shared and dispersed, democracy is possible. Otherwise, it is not possible.

Only secular governments can be democratic. When one or a few religions dominate, the result is always intolerance and a drive by religious leaders to impose their god's dogmas and rules on everyone through the use of political and even economic means. Nothing is more toxic than the takeover of political democracy by either corporate or religious bodies. Overweening economic and religious powers are direct and often fervent threats to democracy.

The worst kinds of government are those that put all power in the hands of a single governing body such as happened with the Soviet Union's Communist Party and in the parties of the four first-named fascist countries, in Mussolini's Italy, in Hitler's Germany, in Franco's Spain, and in Salazar's Portugal. All four of these countries combined political and economic power in one party and, in differing configurations, they also included religion in the mix. The four named fascist countries were Roman Catholic. The Soviet Union treated the communist ideology as a religion of sorts, taught it in schools, and put it in political and commercial fixtures as a part of the ruling complex.

The Republican War Against Us All

The war between the rich few and the poor many continues, especially in the United States. The Republican Party is the mother of this war and it is backed by immense amounts of corporate money and by the military generals and the police chiefs as well.

One wonders at the passivity of ordinary Americans in the face of such offenses and outrages as are now being launched by Republican governors and legislatures all across the country. They are trying to utterly destroy the American electoral system by suppressing and arbitrarily disqualifying voters they don't like and are doing all in their power to subvert the fundamental principles of this country.

The civil rights of women to govern their own sex and reproductive lives are under direct attack and President Obama and the Democratic Party are ignoring these outrages. Previous presidents sent troops into those states that were denying the civil rights of black people but this president and the cowardly Democrats are doing nothing about these civil rights abuses. The right to an abortion is a civil right as is the right to vote without being harassed, blocked, threatened, or persecuted.

In the state of Michigan, the governor and his corrupt legislature have literally cancelled democracy. They are "firing" elected officials and appointing their own personal cronies as virtual dictators over pieces of the pie.

Whoever heard of a democracy in which elected officials can be fired without cause and can be replaced by petty tyrants, friends of a self appointed dictator governor, a virtual king with absolute powers beyond anything ever seen or heard of in any democratic state. Why is the national government allowing these direct attacks against democracy and these virtual rapes of women? Forcing ultra sonic rays into the bodies of women against their wills is a form of rape and it is deeply perverted as well. Women own their own bodies. They are not government property.

This is no longer a democratic country and it never will be again unless the people wake up and destroy the radical and extremist actions of the Republicans. Why are so many Americans, including the president, ignoring what is the most intense attack ever launched against democracy in this country? Are they blind, deaf, and ignorant? Don't they care?

Rich People

Rich people suffer from the delusion that they are enormously important and that ordinary workers and consumers are inferior and contemptible. Sadly, many Americans glorify and almost worship rich people, especially the ones who make themselves into celebrities. No doubt some of this is just a love of money but there is something more. Perhaps many of those groupies feel inferior and think that rich people are all mysteriously talented and deserving of their wealth and celebrity. They want reflected glory and maybe they imagine themselves into the favored environments in which they think their heroes live and strut. And so they bow down before their masters. That's why they vote endlessly for Republicans against their own interests and against the interests of their families.

Commercial advertisers massively feed this hunger for crumbs from on high. Lotteries, reality shows, and talent contests are enormously popular for these reasons. Television comedies as well as sports, police, alien, and space shows all promote these disconnections from reality. We live in a deluded country. We are all observers and fans rather than participants, even in our very own lives. Electronic advances and show-all self exposures, including "selfies," may be of some benefit to society or at least an escape from a dull world, but maybe they are also a detriment and a curse, maybe a fatal one.

Conservative Democrats

Even when differing politicians seem to oppose one another, they still frequently align their overall directions and purposes with the masters of the economic machine that rules this country. For example, I think that the last two presidents put in office by the Democratic Party, Bill Clinton and Barack Obama, did not much depart from the economic principles of Ronald Reagan and the two Bushes. Even though Clinton and Obama were greeted with the bitterest and falsest kinds of accusatory hatred by the Republicans who called them socialist and communist traitors with just about every breath, they were nevertheless grow-the-economy-trickle-down conservatives and University of Chicago Friedmanites firmly dedicated to free market capitalism.

That means they agree with the Republicans that the economic system that rules and should rule the whole world is a system called "democratic capitalism," better understood as corporatism or fascism. The plain fact is that capitalism is not and cannot be democratic. It is, in fact, a hierarchic, authoritarian monolith, an absolutist system ruled from the top down. The United States has a hugely compromised political democracy and, above it, an authoritarian economic system. The economic system is firmly in command and the political system is little more than an empty shell formed around a chimerical image of democracy.

Working people and consumers have no serious part in this country's ruling system on either the political or the economic side. We have a sham democracy ruled almost entirely by the money kings with massive support from the Republican Party and their Supreme Court and with occasional and scattered dissent from Democrats and certain progressive and populist elements on the fringes of political and economic life. In short, this is not a truly democratic country. However offensive the term may be, this is a fascist country though not as intensely and directly murderous as the fascist systems under Mussolini, Hitler, and Franco.

This is an enormous and orderly country with great wealth, the strongest military force in human history, and with very strong police state tendencies. There is much violence and disorder but the population is mostly conformist and obedient.

The United State strongly resembles ancient Rome, ultimately also a fascist state. Both countries were highly successful and dominant and both were, originally at least, somewhat representative of the people under their control. However, neither country was truly democratic or egalitarian. Both countries had democratic beginnings and each abandoned its principles as soon as it became rich and militarily dominant. Perhaps democracy is meant only for small countries or just cities and not for powerful nation states. Being big, rich, and powerful almost always leads to tyranny, it seems.

Libertarians

Leaving aside its commendable though inconsistent opposition to war, the Libertarian movement provides a truly cruel view of the world and a deep contempt for representative governments that seek to use their power to help the least fortunate of their citizens. Indeed, Libertarians are outraged at any sign of altruism or toleration by government for those they themselves consider unworthy. They consider such helping behavior to be an assault on liberty and demand self-sufficiency from all no matter what the circumstances and constraints of their lives.

Ayn Rand admired decisive and entrepreneurial individuals, even vicious dictators and criminals, and hated those she considered weak and ordinary. She truly hated altruism in the Christian religion, indeed in all religions, and glorified those who thought themselves the only measure of morality or embraced her warped view of objectivism. She did not believe in any kind of democracy because it depended on majority vote, which she considered collectivist and therefore socialistic. She stood with aristocrats and rich people and against democrats and the "unfit."

The arrogance and brutality of the Republicans were inherited directly from Herbert Spencer, the originator of the social Darwinist philosophy, from Sir Frances Galton, the originator of the genetics movement, and from Ayn Rand. Ronald Reagan was a sucker for all of this drivel but he didn't understand any of it. He was a dim wit and a symbol of the Republican Party's rush to the far right in the name of the fascist philosophy that underlies the preachments of Spencer, Galton, and Rand.

These beliefs define almost completely the current behavior of the Republicans. Today's Republicans in no way believe in the abolitionist principles of their original party or the belief system followed by Abraham Lincoln, Theodore Roosevelt, and, on the domestic front, Dwight Eisenhower. Though Republicans, those three were liberal democrats in practice as was Franklin Roosevelt, the greatest of the Democratic presidents.

Libertarian Elitism

The reason libertarians want to destroy Big Government is because they want to enthrone Big Business. Libertarians claim that private property is sacred and must never be taxed at all or regulated in any way. However, they are not talking about your house, your car, your clothes, your jewelry, your little money, or your private possessions. They are talking about big property, that is, corporate property. Thus, they are shills for big business and the enemy of democratic government, not just excess government or intrusive government as they claim. After all, democratic government is the only democracy there is. No one sane thinks that corporations or religions are democratic. Nor does anyone sane think that unrestrained individualism can result in anything less than disorder or the absolute dominance of the physically strong and the rich.

Libertarianism leads straight to aristocracy. Libertarians do not believe in liberty as they claim. "Free" markets are not free. "Competitive free enterprise" is neither competitive nor free. One of the purposes of democratic government is to protect citizens against the ravages of irresponsible free enterprisers and individualistic plutocrats. Libertarians don't want to be a part of any community governed by majoritarian vote. They call democracy "collectivism" or "socialism." They want to stand alone and live outside of all community restraints and duties. Their hatred of democracy isn't just a matter of degree. It is absolute.

If all public property and all public enterprise are privatized and if all regulations are eliminated, the only thing left will be totalitarian corporate rule, otherwise known as pure "fascism." The absence of democracy does not increase liberty but undermines and subverts it. Democracy is the only path to freedom short of individualistic isolation and life as a hermit living alone in a cave somewhere according to your own rules and dogmas and armed against all enemies, real or imagined.

Libertarians and Communists

Libertarians oppose all welfare and social service programs and are hostile to civil rights and human rights because, they say, such activities threaten property and the liberty of owners. This is why they oppose anything and everything the government does or might do. They love private power and that means corporate power and the financial interests.

Starting with Ayn Rand, these stances were reactions against the ideology of communism, a workers' revolution against wealth and against the Russian aristocracy, eventually against all aristocracy everywhere. In fact, Soviet Russia was a poor country to begin with and not developed enough to take on all the aristocracy of the world.

Chapter 4. American Beginnings

The Fit and the Unfit

When the English colonialists settled in America, they thought the Indians were deficient in character and civilization. One reason for this contemptuous attitude was that the Indians were nomadic and had no belief in the permanent ownership of property. The English believed that the Indians' barbarity was reflected in their way of dressing—their nakedness and long hair—and also in their "unhealthy" habit of bathing every day. The English themselves rarely bathed and the Indians disliked their rank smell as well as their dishonesty, cruelty, and superior manner.

The Indians thought the English were irrational. They dressed in heavy, thick clothes in the hottest weather and argued over property and status. They tried to subsist by farming alone and made no effort to gather the food that grew everywhere in the forests and teamed in the waters and the air. Even worse, they ate up everything they grew by binge eating just after harvest and kept nothing back for the leaner times in winter and during droughts.

At first, the Indians shared their food stores with the English but the English were never satisfied and demanded more and more. Then, they began to attack and demolish the Indian villages while stealing their entire stock of food. Then, they razed the Indians' fields and destroyed their crops. Thus, they cut off their own source of supply. The Indians, being nomadic, just moved further away to other productive lands and continued to live successfully as before. The English starved and could never figure out that the Indian way of life was superior to theirs. The Indians foraged, farmed, hunted, and fished and knew how to preserve their yields from these activities. The English, thinking themselves superior, refused to follow the example before them. They thought that their god would deliver them from any hardship since they were saved and the savages were not.

The English colonists at Roanoke Island, Jamestown, and elsewhere in Virginia, Maryland, and the Carolinas would have been total failures except for tobacco. The developing English and European markets for this strange product were dependent on a completely bizarre practice (smoking) adopted from the Indians. The Indians did not understand the vast commodification that followed. However, it saved the colonists from their own stupidity and lack of adaptability. The one Indian practice the colonists took up with zest would kill millions of them and their progeny for generations to come.

The early colonies were so punishingly and so badly managed that a good many colonists defected and went to live with the Indians. It was obvious to them that the Indians lived better and had a much freer way of life. The English considered this a betrayal and, when any defectors were captured, they were killed by stabbing, hanging, burning, or breaking on the wheel. Some were staked and shot. There were few women, thus hardly any families and apparently quite a lot of sexual deviancy and some rape of Indian women. Most of the colonists were indentured servants or other lowly people. Consequently, there was a tight class system and the lower orders were driven by cruel overseers to work long hours with little reward. Life expectancy was low, strife and tension high.

The English were defined by their importance back home and by their rank in the hierarchy of the colony. Since wealth and position counted so much, the colonists lived in a rigidly structured community with betters above them and servants below them in ranked order. By contrast, the Indians saw value in more or less equal personal and community arrangements. They were much more democratic and egalitarian than the English. Surely this was a result of the Indians' lack of interest in property and its various commodifications. When people are ranked and valued according to what they own, they cannot be truly democratic. Capitalism does not translate well to wilderness conditions or, arguably, to any peaceful conditions.

When first formed, the United States became successful because it partially threw off the old rigid class system and created a system based on a freer economic and geographic mobility. In a short while, however, the successful consolidated their superior status and the US became the most successful social Darwinist nation ever. That meant a "free enterprise" system based on the idea that competition naturally and justly divides people into the fit and the unfit. The fit are biologically superior as proven by their competitive success and their eminence; the unfit deserve their inferior status and even their suffering and poverty. In this view, the fit are supposed to survive and prosper; "nature's failures" are supposed to go under. This natural elimination of the unfit will improve the race and bring about greater competence and efficiency. This was the conservative philosophy writ large. It still dominates the Republican Party today and is fervently embraced by rich people, and especially libertarians, as a justification for wealth and privilege.

Liberal Democracy Under Attack

Today, conservatives and libertarians believe that nearly all values are commercial and that personal rights are much less important than property rights. Liberals believe the opposite. Like the founders, liberals also believe the community (as a democratic body) has a right to regulate property rights and so-called "free-enterprise" practices in the interest of the whole community. Conservatives and libertarians believe that property rights are sacred and that democratic government is evil when it restricts property rights and acquisitive practices in the interest of personal liberty and community needs. That is why they attack liberals as socialists, communists, and absolutist believers in the rights values set forth in the US Bill of Rights, the Freedom Amendments of the American Constitution, the French Declaration of the Rights of Man and of the Citizen, and the United Nations Declaration of Human Rights. They oppose the civil rights movement in the United States vehemently and never do miss an opportunity to attack human rights as an impediment to their military, commercial, and religious ambitions. They claim that their aggressive beliefs are patriotic and strong-minded and that anyone in opposition is treasonous, weak, and immoral.

In fact, capitalism and Christianity are missionary faiths and each seeks to convert others indirectly by persuasion or directly by force or at least coercive pressures. Fundamentalist Christians are in the business of selling god and compelling others to obey his rules as defined by them alone. Capitalism is no different and no less zealous. It too has a system to impose on others and it isn't just a matter of profit though that too is an imperative. Like Christianity, capitalism provides a totalist way of life and it seeks to impose itself on every human activity. Quite often, there are clashes between Christianity and capitalism but they are usually cooperative and help one another dominate their shared flocks. Though capitalists and communists use one another to frighten and control their own populations, these two also collaborate when it is in their interest to do so.

The habits of mind that possessed the early colonists are still very much in evidence in the practices of our commercialist and Christian masters today. The conservative attitudes of today were inherited from the old royalist system of divine kings and aristocratic lords. That old system morphed into today's' system of privilege based on economic success and eminence rather than royal blood and direct inheritance. The new masters still believe the fit are chosen by god to rule over the unfit but they now believe in an elite aristocracy reverently put in place by "free market competition." There is little difference between today's' internalized colonialism and the systems of external colonialism brought to the new world by the English and European settlers in olden times.

The Manichean system that pits the fit against the unfit remains the same even though the method of control is now largely economic rather than kingly and political. It is money alone that matters now and the wealthy and their accomplices claim that the getting of money is attuned perfectly to god's will and the welfare of the state. Their accomplices consist of the military generals, the police chiefs, and the CEOs and top-level bosses who manage the economic imperium for them and their families. The rest of us are their servants and employees, or so they think.

The media, owned almost entirely by the wealthy, pictures this imperium as democratic and calls all opposition views "extremist," "communist," "socialist," or lawless in some other way. The media is intensely conservative. It is the voice of the ruling class and its job is to deceive working people and consumers so they will believe what their rulers want them to believe. Being obedient is their duty. They are not supposed to ask any questions or offer any dissent. Like the rest of us, they are required to obey and be silent.

Original Intent

The "original intent" of the founders of this country can be read in the words of the Declaration of Independence and the Constitution. Those documents contain universal statements about the rights of man. However, those universal statements were qualified and contradicted by other parts of the Constitution that recognized the legitimacy of black slavery and the inferiority of women. Thus, black slaves were identified as property, not as full men or men at all but as non-human entities without rights or even any power over their own bodies and minds. Although white women were not quite identified as property in the documents themselves, they were denied the right to vote and were treated pretty much as the property of their husbands and as entities with few or no rights that did not derive from their husbands.

The universal statements (All men are created equal...etc.) did not contain qualifiers or exceptions. I don't know if it's possible to know which parts of these documents came first, whether the universal statements or the qualifiers, emerged first in Jefferson's and Madison's minds or, later, in the drafting of the Bill of Rights. However, it seems obvious that the idea of human freedom was in the air and that the qualifiers were compromises and addenda. In other words, they were added to satisfy the slavers. Thus, each slave became three-fifths of a vote and Jefferson's condemnation of slavery was removed from the Declaration of Independence. Still, the original and fundamental thrust of the Declaration of Independence and the Constitution remained clear and universal as ideals.

There could have been no union without the compromise on slavery but that compromise can only be seen as a practical but illogical contradiction to the ideals of the founders. This contradiction led to the Civil War and that war settled the issue in favor of the original and universal sentiments of those documents. The thirteenth, fourteenth, and fifteenth amendments (the Freedom Amendments) returned the Constitution to its original purpose and cancelled slavery. That war also cancelled the absurd idea of an individual state having the right to "interpose" its authority between the national government and an individual citizen for the purpose of denying him his rights, those rights that guarantee his freedom as a citizen of the whole nation, and as well it cancelled the right of a state to "nullify" any national laws it doesn't like.

In effect, the Civil War unsnarled the thicket of confusion and contradiction imposed on the original and universalist ideals of the Constitution by the slavers because of their self-interest. The Civil War not only freed the slaves, it also freed the Constitution from the encumbrances imposed on it by those who distrusted its principles in the first place. That the so-called conservatives of today should continue to argue these and kindred issues on the basis of states' rights, original intent, and judicial restraint (especially the conservatives on the Supreme Court) is absurd. Those who opposed the primary intent and the clear thrust of the American Revolution were the slavers and, now again, their conservative successors, not the liberals.

Jefferson, Roosevelt, and Liberal Democracy

Franklin Roosevelt said, "Necessitous men are not free men." This was an important statement of purpose for the New Deal, an announcement of the government's responsibility to ordinary citizens. Though conservatives and libertarians deny it fanatically, the very freedom of the people depends on the protection of government against the abuses of private power, especially the abuses of predatory commerce and Salvationist religion.

The New Deal provided the fullest expression of democracy ever seen in the United States, or anywhere. It did this under very trying circumstances, circumstances imposed by the Great Conservative Depression of 1929 and then by the war against a rising fascism defined by the melding together of state power and corporate power in Italy and Germany. In both of those countries, the Christian and conservative authorities joined the fascist meld and supported it as a bulwark against the egalitarian and democratic polity aroused by the Enlightenment and the American and French revolutions.

Soviet Russia may have been an accidental offspring of the revolutionary maelstrom caused by the long rule and abuse of royalist and "divine" dictatorships but, in the end, the Soviet system itself became deeply conservative.

Ronald Reagan, hero of the conservatives and libertarians, regularly expressed his hatred for the democratic government of the United States, even when he was in charge of it, and, make no mistake: this was a hatred of democracy itself for Democracy is nothing but democratic government. Very few are foolish enough to believe that private power—corporate or Christian—is in any way democratic. Democratic government has a duty to protect citizens against the abuses of domestic private power as well as against foreign attack.

Conservatives and libertarians have always hated democratic government and, in unguarded moments, they say so. In fact, they long ago adopted a spurious claim from the John Birch Society, the claim that the United States was not established as a democratic state but rather as a "republic." They only extol democracy when they can use it as a cover for their attacks against others. In their numerous aggressions, they always say they are only trying to impose American democracy on others for their own benefit and in accord with an American duty (Manifest Destiny) to spread its political faith across the world. They are dominionist proselytizers on all fronts—political, economic, and religious.

The first duty of any truly democratic government is to working people and consumers, not to owners and bosses. Except when elections and public discourse are corrupted as is the case now (early 2000s), government is responsible to the great mass of people who put it in power. If it does not serve the needs and wants of those citizens, it is not democratic. However, this cannot mean a majoritarian tyranny imposed on minorities and individuals in matters that are personal and intrinsic. That is why we have a Bill of Rights. A majority does not have the right to invade the private and personal lives of fellow citizens or the right to coerce their political, religious, and individual beliefs or to censor their expressions.

People live in communities and they have community obligations that the majority has a right to insist on. However, communities also have an obligation to respect the private consciences and beliefs of individuals and minorities. Such personal and private integrity must be respected no matter how unique or divergent it is. The founders of this country believed in democracy without majoritarian tyranny and they fashioned a government designed to prevent such abuse.

Jeffersonian Liberalism

The conservatives claim to be Jeffersonian. They endlessly tell us that the best form of government is one that governs least, a principle that they violate with every breath they draw. It's true that they oppose the helping and healing power of government; but they love its military and police power. The conservative program is always the same; it consists of imperial wars abroad as well as repression and censorship at home.

Jefferson did not condemn government per se or oppose the constructive use of government to protect the freedom of the people and to improve their lot, as the conservatives claim he did. What he did oppose was military, police, religious, and commercial tyranny and he condemned them equally, whether they came from government or private sources. He wanted no standing armies; he wanted severe limits on military and police power; he opposed the tyranny of organized religion and, most of all, he feared the rising tyranny of banks and industry. Jefferson was no laissez faire capitalist and he was no conservative. In fact, Jefferson was the first American liberal and the descent of present-day liberalism from him is literal and direct.

It may be true, in some ways, that "those governments that govern the least" are best but that cannot mean that all governing controls should be shifted to the hands of CEOs, priests, preachers, police chiefs, and generals. One of the duties of democratic government is to stop those greedy and tyrannical people from becoming our absolute masters and rulers, through the uses of money, big property, Supreme Court abominations, dogmas, guns, jails, and bombs. The self-called libertarians say they oppose foreign wars, but I have never seen one of them marching in the streets with Cindy Sheehan, Jane Fonda, Joan Baez, John Kerry, or any other "peaceniks" when it comes to protesting against any war whatever.

All libertarians are hot to use the police and the military here at home to protect and enable big money, big property, and big profit against working people and their unions and against any democrats. They also believe that guns are sacred property (and maybe also real live people just like corporations) and that gun owners should be allowed, even encouraged or ordered, to shoot people who oppose them politically after being "targeted" by Sarah Palin, Sharon Angle, and their followers. In the hands of fake libertarians, this has become a dangerous place for peace lovers and democrats as well as for peaceful black children being stalked in their own neighborhoods by armed vigilantes or policemen urged to shoot by "stand your ground" laws passed by gun-crazed Republican governors and corporate-controlled legislatures.

The conservative movement has always stood against Jeffersonian liberalism. Alexander Hamilton, John Adams, and Theodore Roosevelt all execrated Jefferson for his liberalism. In colonial times, the conservatives were Tories, sometimes disguised as Federalists or Whigs. Many of them opposed the American Revolution and, when the war had been won, they favored a constitutional monarchy, that is, a strong Hamiltonian central government with a king or a king-like figure at its head. Hamilton was a powerful tool for the banks and the commercial interests and, with Washington's icy tolerance, he set out to capture the American Revolution for this upper class. To a great extent, he succeeded.

I think that Thomas Jefferson was the real father of this country, not George Washington. George Washington provided no ideas and no eloquent words to guide his countrymen or inspire them. The Declaration of Independence was the first great statement of the American idea, the idea that citizens were free and equal and had a right to govern themselves. In writing the Declaration, Jefferson said he was trying to "say things that had never been said before" and called the Declaration "an expression of the American mind." Although he did not participate directly in the creation of the Bill of Rights, being in France at the time, the Bill of Rights was nevertheless another expression of the Jeffersonian idea. More than any other man, Jefferson embodied the spirit of modern democracy.

There were two great factions in America in those early days. Washington, Hamilton, and Adams were the federalists, the conservatives of their time. They wanted a king-like governor and did not trust democracy; but they did not dare to stand against it openly because the Jeffersonian idea was in the wind and the great majority of citizens wanted democracy, not just independence. The federalists also wanted a commerce and industry strong enough to dominate and rule over the nation in concert with a government subservient to commerce. It was Hamilton, backed by Washington and Adams, who fashioned the new commercial empire that would conquer the continent and finally, in our time, the whole world.

Astonishingly, conservatives today claim that, like them, Jefferson hated democratic government and wanted to suppress it in favor of the private power of commerce and religion. In fact, what Jefferson hated above all else was the tyranny of private power; and his knowledge of the world then told him that commerce and religion were everywhere a part of the king's government and in the hands of his royal court. Jefferson wasn't objecting to the future power of a democratic government in the United States. He didn't know what such a democratic government would be like because there was nothing like it in the world then.

Of course Jefferson was suspicious of central governments generally because he feared that they might form alliances with bankers, businessmen, preachers, and priests to the detriment of the people as indeed they have. Thus, he talked often of the rights and freedoms of the people and urged frequent revolutions against tyranny of every kind. To hear conservatives tell it, Jefferson would be on their side and against civil rights, human rights, and the rights of working people if he were alive today. Well, Jefferson was a great supporter of the French Revolution, a revolution that advanced liberal values and opposed autocratic power in all of its conservative and reactionary forms.

Conservatives pretend they are endorsing Jefferson when they quote him as saying, "That government governs best that governs least." Though Jefferson probably didn't know much, if anything, about such isms, his statement can be taken as anarchistic or socialistic. Anarchism is no government at all and socialism is the ultimate decentralization, one that gives the working man and woman control over his and her own work and life without having to obey any orders from owners, bosses, and bureaucrats.

Conservatives themselves believe in a collection of business and religious centralizations and they want all of the real power in private hands; but they want the collaboration of a weak and obedient government in the enforcement of their commercial policies and religious dogmas. It is surely obvious that every company and church is ruled by a central authority of some kind. In any case, conservatives only oppose central authority when it is democratic and thus not under their control.

Though he didn't say it right out and it wasn't so clear at the time, I think it is inherent in Jefferson's philosophy that you cannot have individual liberty unless you have a reasonably strong democratic authority ready and able to protect that liberty against the attacks of local and private power, especially commercial and religious power. Thus, I don't agree—as the conservatives insist—that Franklin Roosevelt's New Deal was anti-Jeffersonian and anti-democratic. The New Deal itself was for the rights of the people and hostile to the abusive power of Big Business and the banks.

Furthermore, the people and the business interests of that time knew this very well. There's no way to tell but I think Jefferson would have been a New Dealer if he had lived during or after the Great Conservative Depression of 1929. Roosevelt himself believed this and considered Jefferson the great hero of the Democratic Party. Conservatives see the Declaration of Independence as being an attack against all "governmental power." On the contrary, it was a direct attack against the King's power, not an attack against any democratic government whatever.

The proof of Jefferson's greatness is in the words of the Declaration of Independence and in his Voltairian respect for truth, reason, and justice in politics, religion, and human endeavor. Tom Jefferson and Tom Paine were the truest radicals of their time in America. Both greatly admired the French Revolution and both supported it strongly, Jefferson in the drawing rooms of Paris just before the revolution and Paine in the streets and eventually in a jail cell. They each had romantic ideas about revolution and thought it a necessary tool in the fight against oligarchy and royal rule.

They each believed in "The People" as a mystical force standing behind the principles of democracy and above their own rulers. Jefferson and Paine were the great revolutionaries and subversives of their times, the champions of self-governance by the masses. The fight against tyrannical and hereditary rule has continued everywhere in the world to this very day and it all started with the Jeffersonians. One of the great breaking points in human history was the American Revolution and the spirit of that revolution and the later French Revolution was Jeffersonian.

It seems to me that conservative demands for weak democracy and strong private power are a vast distortion of the "true meaning of the American Revolution." The founding fathers did not fear and hate the central power of democratic government. They weren't attacking democracy; they were establishing a democratic government for us all. There was, at that time, no democratic government anywhere for them to fear or point to as a bad example, as the Republicans do now when they sneer at France and the Scandinavian countries for daring to be social democrats and not predatory capitalists like them. What the founders feared and hated was the central power of the English king and all kings. In their time, every government on earth was under the power of a king of some kind and virtually every king was in total control of political, commercial, and religious life. The king's power was monolithic and oppressive. That was what the founding fathers were against.

Jefferson and Lincoln are great heroes to me but I recognize that they were both racist to one degree or another. However, Jefferson's Declaration of Independence did not exclude black men when it said that all men are created equal. I don't think that this was an accident. Jefferson wanted to include all men. He was writing a universal document.

Jefferson hated the slave trade and yet he owned slaves and depended on them as support for his lifestyle as a patrician farmer. Jefferson could not have been Jefferson without slaves. This does not excuse his racism but all people live in environments that impinge on them and direct their habits and practices. We all live by what's in the air all around us and we are all flawed and damaged, internally and externally, by the forces that beat against us and shape us. We cannot be entirely individual in what we think, feel, and believe. Prejudices are honed into us, ground into our brains and corpuscles.

Some of us escape or at least somewhat elude the worst of the forces that affront us and invade us. I do not know why some of us turn out to be nobler or at least less intolerant than others. I myself seem almost to have been born liberal and tolerant. I do not know why. None of my relatives shared my feelings and attitudes nor did I have any teachers in the South who influenced my liberal instincts.

I can analyze this state of my consciousness to some degree but I will not do so here in this writing because this essay is not about me, only about what I believe. It is about something bigger and more important than my own internal workings. I want here to talk about Lincoln and Jefferson as archetypes.

Jefferson did not include women when he wrote about human equality. Why? It seems to me that, above all others as a separate definable group, women have been put upon and downgraded far more and for much longer than any others. In fact, men have treated women as inferior beings and servants since the very beginning of human history and perhaps even before that in the persons of animals and divergent protoplasms.

With some exceptions, human males and even earlier forms of men were physically stronger than females. What does sex and motherhood have to do with this? Rape and kidnapping seem to have been weapons of dominance very early on. Then, of course, motherhood placed females in dependent positions, requiring them to carry and then tend to and protect their offspring. Often, they had to stay at home and tend the hearth while males wandered off to hunt and fight. They and their children were often the gatherers and stabilizers.

Males certainly knew that females were important to them and not just as objects of their lust and keepers of the flame at home. Early on, it is unlikely that males and even females at all understood their roles as tools of the evolutionary continuance of their kind. Yet, the impulses of genetic transfer and species continuance were the strongest of all urges and compulsions. Even the hunger for food and the thirst for water did not rise above the drive to continue the line of succession by whatever means possible. And so males did value females in confused and contradictory ways. Yet, women seem always to have been forced into roles of dependence and obedience by men.

The great mystery is why female equality is just emerging now, late in my lifetime. Judging by the last several election cycles (since the early 2000s), Republicans still do not believe at all in the rights of women or in any broad idea of gender equality and fairness. They sneer at women and try to suppress and control their sexual and reproductive lives in degrading and punitive ways. They seem to hate women and are said to be waging a "war on women."

Thus, Jefferson and perhaps Lincoln were unmindful of equality for women. Such concerns were not even a part of their mental maps. It never entered their minds, it seems. As a man, I understand this. I never thought of women as victims until the gender movements emerged and increased my consciousness. I am now in full sympathy with the struggles of women for some reasonable degree of equality. There is no sane reason to keep women down or to deny them rights and standing. What I don't understand is Republican resistance to the right to vote. Thanks to Phyllis Schafley and other Republican anti-feminists, the Equal Rights Amendment failed to get the votes needed to become a part of our constitution. What has followed is the continuing brutality of Republican attacks against the basic rights of women.

Both Lincoln and Jefferson hated the slave trade. Lincoln was born terribly poor and never thought of owning anyone. Jefferson was born in privilege and always benefitted from slavery without believing in it as an institution. I think that both men were noble and decent.

Lincoln was not an abolitionist at first and did not even believe in racial equality. But he became an abolitionist and, despite the lack of immediate effect, his Emancipation Proclamation followed by the Thirteenth amendment made outright slavery in the United States impossible. Sadly, Jim Crow segregation—another form of slavery, muted but cruel—continued for a hundred years more, until our own times.

Jefferson was a slaver and a racist and yet he was one of the greatest voices for equality and justice in all of human history. What strange, wonderful, and evolving men these two of our citizens were. Their faults were human but so were their virtues. Because of such men, we are a lucky country. It's too bad so many of our citizens are still petty and deeply vicious throwbacks to a time before the eruptions of the American Revolution, the nobility of the war against slavery, and the current movement to free women from the oppressions of men.

Jeffersonian Economic Views

The Jeffersonians did not like the overweening power of banks and businessmen and did not want the fate of the people in their hands. In his last years, Jefferson saw the rising of a Hamiltonian state that he called, "a single and splendid government of an aristocracy, founded on banking institutions and moneyed corporations." He said that such a market system would cause citizens to "eat one another" and also said "Banking establishments are more dangerous than standing armies." Jefferson believed in economic equality and participatory democracy with "every citizen an acting member of government."

One wonders how fools like Reagan, Helms, and Gingrich, who claim Jefferson as their own, can possibly explain his loathing for the dominant commerce and corporatism that is worshipped today by the Republican conservatives or his utter contempt for the organized Christianity that those three conservatives tried with all of their might to impose on the people of America.

With the onset of the industrial revolution and with its power over working people already evident, the founders—especially the Jeffersonians— were greatly concerned about the abuses of commerce. The Jeffersonians were hostile to the Federalist efforts to erect a commercial oligarchy to rule over the people. Alexander Hamilton was the architect of this commercial system and Jefferson hated it and railed against it. This is why Adams tried to suppress the Jeffersonians. Jefferson's election in 1800 was called a 'second revolution' because it expired the alien and sedition acts and enfranchised all white men for the first time in human history. This was a great advance for democracy however limited it may seem by today's standards. I want to repeat below some quotes I used in the above chapters simply because I believe those words are enormously important and rarely ever noted or referred to by the Washington and New York ideologues.

The conservatives claim that the Virginians, led by Jefferson, believed that proper economic policy was simply getting out of the way. I don't think that Jefferson saw it that way at all. He wanted to suppress the overweening power of banks, industry, and religion. He didn't want despotic private power any more than he wanted despotic government power. Shocked by the poverty he saw in France, he said, "Legislators cannot invent too many devices to subdivide property. We cannot let this happen in America." He also said, "Another means of silently lessening the inequality of property is to exempt all from taxation below a certain point, and to tax the higher portions of property in geometrical progression as they rise." James Madison, a Jeffersonian to the core, said he supported "laws which would, without violating the rights of property, reduce extreme wealth to a state of mediocrity, and raise extreme indigence toward a state of comfort." In the same spirit, Benjamin Franklin submitted a provision for inclusion in the Pennsylvania constitution which said: "That an enormous Proportion of Property vested in a few individuals is dangerous to the Rights, and destructive of the Common Happiness, of Mankind; and therefore every free state hath a Right by its Laws to discourage the Possession of such property." The wealthy property owners in Pennsylvania voted this provision down.

Alexander Hamilton believed "the American economy required supervision and strategic management at the national level; and that concentrated wealth was a blessing rather than a curse." (Joseph J. Ellis, *The New Yorker*, October 29, 2001) Every Republican and every conservative agrees absolutely with the second part of that statement. Of course, the extreme conservatives (the anti-regulators and privateers) object to any government at all and want to "strangle government" or "drown it in a bath tub" or see it "wither away entirely," as the communists wished, leaving only our commercial and religious masters to govern us all in detail.

The conservatives are being tricky and dishonest when they claim the revolutionary Thomas Jefferson as their philosophical father. Alexander Hamilton, the father of money, was their boy. It's true that, contrary to their pretended opposition to big government, Hamilton wanted big government but he wanted it entirely on the side of commerce and industry and not at all on the side of working people and consumers. Somewhere recently, I saw an account of how, in the 1920s and 1930s, the bankers in New York City hung Hamilton's picture on the wall at the Chamber of Commerce because he was "the one Founding Father who thought and cared a lot about money." Hamilton was the conservative authoritarian, Jefferson the liberal democrat.

Unfortunately, Hamilton's commercial juggernaut—fed by greed, worker and consumer abuse, and narrow self-regard—gained force and speed. Andrew Jackson opposed it later and destroyed the national bank, an instrument of Hamilton's plutocracy; but banks and commercial masters continued to gain power and the economic and political rights of the people continued to erode. It was the Civil War and the creation of a one-party nation after the war that truly empowered the commercial machine that rules America now. There was a brief respite under Franklin Roosevelt's New Deal, which recovered some of the freedoms of the people and gave working people and consumers some new rights and protections. However, the Republican Party regained its place and now rules through a military and police power that didn't exist before the Civil War. Under the Republicans, the instruments of everyday control over the population are corporations and, increasingly, the Christian preachers and priests collecting their own wealth and property at the expense of their flocks and the government.

Jefferson and States' rights

The continuing "Southern Strategy" of the Republican Party includes a strong dedication to the old Confederate claim that the Civil War was about states' rights, not slavery. Thus, Republicans insist that all tyranny comes from the "central" government and not from local and private power. In fact, the greatest abuses of citizen rights have always come from those powers closest to and most intimately connected with the everyday lives of the people and not from distant monarchs. This may be less true today because of the development of tighter systems of police control through better technology.

The old kings ruled through networks of local governments under the control of royal aristocrats; the worst tyranny was local and regional, not national and central. The king himself couldn't touch or even communicate with his distant subjects except through his barons, dukes, lords, and the like. Even the king's control over the morals of the people was carried out by priests who worked in his interests through a parallel aristocracy of ruling abbots, bishops, cardinals, etc.

Seeing the abuses of George II of England and other European kings, the founders certainly worried about the central power of any future kings or other powerful rulers who might emerge, even in our new country. However, they knew that the greatest abuses of power would be at the local level and that local and regional officials would not be accountable to the king or other ruler except in a general and vague way. The notion that the founders didn't realize this and trusted the unchecked authority and voluntary restraint of state, local, and private power strikes me as absurd.

With the rise of Nixon and Reagan, the Republican conservatives began to insist on the argument that the federal government had usurped the rights of the states and was trying to impose racial equality and freedom on the states unjustly (a very strange idea). They even claimed that the thirteenth, fourteenth, and fifteenth amendments were illegitimate because they were imposed on the defeated South by a federal government under the control of Northerners and thus were not democratic. They thought that democracy consisted of the "right" of state governments to suppress the freedom of black citizens and even to kill them.

The cry of states' rights still echoes from the mouths of the Republican conservatives but the Reagan and Gingrich ideologues renamed the doctrine of states' rights and Republicans now refer to it as "federalism' and "devolution." The reason they renamed it is because they are ashamed of their racism and want to hide it from the general population. Republicans have been successful in this ruse and today even Democrats are afraid to call them the racists that they really are.

Despite the claims of some establishment historians and politicians, James Madison and Thomas Jefferson were not for states' rights during the founding. Madison was a fervent nationalist who distrusted the power of the states and wanted them controlled by the central government. He even proposed that Congress be given a veto power over all state laws. Both Madison and Jefferson distrusted state legislatures and their majoritarian abuses of minorities when the Articles of Confederation were the law of the land. Both feared majoritarian rule and supported the idea of a Bill of Rights (proposed by George Mason, another Virginian) in the new constitution.

Later, these two men did support states' rights but only because they saw John Adams and the federalist legislature vote in alien and sedition acts and then saw Federalist Justices John Marshall and Samuel Chase jail Jeffersonians and suppress dissent, including even mild ridicule of the pompous and king-like behavior of John Adams. Because of this monarchical tyranny, Madison and Jefferson favored the rights of state governments to "interpose" themselves between citizens and the abusive power of the Adams government. Later, Calhoun and other racist Southerners adopted interposition as a way of protecting slavery and slave masters from any national legislation; and they also claimed the states had a right to "nullify" any federal enactments they disliked meaning civil rights. Republicans of today continue to advance these same or similar ideas in their fervent and Birchite demands for "states' rights" and even talk of seceding from the union. Madison and Jefferson were not using interposition to protect slavery; they were opposing the federalist tyranny of "His Majesty John Adams."

Today, Republican governors and state legislatures are interposing their extremist laws on the people and they are trying illegally and unconstitutionally to nullify the civil rights of citizens with respect to sexual and reproductive rights as well as to the voting rights of voters. In Michigan, the governor there and his legislature have cancelled democracy altogether; he is firing democratically elected officials and replacing them with his own cronies. Sadly, the national government under President Obama and his attorney general are ignoring these unprecedented abuses; as he lacked the courage to even investigate much less prosecute the known and massive crimes of his predecessor, he is now telling us that there are no Republican crimes and outrages that he will restrain or even condemn because he doesn't want to "look back." In the fight for the civil rights of African Americans, Dwight Eisenhower and John Kennedy sent troops into the South to oppose criminal attacks of state and local officials against the basic rights of citizens. Obama is blind to the voting, sexual, religious, and reproductive rights of citizens and is also blind to his own clear duty as president to protect those rights. What a sad day for democracy.

Chapter 5. Barack Obama and Franklin Roosevelt

Obama Time

In 2007, the Bush Administration presided over a massive economic meltdown, a Great Conservative Recession much like Herbert Hoover's Great Conservative Depression in 1929. The crash was so extreme that all of Wall Street and the Bush Administration panicked and began an enormous bail out for the big banks and the financial community. Barack Obama, elected to the presidency in 2008, inherited this incredible economic debacle and two raging wars as well. As Obama was taking office, jobless claims had reached almost 700,000 a month down from less than 300,000 a month just a year earlier. And from that day forward and still today, the Republicans have blamed Obama for the weakened economy they had themselves created and that was hemorrhaging jobs by the hundreds of thousands while, at the same time, there was a housing crash that was driving many thousands of people out of their homes. Naturally, the Republicans blamed Bill Clinton and black people for the housing bubble as well claiming that black people had been given easy credit that led them to irresponsibly buy houses they couldn't afford.

And so, shocked by the rise of a black man to the White House, the Republicans immediately launched a smear attack against him. When Obama undertook an early effort to initiate a health insurance act that was to provide health insurance for between thirty and forty million uninsured citizens, the Republicans decided to attack that plan as irresponsible, socialistic, economically bankrupting, virtually treasonous, and even deliberately murderous. They called the plan "Obamacare" as a way of tying it to Obama and then proceeded to launch a quite incredible smear campaign against the health insurance plan and the president.

This attack was furious and utterly bizarre; and yet, like so many other Republican wars against social service programs designed to help Americans live better lives, this trashing was successful. In the 2010 interim elections, the Republicans swept into legislative and state offices in large numbers. With their legislative advantage, the Republicans openly announced that they were determined to destroy Obama and every effort he would make to repair the economy, create jobs, and wind down the two wars he had inherited. This two year long attack against Obama was enormously destructive but Obama survived to win reelection in 2012, mainly because the Republicans couldn't find a candidate who wasn't so extreme he sounded crazy.

The Republicans couldn't believe that the American people would keep a black man in their White House after their extreme hate campaign against him and his legislation, many of them insisting that Obama had somehow stolen the election. However, the Republicans retained control of an even more extreme House of Representatives, with the rise of fanatical splinter groups out to shut down the government entirely, tank the economy even more deeply than they had already done, and initiate even more overseas aggressions. A large part of the attack against Obama has been plainly racist. The Democrats, as usual, have done very little to refute the incredible, radical, and inane attacks against Obama and the democratic government of the United States. The future does not look promising for the Democrats in the fast approaching interim election of 2014.

Though still weak, the economy has improved despite Republican subversion, bin Laden has been killed, one of the two wars has ended and the other is winding down. In other words, things are much better and yet the extremist Republicans are winning the propaganda campaign with the help of a radical Supreme Court and with the resulting expenditure of enormous amounts of secret money by the plutocrats. The Republicans are also massively corrupting the electoral system by suppressing the vote, harassing potential voters and by attempting to disenfranchise them, deceive them, threaten them, and gerrymander them out of relevance.

Though the economy has improved immeasurably with unemployment at the lowest level in five years (a little under six percent), there is still much unhappiness with the economy and, irrationally, the Democrats and Obama are getting most of the blame. I do think that Obama did not advance a visible and decisive jobs program and I think that, if there had been a New Deal style jobs program and a Medicare-for-all health insurance program, the people would have responded much more favorably. I think the Democrats would have been much more successful politically and I think the examples set by the New Deal should serve as a model for dealing with similar problems in the future. It's astonishing that The Democratic Party refuses to own its greatest achievements and instead wallows in confusion every time they face attacks from this country's greatest enemy: I mean the Republican Party and its fanatical and extremist followers.

Emergency Jobs Program

Though it amounts to crying over spilt milk, I think there should be an emergency jobs program put in place on a permanent basis. If, at any time, the national unemployment level drops to say, nine percent, then the national government should automatically initiate an emergency employment program under which the federal government would create thousands of minimum wage temporary jobs that would be distributed to and managed by state governors. These jobs would be forty-hour-a week minimum wage government jobs and each appointment would be for not to exceed one year.

These would not be "good jobs" and they would not be skilled jobs. The first purpose of such a jobs program would be to provide employment for those in need and also to put money into the economy as a stimulus. The work to be performed would be what Republicans called "make work" during the 1929 Depression. The people affected would be at the lowest rungs of the economy; a work program like this is certainly better than a welfare program or ruinous unemployment and it would put money in the hands of people in such need that they would be certain to spend it thus stimulating the economy. As long as useful but needed work (not necessarily critical work) is to be performed, there should be no rational objection to having the government supplement the private economy in this way.

What kinds of jobs would be created and where in their states would the governors place these jobs? We have a huge governmental system in America: federal, state, county, city, etc. There is much useful and needed work that can be performed to improve our governmental services and the huge amounts of property under the management of our many governments. Each governor would be expected to canvass his state to determine what work needs there are and where in his state there are areas of greatest need. All such work would be on government property or under an existing government activity. In other words, there would be no competition with the private sphere. This could be done simply. In most cases, only a few phrases or sentences could describe the work to be done: paint city hall, plant flowers or grass or plants, pick up trash, patrol a parkway or other public property, intern as a junior policeman or fireman, perform handyman work, be a teacher's aide, an assistant forest ranger, etc. Almost all governments have some experience with interns. There are plenty of filing, typing, guarding, driving, watching, reading, cleaning, counting, and writing jobs. Surely, responsible supervision is already available in the existing structure of all governments at all levels. The governors would coordinate with federal agencies operating in their states so as to include their job needs and opportunities. This would include national parks and forests, military bases, the Veterans administration, post offices, Indian reservations, federal roads, rivers, harbors, and canals, prisons, public schools and universities, air ports, etc.

Health Insurance

Barack Obama decided on a corporate health insurance plan right from the start rather than a Medicare-for-all plan. Like the Clintons, he wanted to please the insurance and drug companies by guaranteeing large profits in their pockets with no serious competition from a government plan. He also foolishly believed he could get the Republicans to provide some support. The Mitt Romney/Ted Kennedy plan in Massachusetts was the model. The actual writing of the Obama plan was turned over to congress and the shaping of the plan was put in the hands of Senator Max Baucus, a friend of the drug and insurance companies.

Thus, there was to be no Medicare for-all-plan and no option. Like the Clintons, Obama was dedicated to corporate solutions to social service problems and hostile to New Deal solutions. Although The Affordable Care Act was the Republican's own plan, they determined to attack it massively in order to destroy its credibility and to use it to smear Obama and drive him from office. They openly announced that their only purpose regarding everything Obama tried to implement was to oppose it all out. Though they denied they were racist, clearly they couldn't stand the idea of a black man in "their" White House.

Therefore, the Republicans launched a virulent, extreme, and bizarre smear attack against what they called "Obamacare." They said it was socialist and even communistic. They said it was designed to kill people and would establish "death panels" to slaughter the sick and old. They said it was an attack on freedom. They said it was anti-capitalist, though, in fact, it was designed to put billions and eventually trillions of dollars in the pockets of private insurance and drug companies by making health insurance available to thirty million people or more. They said it was a precursor to a national health care system and a government takeover of health care, that is, a plan to force all doctors, nurses, technicians, hospitals, clinics, and everything else medical under government supervision. Actually, it wasn't a national health care plan at all, merely a health insurance plan, one designed to enrich private insurance and drug companies.

These claims were all deliberate lies and they were meant to spread fear, hate, confusion, and panic throughout the population. It was a typical Joe McCarthy type strike against democracy itself and against the government's efforts to cover some of the costs of treating sickness and injury in line with the government's constitutional duty to insure the welfare of citizens. Rarely in American history has there been a more disgraceful and even violent effort to destroy the reputation of a democratically elected president. Such behavior is deeply un-American and even subversive of representative government. Its disruption of democracy is close to treasonous and it was anti-Christian on the part of raging fundamentalists and evangelical Christians who falsely pretended that Christ was a racist warrior like them rather than a healer and a man of mercy and compassion and that health insurance was immoral and not Christian.

Unfortunately, there are tens of millions of people in America who lack the intelligence or the decency to vote against the twisted propaganda of the Republican Party. Therefore, in the interim elections of 2010 and again in 2014, the Republicans won sweeping victories in the House of Representatives and effective control over the Senate as well. This inspired the Republicans to launch still more absurd and abominable attacks against Obama and democratic government. As usual, the Democrats refused to fight back but instead sniveled and retreated. Obama continued to give ground and sucked up to the intransigent Republicans out to cripple the government and mount investigations of trivialities and invented scandals of no credibility at all. The Republicans tried to shut down government entirely (in fact, did so briefly) and raged against the very idea of democracy as usual.

I think the Republican attack against "Obamacare" was avoidable. If Obama had acted quickly to establish a Medicare-for-all health insurance program, it would have been difficult if not impossible for the Republicans to use it as a fat target for their distortions and falsifications. Medicare was and is one of the most popular social service programs in American history along with the Social Security system that itself has been under attack by the Republicans ever since Franklin Roosevelt established it in 1935. Such an expansion of a popular, easy to understand, and easy to write piece of legislation would not have been confusing or hard for consumers to read and understand; in fact, building on the existing legislation, the legislative bill could easily have been held to a few dozen pages. The "Obamacare" act exceeded two thousand pages and was difficult to understand but very easy for Republicans to misrepresent and lie about. I think it would have been politically impossible for any Democratic congressman or senator to vote against a Medicare plan and seriously difficult for very many Republicans to vote against a bill well understood and liked in their districts and states.

Obama and the Democrats dug their own graves when they advanced a corporate health insurance plan that was much too long and complex and so very easy to mangle and maul.

Such a bill needn't have included any mandate or tax penalties for non-participants, two very unpopular parts of the "Obamacare" plan. In fact, such a plan could have been voluntary. Young people could have been induced to sign up without a direct requirement punishable by a tax fine. One inducement that occurs to me is a co-pay increase year-by-year after age twenty-six. For example, a person who doesn't sign up by age twenty-seven would have his or her co-pay increase by, say five percent and by another five percent increase for each following year of non-participation. Furthermore, the co-pay arrangement could be flexible—raised or lowered—if cost shortfalls or surpluses required such adjustments.

Another possible model for a universal insurance program (other than Medicare) was the Federal Employees Health Benefits Program (FEHBP). This health insurance program was established for federal government employees fifty-five years ago. It is an excellent program similar to Medicare but it is for federal employees only just as Medicare is for old people only; but the Republicans hated it when it was established and have been attacking it ever since as indeed they have been attacking any and all benefits for civil servants ever since the nineteenth century.

Republicans hate the civil service system and have long tried to destroy it and return it to the old spoils system. Thus, the problem with emulating that insurance system and making it available to all Americans is its much greater vulnerability to Republican attacks. Though that system is more or less voluntary, virtually all civil servants are covered by it. It is quite expensive, even though the costs are shared by employees and the government. It would be much more so if it were made available to all. Thus, it would have to include some kind of incentive (as does "Obamacare") to induce young people to enroll.

Some Democrats proposed making FEHBP the model insurance program available to all (rather than "Obamacare") but they were dissuaded because of the massive Republican hatred for government employees.

The huge swirl of discontent aroused by the vicious smears, lies, and distortions of the Republicans is still with us now, two years into Obama's second term. Now, the Democrats have lost their bare majority in the Senate and will still be far outnumbered in the House. The political miscalculations of Obama and the Democrats will continue to have evil consequences for governance in the last two years of Obama's time in office and for years thereafter.

As of April 2014, ten million people have signed up for "Obamacare" and so the Plan can be called a limited success but a majority of the people still oppose it and there has been a terrible political destructiveness that will damage the government for years to come. By the way, there are still thirty million or more who so far have no health insurance at all, because Republican governors have refused to accept money from the federal government for the expansion of Medicaid. These refusals can be laid at the door of the Supreme Court that placed Medicaid extensions in the hands of state governors and thus in the hands of the obstructionist Republican Party. As a result, millions of Americans are suffering and dying right now because Republican "death panels" refuse to allow them to protect themselves and their families against sickness and disease. Is the Supreme Court itself a "death panel?"

The Rise of Republican Conservatism

Ironically, the conservative scourge began in earnest with Abraham Lincoln who was the first man to become president under the sponsorship of the Republican Party and yet he was a thoroughgoing liberal. Although he had to fight a great war and had to be ruthless at times, he believed fervently in both civil rights and human rights and even believed that working people had rights and dignity. But Lincoln was murdered by a Southern fanatic and then the Northern conservatives seized control of the Republican Party and turned it into an instrument of corporate capitalism and Jim Crow racism. Abraham Lincoln has been rotating in his grave ever since.

The social Darwinist philosophy, incorporated into the Republican Party after the war, restored the old hereditarian belief in a ruling nobility but hitched it to the divine right of capitalists rather than the divine right of kings. Of course, social Darwinism was a conservative philosophy. It was invented by Herbert Spencer, an English philosopher greatly admired by corporate owners and other such predators throughout the Western world. Herbert Spencer was not a real Darwinist despite the name of his philosophy. Charles Darwin was himself a scientist, Herbert Spencer a thoroughgoing corporatist. What Spencer really believed in was the Lamarckian inheritance of acquired characteristics rather than Darwin's benign natural selection. Spencer merely used the concept of natural selection and the social Darwinist term "evolution" in a distorted way to justify the predatory behavior of the corporatist plutocrats and to demonstrate the supposed superiority of their ruling class. Spencer himself invented the phrase "survival of the fittest" and used it to explain away all manner of economic and political tyranny against the weak and downtrodden.

Spencer's philosophy held that members of the rich and privileged classes deserved everything they had no matter how they had acquired it. Spencer believed that the capitalist system itself was perfect and that success and failure under it were always deserved. Competition was the engine of capitalism and success was all a matter of evolution following its natural course. The superior beings of the plutocracy rise to the top in a natural fashion and the inferior beings of the lower classes sink down and die out as they deserve to do. This extinction of the unfit is necessary to human progress and happiness, and nothing must be done by governments or anyone to alleviate the suffering of the poor or to slow down their elimination. The physically, intellectually, morally, and economically feeble must be weeded out by nature and it is the job of governments to help them disappear from the face of the earth. "Nature's failures" must not be allowed to propagate and prosper. Naturally, the social Darwinists believed that white Europeans were superior to everyone else; Aryan males were on top with their wives and daughters only a step behind them in supremacy.

Though it began in England and on the European continent, social Darwinism reached its apex in the United States; and, of course, it is still going strong today. It was a godsend to the laissez-faire capitalists and freed them from all restraint and any pangs of conscience about their rapacious, greedy, and murderous behavior toward workers and poor people. However vicious they became, their new philosophy said that there was absolutely nothing they could do to the poor that was not deserved and fully supported by god's great genetic and evolutionary plan in the sky. Capitalism was the path to heaven and only the rich could get through the eye of the needle and past the pearly gates. God's grace was reserved for the successful alone. If you wish to see and hear this philosophy explicated every day, tune your television set to the *Fox News* channel.

Another Englishman named Sir Francis Galton, the founder of eugenics, did studies that "proved" the existence of a superior class based on breeding. Though he was more interested in biology than economics, his studies supported and complemented the social Darwinist philosophy of Herbert Spencer. Galton believed in programs of sterilization and genocide and he insisted that the unfit and unsuccessful had to be eliminated as they were a threat to the betterment of mankind. Naturally, it was the conservatives in the United States who embraced his ideas most ardently as they did the companion ideas of Herbert Spencer. They were greatly worried about the menace of the feeble-minded underclass and the threat of the unfit just as they are today.

Early in the last century, the conservatives (Democrats and Republicans both) decided to purify the race by sterilizing those they considered subnormal or a burden on the state. By 1917, the conservatives had passed sterilization laws in thirty-three of the forty-eight states in the United States.

These laws were to continue in effect for almost seventy years. Under them, tens of thousands of poor people were sterilized and millions more were intimidated and terrorized. The sterilized included orphans and children from broken homes, lepers, paupers, the homeless, epileptics, the physically handicapped, the mentally retarded, alcoholics, syphilitics, prostitutes, disobedient and unwanted children, "moral degenerates," young girls who had been raped or who had children out of wedlock, and just anyone the conservatives defined as unfit, impure, or shiftless. The conservatives felt it was their patriotic and Christian duty to neuter or exterminate everyone who did not meet their criteria or obey their rules and dogmas.

The Lynchburg Colony was an orphanage that functioned for many years as a sterilization factory for the conservatives. More than eight thousand children were sterilized at this orphanage alone and it became a model for other states and other countries interested in cleansing their populations. In 1927, certain sterilizers deliberately precipitated a court case for the purpose of legitimizing their eugenics program once and for all. This case was known as *Buck v. Bell*; and the Supreme Court approved it and has never expressly overruled it. Carey Buck was a young girl who had been raped and then declared unfit as a result. A committee at the Lynchburg Colony felt that Carey Buck's being poor and having been raped was proof that she was defective and needed sterilizing. Their evidence of inferiority convinced the Supreme Court that forcible sterilization was constitutional based on the previously established power of states to vaccinate children. Thus, the Lynchburg Colony continued to sterilize unfit children until 1972 as did many other orphanages and poor houses throughout the nation.

At Lynchburg, Orphans labored for long hours on farms and in the mess hall. These children were often farmed out like criminals or slaves and required to work for farm bosses who greatly abused them. The disobedient were thrown into darkened blind rooms with no beds, no running water, no lights, and no furniture or bathroom facilities except a bucket. Their heads were shaved and they were often beaten with straps, boards, or heavy keys. Some were simply murdered.

Just a few decades ago, the American Civil Liberties Union sued the state of Virginia in the interests of some of the abused and sterilized survivors but the officials of the state fought them tooth and nail. Republican Governor Galton, refused to release the records of the Lynchburg Colony, refused to apologize or express regret, and refused to compensate the victims of the state's eugenics terrorism. Now once again, in our time, the conservatives, under the leadership of Congressman Nut Gingrich, tried to resurrect just such orphanages for the "unfit." Nut's main associates in this attack against poor children and their parents were Charles Murray, William "Comstock" Bennett, and Ronald Reagan.

When Adolf Hitler came to power in Germany in 1933, one of his first acts was to initiate a eugenics program by passing a sterilization law modeled after the one that enabled the Lynchburg Colony. In short order, Hitler sterilized half a million unfit Germans. The Lynchburg conservatives praised him and urged him to apply the "pruning hook" with vigor. They complained about their own nation's comparative caution, saying "The Germans are beating us at our own game."

The conservative philosophy of those times was exactly the same as the conservative philosophy of these times. Nothing has changed. Of course, the conservatives have cleaned up their language and now use more benign-sounding terms to justify their war against the "unfit" and the "unsuccessful." For example, they continue to attack poor people, welfare mothers, children, the sick, the homeless, the jobless, and minorities but now they call them the "special interests" and say that they should be deprived, punished, and abused for their own good and for the protection and profit of the middle class.

The Great Conservative Depression

When Franklin Roosevelt first came to power, the nation and the world were in terrible economic trouble. The Great Conservative Depression of 1929 resulted from many years of conservative misrule but it did not hit full-force until Franklin Roosevelt's predecessor, Herbert Hoover, became president in 1928. Then, in October of 1929, came Black Tuesday and the biggest stock market crash in Wall Street history. This marked the official beginning of the Great Conservative Depression and it spread throughout the world.

Herbert Hoover blamed the European countries for unbalancing their budgets and for spending money to feed the hungry and provide "make work" for the jobless. The Germans blamed war reparations and the British navy. France blamed Great Britain and the United States for exporting unemployment through their practices of automation and mechanization. The British blamed Wall Street for being rich and for not being in London. For some reason, the president of the Wall Street stock exchange blamed a rich Englishman named Clarence Harty. Clarence Harty blamed the downward spiral of the business cycle. The Marxists blamed overproduction. The bosses blamed lazy, shiftless workers, and the communists. The economists blamed inflation and cited the bad historical examples of the Tulip Mania, the South Sea Bubble, and the policies of John Law. Some conservatives even blamed the weather and sun spots. Naturally, all conservatives everywhere agreed that mostly it was the fault of unions and government regulations. Lionel Robbins, a conservative professor at the London School of Economics, warned that governments must do absolutely nothing to feed the hungry, house the homeless, or provide jobs for the poor lest it create a really serious problem. He admitted that doing nothing would cause a lot of suffering and death but said that doing something would be infinitely worse. Why, it might even unbalance everybody's household budgets and force the rich to sell their summer palaces and their gold teeth.

These reactions must be understood in the historical light of conservative philosophy. Conservatives worship capitalism. It is their religion. They believe it is not only sacred and magical but entirely self-correcting as well. Both god and Mother Nature ordain it as the one and only economic system appropriate for this world. In fact, even heaven is capitalist. The only economic sin is to interfere with the pristine independence of capitalism. Left alone, the system will always work perfectly even if it does take a few decades, even if a few million poor people have to starve, even if it does cause mass unemployment and vast suffering. Of course, this is the old social Darwinist idea again, always a part of the conservative belief system. Competition will justly wipe out the unfit and the fit will survive and prosper. The suffering of the poor is necessary and desirable. Morality is in the capitalist machine, not in humanity. Everyone must bow down to the god of capitalism, and no one must ever question it or interfere with it in any way. Those who do so are the enemies of god and the state and they must be silenced before they arouse the people against their capitalist masters.

Obviously, Herbert Hoover was a conservative. He loathed the idea of government aid to starving people. It was a misuse of government. After all, government wasn't for poor people. He praised self-reliance and said that free food would only spoil the hungry and foul the machinery of capitalism. He was a trickle-down man all the way. He believed that the government should give millions to the rich and their horses and that a few dollars and a few oats would trickle down to the poor and their mules. The government didn't even have the right to regulate the trickle-rate or measure it or even mention it. That was entirely the business of business. Herbert was a purist. He just couldn't waste the government's time worrying about lazy and no-account hungry, jobless, and homeless people. They were their own problem. Besides, all of those troublesome poor people were causing poor old Herbert to suffer from a terrible stress and he just had to get out on the White Palace lawn to play medicine ball with the conservative senators and the fat-cat industrialists. It kept his big stomach down when he was eating too high on the hog; and, being a man of some of the people, he believed in playing ball with the rich masses. It was called "Hoover Ball" by the poor masses.

Herbert Hoover's Secretary of the Treasury, Andrew Mellon, thought that the depression was a good thing because it would "sanitize" the economy and have a good effect on the whole country. It would purge away the incompetent and lazy. It would make way for hardworking, efficient people. The victims were just paying for their economic and moral sins. They deserved their fate. Vice was always automatically punished by the noble capitalist system. The good would survive. The bad would go under. The nation would be purified and cleansed. Conservative realism would triumph over liberal sentiment if only democracy and compassion could be kept out of it.

The great Wall Street crash of October, 1929 became the symbol of capitalism's greatest economic failure. By mid-November, stock market prices were forty percent lower than they had been in September. In June of 1930, Herbert Hoover said, "The depression is over." The next day things got worse. By the end of 1930, thirteen hundred banks had failed and in early 1931 eight hundred more failed. Hoover called for tax increases, cuts in government spending, and a balanced budget. He provided no help for the jobless, starving people but loaned millions to the banks. Nothing trickled down. In 1931, a total of twenty-three hundred banks had failed. Then the entire banking system collapsed.

When the Great Conservative Depression came to the United States, the South had already been in a depression of its own for ten years. In 1930, a draught came to half of the nation's states and agriculture was devastated. The capitalists laid off one-third of the nation's entire work force. There were twenty million unemployed in a nation of only one hundred and ten million people.

In Detroit one day, Henry Ford fired forty thousand workers. Against conservative sentiment, the city government was feeding thirty thousand people a day. It wasn't enough. One person was starving to death every seven minutes. There were one hundred and fifty evictions a day and the streets were full of homeless people. Even as the conservatives ignored and insulted the hungry and homeless, the communists supported them. Naturally enough, some found communism appealing since it was their only alternative to being starved to death by their own government and its business partners. At the River Rouge plant, religious groups joined with the communists to organize a peaceful protest march. Henry Ford's security force and the police together assaulted them with freezing water, gas, and gunfire. Four were killed and twenty were wounded. Historians call this incident "The Massacre at River Rouge." The communists and sympathetic Christians organized the funerals. Millions of working people mourned.

Meanwhile, in the state of Arkansas, 150,000 tenant workers were on the verge of starvation. The lucky ones had dogs to eat. Hoover refused to help them. Some died. In England, Arkansas, five hundred starving tenant farmers marched peacefully on the stores in town begging for food. They were not violent but the newspapers called it a riot. The government would not help them and neither would any of the business owners. The Red Cross helped a few and the rest went home to face starving families empty handed.

The tenant farmers formed a union and 25,000 joined. They called a cotton-pickers strike. The planters passed ordinances outlawing unions and free assembly. All the conservative governments of the South had long charged a poll tax of one dollar to prevent poor and black people from voting. Naturally, the conservatives controlled the entire political structure and owned all of the property. And of course, the local sheriffs and the state militias were all controlled by the bosses. They sent nightriders after union organizers, union members, and their lawyers, all of whom were described as "communists." The police and their vigilantes used guns, straps, knives, and ropes to punish and kill the helpless farm workers. They evicted them from their homes and drove them out of town. Local law officers murdered union members, shot them in the back as they met in a church. Some were lynched and their bodies dumped across the border in Tennessee. Blacks and whites served as equals in their Southern Tenant Farmers' Union. Of course, that enraged the conservatives and was one of their excuses for violence and injustice. It also convinced them all the more that the whole thing was a communist plot. After all, only communists believed in civil rights and racial justice. The union was destroyed by force and the planters triumphed. But Franklin Roosevelt was riding slowly to the rescue.

In September of 1934, there was a nationwide walkout by 400,000 textile workers to protest starvation wages, increased workloads, and the tyrannical imposition of a slave-like life on working people by the big bosses. In a town called Honea Path in South Carolina, the mill owners ran the town, owned all of the housing and stores there, and controlled the police. Mill workers had no rights at work, at home, or even in the streets or fields. They were mere chattel and the bosses regarded them with a vicious contempt. On September 6th, the mill workers assembled at the mill to sing "We Shall Not Be Moved" when the bosses ambushed them with their police and began shooting unarmed working people. Seven men were killed and seventeen were wounded. The superintendent of the mill had installed a machine gun but it malfunctioned just as the police tried to turn it on the peaceful workers. Had it worked, hundreds more would have been killed. There were no prosecutions and no convictions. The mill then blacklisted all of the strikers. From then on, no one in the town or the entire state was allowed to mention the strike or even say the word "union." Vestiges of that censorship continue to this very day. Now a movie has been made of the massacre but it cannot be shown in the town of Honea Path, whose residents continue to be tyrannized by the mill as well as by local churches and businesses. Now, more than sixty years later, a few of the townspeople are trying to erect a red granite marker in the town square to memorialize the murdered workers. The words on the marker are the last words of one of the dying strikers, "We died for the rights of the working man." The conservatives still rule the town, the state, and much of the nation; and the workers still have very few rights.

Aliquippa, Pennsylvania, was a town built and owned by a powerful steel business called the J and L Company. The workers there were English, German, Serb, and Slavic immigrants as well as members of the darker races imported from the South. Of course, the town was strictly segregated by class and by race and it was violently antiunion. "Big Tom" Girdler was the company president and he described the town as a "benevolent dictatorship." The company owned everything and everyone, including the city police who worked with the company's private Gestapo to intimidate and control everyone. Those who disagreed with any aspect of company policy or expressed any anti-conservative views were jailed or committed to one of the state's insane asylums. This was only one of many company towns throughout the nation and all of them were slave towns operated entirely for the benefit of the upper class owners and their grim bosses. The attitude of the industrial owners and their supporters was that working people were their economic servants and their enemies. The bosses feared that the workers might revolt at any minute. Therefore, they stockpiled weapons to attack any rioters, strikers, or other troublemakers. The industrialists saw everything in the working world as a plot against them and a threat to their rich way of life. They cooperated with one another in their use of threat and force and violence. The J and L Company even sent its police force to a nearby town to attack strikers there where they killed one man and wounded twenty others. It was just another day at the plant for the conservatives.

Then, Franklin Roosevelt asserted himself and a law called the Wagner Act was adopted. This act guaranteed workers the right to bargain collectively through their own representatives, outlawed discrimination against union members by conservative bosses, and forbade the bosses from sponsoring sweetheart unions of their own. This was the first time that workers had been allowed any rights or protections by the government; and the conservatives, used to government collusion with their tyranny over workers, were outraged. Their hatred of Franklin Roosevelt spewed out all over the country and they prepared for industrial war.

"Big Tom" moved to Chicago when Republic Steel hired him to head up its operation and to lead "Little Steel" against John L. Lewis, a famous union leader of rising strength. Right away, Big Tom bought $50,000 worth of weapons and initiated a smear campaign against John L. Lewis as a communist and worker's devil-leader. Then, on May 26, 1937, the workers struck and began picketing. Big Tom surrounded the strikers with his police force. The police opened fire and began shooting people. They killed ten and wounded thirty more. Then, they threw the wounded into their police wagons and kicked them all the way to the jailhouse. Big Tom's journalists said it was a riot by the strikers and that the communists had instigated it. This propaganda and the police assault broke the strike but caused a congressional hearing to be conducted by liberal Senator Robert LaFollette.

In the hearings, Big Tom swore that the workers had rioted when John L. Lewis and the communists agitated and aroused them. It was all a plot against the United States. A documentary film that had been suppressed by the industrialists and their lackeys in the press was uncovered and shown in the hearing. ("Republic Steel Strike Riot: Newsreel Documentary" produced by Paramount Pictures/ see the Memorial Day Massacre, National Film Registry). It proved that Big Tom had lied, that there had been no worker's riot, and that the police had simply assaulted and murdered the workers without provocation. After the hearings, union elections were held and the union won. It was a great victory for working people and a defeat for the conservatives. Afterward, the Northern states actually began to protect the freedom of assembly and began to guarantee workers' rights of organization and association. However, in the Southern states, backward as always, it would take two decades before workers and citizens gained any rights and any protection against the tyranny of conservatism and the bosses. To this day, unions in the South are illegal and are considered communistic.

After the First German War, a grateful Congress promised bonuses to the veterans but, being conservatives, they delayed payment until most of them would be dead, namely in 1945. However, in 1931, many of the veterans were starving like everyone else and they wanted their bonuses. Congress was reluctant but, nevertheless, a bill was introduced. To encourage Congress and to petition for their money, veterans began marching to Washington from everywhere in the nation. On the way, they were often harassed and hassled by the police for being poor and disgruntled but they came on. They marched and marched until there were thousands of them waiting for Congress to act. The city police sent them to the Anacostia Mud Flats because no rich people lived there and it would be easy to cut them off and block their way to the city by closing the bridge over the Anacostia River. You see, the police and the Congress were afraid of the veterans. Untroubled, the Bonus Army established a tent city on the mud flats. They lived in cardboard shacks, many with their wives and children, and scrounged whatever they could find to eat. White and black veterans lived together in harmony in their little city but Washington itself was rigidly segregated, thanks to Woodrow Wilson. Naturally, the sight of black veterans living with white veterans outraged officials in the government and the white police force. All the while, Herbert Hoover was constantly urging Congress to defeat the bonus bill.

The Senate defeated the bill. That brought many more veterans to Washington until there were more than 20,000 of them. They came downtown and marched around the Capitol building asking for their bonuses. The press called it "The Death March." The members of the House and Senate sneaked out the back door. A retired general named Smedley Butler was a Marine hero who had won the Congressional Medal of Honor twice and sixteen other medals in battle. Still, the conservatives hated him because he had criticized his own military as an arm of unjust colonialism and had become a symbol of opposition to conservative tyranny. His speech of support helped the veterans across the nation but not in Washington where the Republicans were growing tired of free assembly and the right of veteran citizens to petition their government. Washington didn't care what the country thought or what the veterans wanted, needed, and were entitled to.

Conservative officials of the government and the press began to attack the veterans as communists. Of the 20,000, about two hundred of them actually were communists and they did indeed support the veterans and the bonus bill. Thus ideologically aroused, the police began to arrest veterans for no apparent reason. Some bricks were thrown, the only weapons the veterans had, and the police shot and killed two veterans. Smelling blood, Herbert Hoover panicked and called out his army to attack its own heroes. General Dugout Doug Macarthur was put in charge and he had Dwight Eisenhower and George Patton by his side. Doug brought tanks and the horse Calvary to attack his countrymen and fellow veterans. Using tear gas, sabers, and bayonets, they cleared the city of veterans hacking away at them with their blades. Armed with tanks, the courageous army then crossed the bridge and marched on the veteran's camp. There the soldiers bravely trapped many unarmed veterans and six hundred women and children in their shacks that they then proceeded to set on fire. The soldiers destroyed the homes and possessions of the veterans and drove them headlong from the seat of the government for which they had fought in the Great War. Now refugees in their own land, they straggled home poorer than ever but well informed about the nature of their government and its army.

General Douglas MacArthur said that the disloyal veterans, inspired by the communists, were trying to overthrow the government. Herbert Hoover agreed with him and continued to oppose bonuses for the hungry veterans and help of any kind for the starving, homeless millions. And, of course, to this very day, communism continues to be the all-purpose scapegoat for conservatives to blame for every sin and every problem. Even the end of communism has not silenced their blame game. But they have now added "terrorism" to their vocabulary of hate and accusation.

The atrocities described in these pages are typical of the acts the capitalists and their Republican government regularly performed against working people both before and during the Great Conservative Depression. In the United States, the conservative movement has always been at war against working people and the poor. Every version of conservatism is social Darwinist at its root. It is not possible to be a conservative without believing in a superior over-class whether it be called the oligarchy, the plutocracy, the owners, the bosses, the rich, the fit, the job creators, the successful, or whatever term the conservative mind might provide to describe the commercial aristocracy that rules the United States.

The New Deal

Franklin Roosevelt was himself born rich and raised in high circumstances. Yet, he became the champion of the little man against the big man. He came to embody the liberal ideal of fair play and economic justice for working people as well as compassionate support for the less fortunate. As a young man, Franklin was a rising star in the political firmament when a dread disease, polio, struck him down and crippled him forever. He never walked alone again. Perhaps his affliction in some way explains his identification with the oppressed and downtrodden. He had been born a rich conservative; disease made him a liberal democrat.

Upon gaining power, Franklin Roosevelt quickly impounded gold and silver, devalued the dollar, and declared a bank holiday. In short order, he appointed government conservators and solvent banks were allowed to reopen. Then, he regulated the banks and the stock exchange to prevent further abuses of power. The money crises was thus ended and trust was restored with an understanding between Roosevelt and the people that democratic government would supervise the capitalist to prevent them from cheating any more than was necessary to preserve the capitalist system. You see, Roosevelt saved capitalism from itself. The capitalists were not grateful, though, for nothing is harder for conservatives than the thought that they are subject to democratic control and are not the absolute masters of their own and everybody else's fate.

Roosevelt created many relief agencies to serve the needs of the people and to reform the selfish, tyrannical empire the country had become under the long rule of the Republicans. He created a Civilian Conservation Corps (CCC) that provided three million jobs for young, unemployed men to work on such projects as flood control, reforestation, road building, and water conservation. He created the Federal Emergency Relief Administration (FERA) and the Public Works Administration (PWA) which provided jobs and helped the people with slum clearance, improvements in rivers and harbors, and in the building of low-cost housing, hospitals, public schools, highways, and many other public buildings and structures. There were 35,000 such projects and all of them were successful to one degree or another. In addition, the Civil Works Administration (CWA) put four million to work on worthy neighborhood projects. The National Youth Administration (NYA) provided part-time work for some five million high school and college students in need and provided vocational training for many others. The Works Progress Administration (WPA), in total, provided work for 8,500,000 and benefits for some thirty million. The liberal, Harry Hopkins, ran the WPA and put four million to work in just the first few months of that agencies existence. He set up day care centers and initiated school lunch and literacy programs. "Social engineering" screamed the Republicans. Harry Hopkins put one-half of the eighteen million unemployed to work through this and related organizations. The projects carried out were road and bridge building, construction of airfields, serving school lunches, operating vocational schools, collecting historical and sociological data, decorating public buildings, giving plays and concerts, etc. "Permanent welfare state," whined the Republicans. You see, Republicans do not like the welfare of the people and do not like any engineering, social or otherwise, that serves the interests of poor and working people.

Over the course of the depression, these relief agencies put millions upon millions of people to work and provided services, improvements, and resources that are still serving this nation today. The work done in these projects was carried out, for the most part, by unskilled workers supervised by the government. The Republicans bitterly and fanatically attacked each project and complained, without evidence, of incompetence and inefficiency. Nevertheless, the fruits of this work still survive and will survive for a long time to come. Everywhere there are parks and forests, rivers and lakes and ponds and harbors, hospitals and schools, roads and highways, housing units and office buildings, and much more besides. Meanwhile, most of the capitalist work of that time has fallen into disuse and ruin and the buildings and structures they constructed have toppled down and turned to dust.

Predatory capitalists are big braggers and complainers but they are very small achievers.

Franklin Roosevelt also passed laws that prohibited child labor, established minimum wages, reduced hours of work, and controlled unfair competition. He established a Federal Communications Commission (FCC) to regulate radio broadcast and telephone and telegraph companies in the interest of the people. He established the Tennessee Valley Authority (TVA) that erected dams and power plants and sold electricity to millions of consumers at rates one-half of those charged by the private power companies. The TVA also gave jobs to the unemployed and carried out valuable experiments in irrigation, scientific farming, and flood control. The Rural Electrification Administration (REA) brought electric power initially to two million consumers and, in a little more than a decade, to 78% of all farms. Now everyone has electricity. The Home Owners Loan Corporation (HOLC) refinanced mortgages for some millions of homeowners about to lose their homes to the conservative landlords through foreclosure and gave many loans for home improvements. The National Housing Act (NHA) assisted with slum clearance and helped in the building of low-cost housing for the poor and homeless.

To promote social justice and provide security for the old and worn, Roosevelt obtained passage of the Social Security Act of 1935. Under this act, working people were entitled to monthly pensions at age sixty-five and, by 1949, forty three million were covered. Now nearly everybody is covered. This act also provided unemployment compensation, public and old age assistance, help for the blind, support for dependent children, child health services, and public health assistance. Naturally, the Republicans hated social security and they tried their best to defeat it so that working people would be dependent on them. The Republicans understand all too well that safe and secure people need not be compliant and servile. Although they pretend otherwise for fear of being voted out of office, the Republicans still despise the social security system and, whenever the voter's backs are turned, they try to undermine it and destroy it through privatization schemes. That they have not yet succeeded is a great tribute to the foresight and wisdom of Franklin Roosevelt and the resistance of the people.

The bitterness of the Republican conservatives toward Franklin Roosevelt knew no bounds. They called him a "traitor to his class" and referred to him contemptuously as "that man in the White House." Because he dared to reduce their privileges and their power, they said he was a tyrant, a fascist, and a communist. Their understanding of such terms was surely strange if not downright bizarre. To them then, and still today, democracy was tyranny and tyranny democracy. They had no sympathy for or understanding of such concepts as justice, fair play, and simple human decency. They were and are a cruel lot and nothing matters to them except their own narrow interests, their possessions, and their private power.

Franklin Roosevelt responded, "They are unified in their hate for me and I welcome their hatred." He called them "economic royalists" and said, "Organized money is dangerous." He referred to big business as "private government" and the "regimenter of the people." He warned the people "the liberty of a democracy is not safe if the people tolerate the growth of private power to a point where it becomes stronger than the democratic state itself." He warned against "ownership of government by an individual, by a group, or any controlling private power." The conservatives loathed and despised Franklin Roosevelt but the poor everywhere had pictures of him on their walls. Wherever he went, the people cheered and the conservatives slunk back into their castles and golden grots hanging their heads.

Franklin Roosevelt put an end to the tyranny of the corporate owners in his time but unfortunately his reign did not change things permanently. After his death, the Republicans and their masters emerged from their private grots once again and began to attack the programs of Franklin Roosevelt's New Deal. Many of those programs have been destroyed and many others weakened but the Republicans have not quite consolidated their recovered power. Not yet. Though much weakened in our present age, the liberals continue to fight for justice and a fair deal for the people. Their dream will never die.

For many years, Franklin Roosevelt led the fight against tyrants at home and abroad. Then, just as the Second German War was ending, Roosevelt died. The Republicans rejoiced but the people wept. Their benefactor had died and they did not know what the future held for them. The Republicans knew and licked their greedy chops.

CHAPTER 6. LUG AND LUD: A CAPITALIST AND CHRISTIAN FABLE

(Extracted from an unpublished novel called *Man of Light*.)

Graham Cracker was just about ready to sail for home but he decided to stop off at the coastal islands for a little R and R. He didn't know that the two islands nearest Loveland were in the hands of two brothers who had become enemies and kept their island colonies in a perpetual state of hostility toward one another. Though there were numerous little raids back and forth between them, there wasn't a real war. What there was was a cold war.

Now, cold wars are a modern invention. They are better than hot wars because they allow the leaders and the military class of a country, or an island, to maintain a profitable state of emergency for years on end without actually using up important resources or sacrificing enough lives to make the working class really angry. It's great for the economy and it allows leaders and their followers to call themselves patriots without ever doing anything the least bit patriotic. Whole populations can be kept armed, angry, and alert for decades on end just by mentioning the imaginary threat of a cold-war foe. Better yet, the cold-war threat can be used by the ruling class to attack its political opponents at home as traitors and enemies of their own country. It seems that conservative populations love to hate their enemies and, of course, their enemies are just anybody their leaders cuss and call bad names. There is nothing better for national unity and prosperity than a good long cold war.

The story of the two brothers in charge of the two hostile islands is kind of interesting if you are into cold wars and such arcana and, of course, we are. Unbeknownst to Graham Cracker, Mother Church and Father Dollar had once been lovers and had, as a result, produced two illegitimate offspring. They were twins and the shamed parents had named them Lug and Lud. Then, as a means of covering up their illicit affair by concealing the evidence, they shipped Lug and Lud off to the continent of Farbelow Us for adoption. Thus, Lug and Lud had grown up in the family of a Christian industrialist who built war machines for a living. The industrialist was very rich, of course, and the twins had a conventional and conservative upbringing. However, they had not turned out well. Lug was obsessed with machinery and Lud hated it with a bitter, destructive passion. The children fought all the time. Lug was always building cute little machines and Lud was always attacking and destroying them as fast as Lug could build them. Lug loved money and material things. Lud was an idealist and an ascetic.

Lug and Lud had parted company when they reached their twenty-first birthday and came into their inheritances. Then, they left their home on the continent and, with a few mercenaries, each one captured an offshore island of his very own. Lug's mercenaries were mostly robots and other machines and Lud used the natural power of religious zealots and creatures of the forest to help him achieve his island empire. Lug's island state was corporatist with him as the CEO. Lud's state was theocratic with him as the head priest. Of course, Lug was a capitalist and Lud a kind of communist-Christian naturalist.

In the founding of their island kingdoms, Lug and Lud established ruling philosophies for everyone to live by. Lug's was called the New Industrial Freedom and its aim was to guarantee a closely supervised lifetime of hard labor as a pathway to efficiency and profit. Metaphorically speaking, Lud established a shining city on a hill in the name of the Great God of Some of Us. Lug's first act was to post an organization chart on the first tree he came to. Lud's first act was to plant a tall cross in the dirt. Lug believed in small government and big business and, of course, Lud believed in small government and big religion. As different as they were, they shared a strong hatred for government, especially government that interfered with the workings of their ideologies. They knew that democratic government was the most dangerous of all governmental systems because it was the one most likely to weaken their power.

Unlike his brother Lud, Lug had scouted ahead and had selected his island because of its plentiful supply of raw materials he could use in his trade. There were plenty of steel and plastic trees for him to cut down and shape into machines. Lug brought a dozen machine-making machines and two-dozen machine tenders with him and he knew there were about a hundred aborigines on the island and that they had mules and goats enough to harvest and transport raw materials to wherever he needed them. He knew there might be a problem obtaining machine fuel but there was plenty of sunshine and he was confident he could harness it and turn it to good use.

Lugs Island was pretty much a normal island. It had traditional animals, trees, plants, and plenty of freshwater lakes. There was nothing odd or unusual about it except Lug's plans to turn it into a factory town. You see, productive industrial communities have a habit of eventually turning themselves into uninhabitable quagmires.

You'd better believe that there were no machines on Lud's Island unless you count the island itself as a machine. Eons ago, something strange had happened in the creation of this island. It rose right up from the bottom of the sea and brought all kinds of oddities with it. As soon as it emerged, volcanos began erupting and great lava streams ran hither and yon until lava covered just about everything. Then, a hundred geysers shot up and, strange as it may seem, most of them spewed an icy liquid all about them until icebergs and boiling lakes sat there side by side confronting one another with their opposite natures. They learned to live together and the whole island divided itself into zones of hot and cold. In mid flow, hot streams, milky with lava, turned into cold streams, tinkly with shards of ice. One side of a boulder would glow red with violent heat and the other side would be shivery cold to the touch. It would be raining in one place and in another, only a few feet away, it would be sleeting or snowing. Glaciers formed and right beside them were roiling lakes of fiery water.

Great rocks jutted up and pink and blue coralines multiplied and fused together into strange patterns. Waterfalls fell down long escarpments and all the way to the sea. A little moss grew here and there but not much else. Slowly, certain unusual life forms either evolved right there on the island or emerged already-formed from deep pits under the sea. Perhaps they rose up from ancient seabeds and came to the island through the many deep perforations that marked its surface, but then again perhaps they were created original by fire and ice in a quick evolutionary jump.

Some animals called thermafrogs were spewed up by the thousands in the icy spouts of the cold geysers. These animals were so cold that they instantly frosted everything they touched. Thermafrogs didn't move very fast; in fact, they managed only about one short hop a week, but it was enough to keep the lot of them in a state of apparent undulation all the time. Their croaking was slow and low and produced a constant sound, a kind of mumbling hum. They were so thick that Lud's people had to kick them aside as they came ashore. They threw many into the sea and children used them as footballs and hockey pucks. One man tossed a few into his sandwich box to keep his Pepsi cold and his Twinkie fresh. The idea spread and people began building little boxes to cool their drinks and preserve their vegetables. This is how the ice chest was invented. Then, someone discovered that thermafrogs were good to eat. They had to be cooked for fourteen hours on a hot rock before they became tender enough to chew. Even then, they never got warm, even when they were well done. Nevertheless, they made an excellent cold dish and were usually eaten as an appetizer.

Thermafrog eyeballs were sometimes used by children as marbles and necklaces but they were too cold and clammy to be much fun. You could make attractive shoes and hats out of the skin and they were comfortable enough in the hot zones but nowhere else. No doubt thermafrogs could have been turned into Freon and cocktail ice for export, but Lud discouraged commerce and trade. As a result of these consumer efforts, the thermafrog population was gradually reduced until finally a citizen could walk a few yards without encountering any.

There was an island plant called the florarose and it was as hot as the thermafrog was cold. These plants grew in the still hot but cooling lava beds, and soon they began to spread to all of the warm zones of the island. They had bright red flower heads, as big as those of sunflowers, and a thymy smell. They were always warm and nothing could make them feel cool. The florarose was edible and nourishing but not very tasty unless you liked hot, coarse, minty salads. Still, the islanders had to eat them. They were the only vegetables on the island other than true weeds. The florarose was considered the official flower of the island colony. It made a very good heating pad and would have been a satisfactory mother hen if the islanders had had any eggs to hatch. Because they were warm, some people liked to hug them and talk to them and a few lonely people actually slept with them at night.

The island also had a fish called the ichthyop that at first swam laboriously through the lava streams with its mouth wide open. Somehow, over time, it managed to thin, cool, and clean the lava until it became a fine, warm liquid, a kind of mild broth. I kid you not: this broth was delicious if you strained and salted it enough. After having converted the lava to broth, and even as the islanders watched it evolve, the ichthyop gradually changed from a murky brown to a deep blue color. Of course, it had a wonderful taste and it did not have to be cleaned, scaled, or cooked. It was always ready for the table, just as it was; all it needed was catching.

And, yes, there was a unique bird on the island. It was called the ornis and no one knew where it came from. Nevertheless, it obviously was a part of the island's ecosystem. The ornis was the same color as the florarose and had its same minty smell; it was cold to the touch like the thermafrog; and its big, corkscrew beak was the same blue shade as the body of the ichthyop. The ornis may well have originated elsewhere and flown to Luds Island but it certainly did adapt quickly to local conditions and appearances. It was a large, swift bird with a wingspan of about three feet. The only sound it uttered was "chut, chut, chut," but its wings whistled a catchy little tune when it was in flight. One odd thing about the ornis was that it flew upside down except on rainy days. It was not edible or useful in any way but it certainly did catch the eye.

Lud's people soon came to believe the earth was their mother and that it would take care of all of their needs. Perhaps they were right. There was food enough and the very surface of their island served them well. There were certain areas on the bare ground that were very hot; some of them even glowed red but others were less intense. These were all called "hot spots" and they were used for cooking and foot warming. You could fry cook right on the surface and the islanders soon learned to split open the earth at a hot spot to make neat little ovens in which they could bake their bread. At other places on the island, there were "cold holes" that were used as refrigerators and freezers.

Right in the middle of the island, there was a gigantic hole that blew air that was sometimes hot and sometimes cold. It had big, ridge-like lips that expanded and contracted in no clear pattern and for no obvious reason. The islanders didn't know what to make of it. Some used it as a garbage disposal and others as an oracle into which they threw their various sacrifices and to which they swore their oaths. It was called the oraflex and it served as an assembly place and a kind of public square for the island community.

Lud was very disappointed when he found that there were no natives on the island for him to conquer and convert. Nevertheless, right from the start, Lud's people believed there was an invisible presence among them. No one ever found any real proof but everyone thought that a mysterious people did live there with them. Things were always disappearing, many claimed to hear gentle laughter in the night, there were sometimes unexplained imprints on the ground, and quite often they could hear the muted sounds of footfalls.

Lud brought nineteen human followers with him and more than a hundred simians. The anthropoids behaved just like all the other Christians but they couldn't talk and didn't know A from Z. There was hardly any native life at all on Lud's island except, of course, the thermafrogs, the floraroses, the ichthyops, and the ornises. The ground was mostly bare when they arrived but the earth was fertile. In fact, as soon as they landed, weeds began to pop up everywhere they set foot. Lud had to make a law requiring everyone to walk backwards so they could weed behind them as they went along. Otherwise, they would have been ass-deep in weeds.

Lud's people had no housing. There were no trees to build anything out of and they only had a couple of eoliths for tools. Therefore, they lived among and under the rocks and some even slit open the warm earth and went underground. In one way or another, the island provided very well but the islanders didn't have any supplements to keep them healthy. The simians took to licking the rocks and the humans soon realized that this was how they obtained their salts and minerals. Of course, they followed the lead of their brothers and became rock-lickers themselves. Visitors thought Lud's people rather odd. Backwards walking and rock-licking just were not accepted as culturally correct in the outer world. These were not conservative things to do.

Lud was excitable and maybe crazy but he wasn't stupid. Therefore, he knew full well that he needed some kind of economic management. Thus, he imported one of those economists from the Chicago School and appointed him to the position of Corrupt Faggle. It was the Corrupt Faggle's job to manage the island's economy and to lie, cheat, and steal for everyone else. He was the island's only capitalist and he was allowed to make a big profit, up to twelve cents a day. No one else was allowed to make a profit at all and, relativity being what it is, the Corrupt Faggle became very rich and important. He was kind of the opposite of a scapegoat. He was the designated profit monger and he allowed everyone else to focus exclusively on life and religion. The citizens were very grateful and appreciative of the Corrupt Faggle's financial expertise.

Because of his holiness, Lud had developed certain magical powers. He could wither grass with just a glance but, of course, there wasn't any grass on the island and so this power was largely useless. Eventually, he did learn to wither weeds and move rocks a few feet at a time with a stern look. He could also catch fish without a fishing pole or even a hook. He just called to them and they crawled right up out of the water and flopped at his feet. This power was not all that useful either since there were plenty of ichthyops available to everyone and the ichthyop was a better-tasting fish than any Lud could call up from the sea.

Lud could also turn small rocks into loaves of bread and boxes of cigars. This would have been a very useful power but the bread wasn't very good and no one would eat it. The cigars were of good quality but there wasn't a single match on the whole island and no one had yet figured out how to light a cigar at a hot spot. Lud rarely used his powers because no one had any use for what they produced. He did kill a few weeds and sometimes he would move a stray rock or two and people did appreciate it. Nonetheless, the people of the island didn't pay that much attention to Lud anymore. It was kind of sad.

*

By contrast, Lugs Island was rather a dull place but, at least, it was more or less normal. On Lugs Island, there most definitely was an upper class. For the benefit of this upper class, every last thing was machine driven but a lower class was still needed to polish and maintain the machines and to do all the little things that servants do to make their masters feel important and superior. Most of the members of the upper class never moved a muscle from dawn to dark. They became so lazy that even Lug regarded them with contempt, but he needed a leisure class to consume all the things his machines were producing and he needed the lower class to service the machines and the upper class.

Lug himself considered the machines the real upper class and thought they were superior in just about every way to people. Lug would have designated the machines as the leisure class by edict but they had no capacity for pleasure or idleness and did not consume very many goods. Lug loved his machines but they really didn't return his love. He thought they did, though, and eventually he turned them into objects of love and worship for all of his island citizens. But that was many years down the road, after his big crack up. That's not really a part of our story but it's interesting to know that Lug eventually built an ultimate machine, shot it up into the clouds, and made his citizens worship it as their God. They really didn't very much mind. They needed some kind of a God and one was as good as another, just as long as they got some awe and fear out of the deal.

In his youth, before he went balmy, Lug was very inventive. First, he invented a box for carrying fruits and vegetables and named it after himself. Then, he invented the lugsail at the request of a friend with a boat and its use became widespread. Then, he got a patent on the lug nut and began to accumulate some capital. After that, he produced machines and machine parts by the thousands and became quite well known in the industrial world. There were always mixed feelings about Lug, though. Some thought him a capitalist hero and a man of genius while others thought he was a clumsy fool and a blockhead. You see, in those backward days, some people didn't think that machines were as important as people and the Supreme Court hadn't yet developed its theory that industrial machines and corporations were actual people.

Now though, Lug needed an invention to sustain his machine economy. He had no fuel to make his machines go. On the mainland, he had used imps as batteries but there were no imps on the island. He had a few imps in the machines he brought with him to the island but they had just about discharged themselves.

One day, in a certain shady place, Lug was strolling along with his nose in the air, thinking about his problem, when he tripped and fell into a big hollow log. When he got up, his hands and knees were all aglow with sunlight. This seemed odd because he was standing in the shade at the time. He realized that this residue of sunlight had been stored somehow in the hollow log. He looked in the log and there, down under some water and among some strands of moss, he saw a whole colony of maggots and they were as bright as sunlight. In fact, they were sunlight. Somehow, the combination of shade, water, moss, and hollow log had enabled the maggots to absorb sunlight and become energy cells. Lug stayed there for twenty-four hours to observe the log and the maggots. He discovered that, for four hours in the morning, sunlight covered the log with a peculiar intensity. Lug noticed that the vines way up in the trees acted as a kind of filter and magnifier for the sunlight. He decided that this filtering process was responsible for the sunlight's peculiar intensity. He didn't understand the scientific causes and effects at all but he was sure he did know the conditions needed to produce charged maggot cells.

He brought in a crew of aborigines and had them drag a hundred logs into the area under the light source. He ordered them to fill each hollow with water and moss in the same pattern as in the original hollow log. Then, he had them collect a hundred million maggots and place a colony or two down in the moss in each hollow log. Then, Lug pitched his tent and set up an observation post. He had to wait twelve days but, finally, the experiment succeeded. In forty-eight of the logs, Lug found charged maggot cells. He never found out why fifty-two of the logs failed but the ones that were successful supplied energy enough for his purposes.

Lug dealt with the aborigines on the island in the usual capitalist way. He took control of all the food, water, and land and made access to it a condition of employment. Of course, just about everybody then had to go to work for Lug. A few held out but Lug and his bosses labeled them as shiftless, lazy, and no account and they soon became pariahs and criminals even in the eyes of their own people. Lug thus created his own reserve work force and kept them in their place by forcing them into lives of dependency and crime. As they sank into sloth and degradation, Lug began to attack them in his newspaper as welfare cheats, sexual sinners, and despoilers of the island's values. All in all, Lug said they were unfit and unclean and, to prove his humanity, he urged his subjects to establish punitive programs to uplift them and improve their morals. You see, a degraded subclass is essential to the proper functioning of capitalism. Without scapegoats to distract them, working people tend to notice the crimes and abuses of their bosses.

*

When Graham Cracker and his fleet arrived in the waters between Lugs Island and Luds Island, they decided to split up with half of the ships going to one island and half to the other. Most of the young knights in Graham Cracker's party preferred to remain on the beach of Luds Island so they could swim in the lagoon, sun bathe, and play ball. They had had enough adventures and just wanted to hang out. Though he disapproved of leisure and fun, Graham Cracker made an exception and let them have their playtime. He, Chris, and Mother Church took a few volunteers with them and headed inland to look for the religious colony they had heard was living there on Luds Island. Graham Cracker was favorably disposed toward the inhabitants because he had heard that they were good Christians and mostly white in color.

Graham Cracker was shocked to find out what kind of an island he had landed on. He kept stepping on hot spots and scorching his feet and then he fell headlong into a cold hole and came out covered with frost and icy water. He found a warm zone and was drying out nicely when an ornis flew by upside down and brushed him with a big wing. He lost his balance again and fell right into a pile of thermafrogs. Their cold and clammy touch disgusted him and he kept wiping his skin with his big red bandana. How could anyone live in such a place, he wondered, especially a holy colony of worshipful Christians. He really thought that this island was more like hell than heaven, but he soldiered on.

Soon, Graham Cracker's party arrived at the oraflex which they thought frightening with its big mouth yawning open and snapping shut as steam shot into the air, blinding them, and ice shards showered down violently on their unprotected heads. They backed away and were watching from a safe distance when a gaunt white man in rags walked right up to Graham Cracker and chucked him three times under the groin, grasping his testicles, lifting them up, and letting them fall down again. At the same time, he said, "Welcome, pilgrim, welcome."

Graham Cracker jumped back in fright, his jaw slack, his eyes bugging out. He tried to speak but he could only sputter and stammer. He backed away some more. Graham Cracker's behavior irritated the man in rags and he shouted, "Are you such barbarians that you do not even greet your brothers? Have you no manners or etiquette?"

Graham Cracker then realized that the testicle gesture was some kind of greeting, like a handshake, and he replied, "I'm sorry. I don't understand your customs. Rest assured that we come in peace."

The man responded, "Ah well, are you good Christians?" Graham Cracker assured him they were and identified himself as a minister of the Lord. The man was pleased and said, "Good, good. We welcome you with all our hearts. You shall have our hospitality. And God's."

Somehow, the testicle greeting established a warm bond of friendship between Graham Cracker and Lud. The visitors remained for three days, during which time Graham Cracker and Lud talked long into each night about their godly beliefs and hopes. On their last night together, nature once again accosted Graham Cracker unjustly and made him wonder if Luds Island really was a holy place.

As they sat around the oraflex, imbibing its wisdom, there came a noise in the dark. There were several footfalls and a tinkle of laughter just beyond the fringe of light cast up by the oraflex. Graham Cracker rose up in anger at the effrontery of this rude interruption and stepped out into the night just beyond the protection of the oraflex's halo. Then something, or someone, pushed him and he reeled back again, whirling and turning, until he arrived at the lip of the oraflex, paused there for a moment, and toppled in. Aghast, his companions arose and approached the mouth of the oraflex. The oraflex seemed to be chewing, but then it opened again and burped Graham Cracker up with a gurgle and a splat. Graham Cracker fell face down and lay there in a daze. His clothes were all gone and so, after he revived, Lud and his simians dressed Graham Cracker in a seaweed skirt and draped a florarose garland around his neck and shoulders.

Graham Cracker slept a troubled sleep that night, dreaming the oraflex was the entrance to hell and that it was about to claim him for good. The next morning he was sad to leave his new friend but glad to be leaving the oraflex and the weirdness of its hellish environment. From that day on, Graham Cracker carefully avoided every hint of a hole in the ground, however shallow, however innocent. He even gave up sex.

*

The other half of the fleet had anchored on the opposite side of the straights in the lee harbor of Lugs Island. There was an organized beach on that island with concession stands, bathhouses, and a couple of fast food huts. Everything was machine driven and you had to deposit money in slots to get anything to work. However, there was an aboriginal caretaker on duty and, while he didn't speak a language anyone could understand, he could point, smile, and give change. After some refreshments, Father Dollar, Sir Plastic Jesus, Buck Ocool, Elvin Harf, and a few young knights headed inland. Everyone else remained at the little park near the concession stands where there were some ball fields, a pier, a peep show, a brew hall, and some slot machines. Just as Father Dollar and his party were disappearing, the young knights on the beach discovered a whorehouse back in the weeds, but it was rather unusual, that is, all the whores were machines. Nevertheless, it did a good business that sinful day.

After walking through the woods for just a few minutes, Father Dollar and his party came to a paved road in a good neighborhood. Everyone there had a nice house and, nearby, their machines lived in palatial hangers and tastefully decorated Quonset huts. This was obviously upper-class territory.

Lugs Island had a middle-class and a lower-class neighborhood as well. The middle-class neighborhood adjoined the upper-class neighborhood but, of course, it was plainer. The lower-class neighborhood was strictly for aborigines and it was located on the other side of the island and hidden in the thick woods. Naturally, the aborigines still lived in their ancestral grass huts and still ate their traditional fare of dung beetles, fish heads, and creasy salad for breakfast, lunch, and dinner.

Every upper-class family owned a machine or two while members of the middle-class were not allowed to own the machines they spent their working lives servicing and operating for the upper class. Of course, members of the lower class were not allowed even to touch a machine because they didn't know anything about machinery and didn't understand push buttons and levers. You see, machinery confuses the minds of members of the lower class and corrupts their morals. It's harder for an uneducated person to benefit from a machine, or anything else expensive, than it is for a Cadillac to get through the digestive system of a gnat.

In the few years since he first came to the island, Lug had learned a lot. He was now making some really good machines, so good that they looked just like people. In fact, Lug called them "virtual people." They were a little stiff legged, their thumbs didn't work just right, their voices were kind of scratchy, and their eyeballs quite often got stuck in their sockets and wouldn't roll around like they were supposed to. Just the same, you had to look twice before you could tell that the machines weren't actual people. There were three or four hundred of them by now. Lug put about a fifth of them in the upper class and promptly forgot he had done so. Lug had given these upper-class machines great big consumer glands and had programmed them for leisure-time behavior, especially for conspicuous-consumption activities. Even so, they never became the insatiable consumption machines that real people are. After all, they were just machines, not bottomless pits. These virtual people were fully integrated into the upper-class neighborhood into which they had been injected. You see? Integration does so work.

As Father Dollar and his party marched single file down the upper-class road, a lugmobile pulled up behind them and Lug himself got out. Lug was accompanied by two armed police machines and they really looked mean. Lug said, "Halt! Where do you think you're going? This is private property and you don't have a permit."

Father Dollar answered, "We are capitalist entrepreneurs and we come here merely to explore opportunities and make friends. We are not your competitors."

With that, Lug said, "I can see you are not our enemy from that other island. We've had much trouble from them and you can never be too cautious in a capitalist democracy like ours. Those others only want to take what we have and drag us down to their nasty level. Nevertheless, we are always glad to see friendly strangers and we welcome you as tourists. You can stay in our guesthouse for a few days if you like. There is only a nominal charge."

"Thank you, sir. I am Father Dollar, this is Sir Plastic Jesus, and these others are our employees." Of course, Father Dollar knew who Lug was just as, on that other island, Mother Church knew who Lud was; but neither of them was going to reveal anything. Lug did not know that the man he now welcomed was his father nor did Lud, on that other island, know that he was hosting his own mother. Can any man ever know how many rivers of strangers' blood flow in his own veins?

Lug used his maggot-cell phone to call for a lug bus to take his guests to the guesthouse. He rode along with them. On the sides of the road in several places there were dozens of rusty and dismembered machines. When Lug saw Elvin and Buck staring at the ruined machines, he said, "That's the work of savages from that other island. They hate machinery and regularly conduct raids against our peace and order. Prosperity and progress mean nothing to them. They are communist barbarians and are simply indulging in class warfare." Although Lug hadn't mentioned it, in the past he had himself launched many raids against that other island and had even tried to harm his own brother, Lud, by planting a deadly sneezing powder in his beard and dangerous fire crackers in his cigars. Lug had not succeeded in disabling or killing Lud but it had not been for lack of effort.

In truth, Lug's raids against Luds Island had been just about useless because there was nothing on Luds Island worth destroying. Worse yet, the hot spots and cold holes there were always tripping up Lug's raiding machines and disabling them. And the oraflex was the worst of all; it could gobble down three or four machines all at once. A big reason for this was that Lug's machines were honers, that is, they were engineered to seek out contrasting bands of heat and cold.

On the other hand, Lud's raids against Lugs Island were quite successful. Lud's people had learned how to use thermafrogs and floraroses to foul up and short out Lug's machines. You could throw a Thermafrog against a machine and it would stick. Apparently, the machine's heat instantly fried the cold Thermafrog and fused it right to the metal. Then, the Thermafrog frosted over the machine's electrical connections and shorted out its circuits. As for the florarose, you simply stuck one on the machine with a piece of masking tape or hung it loosely around the machine's neck or its shoulder. The heat of the machine then caused the florarose to grow so rapidly that it soon covered the machine and bound up all of its joints and moving parts. Thus hogtied, the machine fell down in a heap. And so Lud was winning the cold war but, of course, he wasn't really winning anything except revenge and moral satisfaction. Furthermore, it took considerable energy to keep the raids going for, you see, Lugs Island had a strong productive capacity and the workmen there could replace the machines faster than Lud's people could destroy them. Still, Lud kept on attacking even after Lug himself stopped retaliating and decided to simply increase his production. Actually, the cold war was good for Lug's economy and it kept patriotism at a high level. Although Lug enjoyed hating Lud, he came to feel that Lud's attacks were necessary and desirable. You see, brothers are sometimes useful, after all.

Lud was not using original Christians to carry out his raids or he might have been a little less fanatical. He had trained his simians to do the dirty work. To start a raid, he just put a dozen or so of them on a log and pushed it out toward Lugs Island. Once ashore on the island, they did the rest. They were very good at scampering around near the stomping feet of a bunch of machines without getting squashed. Sometimes, they even climbed up a leg or an arm and sat there on a machine's head or on one of its shoulders. Thus, it was very easy for a simian to reach into his shoulder sack and get a thermafrog or a florarose to attach to the machine. In quick order, the simians destroyed hundreds of machines and never took a single casualty of their own. They were much more effective at this kind of warfare than the machines were and they didn't require any fuel or upkeep at all. Maybe Lud was right to prefer animals to machines.

Father Dollar found a kindred spirit in Lug. They talked a good deal about free markets, supply and demand, money flow, goods and services, quality control, and the bottom line. Lug gave Father Dollar a tour of his machine factory and allowed him to inspect a fleet of new machines. Father Dollar thoroughly enjoyed himself and made copious notes about matters he hoped to include in a book he was writing called "The Joy of Capitalism." Father Dollar thought Lug a free-enterprise hero and a gifted inventor. How good it was for him to escape the frivolity of Graham Cracker's mindless religious crusade. Father Dollar thought that Graham Cracker had wasted a great opportunity for gaining new markets and new customers for the KBS in Farbelow Us. He was certain that, if he had been in charge, things would have been different and much more profitable. He was certainly glad that this summer crusade was about finished so he could return to the comfort of his Wall Street penthouse and the pleasure he drew from serving on his numerous boards and commissions. You see, the actor playing Father Dollar had gotten into his part so deeply that he had forgotten who he really was.

All the crusaders from both islands returned to their ships more or less refreshed and eager to sail for home. There were favorable winds and the weather was good. The trip home was uneventful. In port, Graham Cracker and his senior staff said goodbye to the student knights and dispersed to their several hearths and resting places. The student knights returned to Munchausen in high spirits, having survived and benefited from their first foreign crusade. Now, they were truly men of the world and knights for all seasons.

Chapter 7. Military and Police Power

Our Wars

Just about every American war has been falsely represented as a defense of the homeland and a fight for democracy. In fact, nearly all of our wars have been brutal and unprovoked attacks against other, weaker countries.

Over and over again, it is said that we must "support our boys over there" and that anyone who doesn't support the latest war is a traitor who is responsible for the injuries and deaths of our patriotic heroes. Opposition to these wars and any truthfulness about their purposes, aggressions, and atrocities is furiously put down and the "peaceniks" are vilified, jailed, and assaulted in the streets. The warmongers can't bear the thought that those Americans who fight their wars are anything less than noble patriots and crusading Christians protecting the rest of us from the evil attacks of foreign enemies out to invade our country, destroy our way of life, and enslave us.

All of this propaganda is quite insane. Even complete morons ought to be able to see that those who oppose war want to save the lives of our boys over there and that those who support war are directly responsible for their deaths and for the deaths of those they kill. As idiotic as this war propaganda is, however, it is fully embraced by nearly everyone. It flows from the television tubes, the radios, and the newspapers like lava from a volcano. Its intensity and fury is startling and obscene. Nothing is more shameful and less patriotic and Christian than this warmongering fanaticism.

The latest example of an unjust war, of course, is the murderous attack by George W. Bush against the innocent people of Iraq. To justify this war, every lie imaginable was manufactured and relentlessly pumped out by Bush and his aides. They said the Iraqis were responsible for the September 11th attack although none of the attackers were from Iraq and no Iraqi had anything whatever to do with the attack. They said that Saddam Hussein and Osama bin Laden were pals and that Saddam had helped bin Laden plan the attack although these two hated one another bitterly and, in fact, had never had any dealings at all. They said that Saddam had a mighty arsenal of weapons—more than 500 tons of poison gasses, a vast nuclear capability, and a highly sophisticated delivery system that could hit Washington or London within forty-five minutes.

In fact, Iraq possessed absolutely none of these weapons or any delivery capability at all. Iraq was, in truth, a completely devastated and weak country that had been utterly destroyed by more than twenty years of wars all of them either caused and supported by the United States or waged by it against the people of Iraq. Furthermore, no Iraqi, including Saddam Hussein, had ever made an attack against a single inch of American territory and had never threatened to do so. Neither have any Iraqis ever made an attack against a single American citizen except in self defense against those who assaulted them, their families, their friends, and their country on their own streets and inside their own homes.

After having lied this country into an invasion of Iraq and a cruel and incompetent occupation, the truth about Bush's WMD fabrications came to light—after which he began to lie about his lies. Then, he said, Saddam was a personification of the devil himself and, ignoring the fact that we helped him do it, Bush told us that Saddam had tortured and killed his own people. Thus, Bush said, his attack against the people of Iraq was actually a defense of the people of Iraq. He was killing them by the thousands to save them. Furthermore, Bush said, the Iraqis themselves supported his murderous war against them and their families and yearned for a Bush-imposed "democracy" managed entirely by giant American corporations and the US military.

This is where we stand now (2004)—with the American people about to return this dishonest, cowardly, and violent man to power for another four years so he can continue the killing and even extend it to as many as fifty or sixty other countries, according to his and Dick Cheney's own statements. Thus, clearly, a vote for Bush and Cheney will be a vote for many other wars against other innocent peoples who have never threatened or attacked us at all.

The simple truth is that we do not live in a decent country and the American people are not a decent people. They deserve George W. Bush and his never-ending wars. Let the killing and dying continue.

Total Surveillance

Now that Barack Obama has forgiven all of the crimes of the Bush/ Cheney gang, he has decided to continue their war on terrorism as well as their surveillance program. What kind of a democracy conducts a campaign of total surveillance over the messages of its entire population, more than three hundred million citizens, and including near total surveillance over the rest of the human race? Can such fanatical and indiscriminate behavior possibly increase the safety and security of the people of this country? The truth is so-called "terrorism" is an abstraction impossible to identify and exterminate by such massive and blindly exhaustive measures as those being used now. Violence is an indestructible and erratic but ubiquitous part of the human arsenal that cannot be extinguished or even accurately labeled or found inside the secret minds and hearts of political attackers. Efforts at such minute point-and-kill actions based on patterns, locations, associations, rhetoric, and affiliations are quite insane and they cannot ever combat any more than a tiny handful of potential enemies set on and capable of suicidal attacks against a collection of targets of almost infinite size. The U.S. consists of more than three hundred million ever-moving people and billions, probably trillions, of possible targets that themselves move and shift, form and disperse, dwindle and relocate all the time. I refer to large collections of people meeting with other people along with the enormous number of buildings—homes, offices, schools, cars, buses, trains, planes, ships, banks, military bases, police barracks, stadiums, arenas, field houses etc., etc., etc.— that make up the content of the American nation. The numbers are immense and the number of imagined enemies almost as large.

This country cannot possibly identify likely or even potential violence in this way and it certainly cannot act against such possible violence in a carefully narrow, timely, just, and accurate manner. These incredibly stupid efforts to predict violence before it happens and to label enormous collections of possible attackers by classifying everything remotely connected to their persons, families, tribes, movements, patterns of activity, guessed-at intentions, races, beliefs, dress, habits, cultures, etc., can only be described as senseless and counterproductive. Killing an occasional cipher or even a so-called high value target will do nothing to reduce the dangers from so-called terrorists. In this process, we are manufacturing new terrorists, new enemies every day. We are not solving the problem; we are making it much worse. And it's all about politics, all about avoiding any appearance of weakness or missed defensive action by politicians and other officials so that competing partisans can blame somebody else and can claim a toughness advantage over some competitor or domestic opponent. Al Qaeda and bin Laden accomplished their mission in spades. How the Americans reacted to the September 11th attack has caused thousands of times more destruction and distortion than all terrorist actions put together.

The so-called "war on terrorism" is pretty much a rerun of the cold war. The difference is that we have a much bigger collection of terrorist enemies now than we did when we were indiscriminately attacking mostly imagined communist enemies. Almost all of the communists the politicians—almost exclusively Republicans—were attacking during the cold war were completely innocent fellow citizens, namely Democrats, always liberals, and almost without exception government employees, civil servants. The Republicans hated their own country and their partisan opponents, and their war against communism had very little to do with communism. In other words, they made it up for political advantage and to satisfy their raging hatred of the democratic government of the United States. It was not a foreign war; it was a domestic war. This war on terrorism is similar and equally harmful to this country and to innocent people all over the world. And it is bloodily stupid besides.

Fake Patriotism

Anybody who falsifies his country's history in order to deceive citizens into believing patriotic things is disloyal. Believing in and acting on lies, even to the point of giving your life in battle, makes a citizen a fool, a dupe, and a victim. False prophets are not only crooked and corrupt; they are also subversive and traitorous. So-called patriotic organizations—like the American Legion—regularly falsify their country's history, especially its war history, and lie to the public while waving flags, displaying trophies and emblems, and uttering vapid words of self-praise and militant glorification. The false patriotism of such people is always accompanied by oaths in favor of every war, no matter how unjust, and includes bitter attacks against everyone who disagrees or anyone who dares to tell any part of the truth about the many atrocities and errors of America's militant warriors and its knee-jerk pro-war politicians.

The fact is, no country and no other organizational entity can ever improve itself and become even moderately just and decent until it looks at, tells about, and criticizes its own errors and offenses. Nothing is more patriotic or morally useful than the truth, especially the negative truth. To lie incessantly about yourself and those organizations to which you belong is an arrogant sin and a crime against reality. Self-improvement cannot come from self-delusion. You cannot correct a mistake unless you know you have made a mistake. Real patriotism can only be based on truth-telling and honest reform. Patriotic lying is just a way of undermining democracy and a nation's honor in the interest of the corrupt pride of old warriors and other false loyalists.

Bombing Civilians

How did it make sense to bomb the civilian populations of places like Iraq, Serbia, and Afghanistan as a way of punishing the dictators of those countries? Were Hussein, Milosevic, and the Taliban so tenderhearted toward their own people that they would obey the US in order to lessen the suffering of their own citizens? Were they more compassionate than our own leaders? It seemed so or, at least, our own leaders seemed to think so.

Without question, Hussein, Milosevic, and the Taliban had many enemies among their own people. Why did we bomb those innocents, people who were on our side and against their own leaders? When you bomb a whole people, when you kill members of their families and their friends, you turn them all into enemies and patriots. You turn them all into supporters of their own country's leadership, evil though it may seem to them. Not only do you make enemies of them for today but for all time. You can't attack people unjustly and not arouse their hatred. Bombing somebody, invading their country is not a rational way to punish their leaders or make the population democratic and pro-American. Democracy does not grow out of the barrel of a gun and bombs do not spread good will toward men and women or establish any version of civility. When at long last will the world's people outlaw the senseless and counterproductive bombing of innocent civilian populations?

Our Military System

There is nothing the American military doesn't have. It is a culture entire unto itself. It is one of the largest dictatorships in the world. It has its own pay and retirement systems, guaranteed medical care for everyone, its own hospitals and doctors, its own night clubs and bars, its own ships, busses, trucks, trains, planes, and cars, its own beaches, golf courses, and swimming pools, its own radio and television stations, its own sports teams and stadiums. It even has its own businesses, its own advertising and propaganda arms, its own internal police agencies and international spy operations. In fact, each branch of the military has its very own internal army, navy, and air force. Excepting entire large countries, only the Catholic Church is richer and more dictatorial than the American military.

Invading Panama

When George Bush the elder invaded Panama, his hidden purpose was strictly political; he thought the war would be popular and that it would help him win another term. He learned from Reagan that a quick, cheap war is a good political tactic, no matter how many innocent people are killed.

With the conquest of Panama under their belts, Bush then told us that all of the Latin American leaders who had condemned our invasion publicly were secretly in favor of it. We had every reason to believe our leaders were lying to us again but, for the sake of argument, let's suppose it was true that the Latin American leaders secretly supported the American attack. Then, we have to ask: What reason could there have been for their pretended opposition to our attack. Who were they afraid of? It was quite clear: They were afraid of their own people. There is no other possible conclusion. The people of Latin America were against the invasion and, indeed, against all aggressions by the United States against Latin countries.

Courage

The concept of courage serves the establishment very well. If soldiers themselves make attacking a point of honor and retreating a disgrace, then self-sacrifice becomes the norm and self-preservation cowardly. I wonder if, in the dimness of the past, some maximum leader calculated this point and instituted the idea of honor and courage just so the warriors would serve the mission of the leader. Honor and courage have long since become great virtues in and of themselves without any recognition of the ultimate goals they are used to advance. Even Nazis, communists, and other such villains have their honor and courage, and our side sometimes admits that they do. Of course, if the other guy is courageous and you kill him, then you must be even more courageous than he was.

Thus, the two sides reinforce their shared devotion to the code of honor raised up every day by the world's military forces. It is soldiers who sometimes praise the enemy, never politicians or any of the other safe patriots back home. For them, courage and honor are reserved for the home boys, never for the Nazis or the dirty rotten communists lurking sneakily in the jungles disguised as brave men and women out to defend their country at any cost. We are brave. They are fanatical.

War Mongers

Soldiers at war don't and can't admit the truth, even to themselves. The truth is that they are almost always fighting for a bad cause and they are almost always killing people at least as good and as innocent as they think they are. They are the victims of politicians and generals who lie to them about their duty and the nobility and necessity of the cause they have been persuaded or forced to kill and die for.

Even when you are the obvious attacker, the invader, the occupier, the aggressor, you will not be able to think well of the people who justly resist your attack. When they threaten your life or wound or kill your comrades in self-defense, you will become hostile to them and you will hate them. It is inevitable. It is the trap soldiers are caught in even against their natural tendency to be just and not to wantonly hurt and kill others. It is a soldier's duty to kill on command and it doesn't matter how dishonest the command is or how unjust the attack is. He is required to obey on pain of imprisonment or death.

It is a favorite trick of politicians and other war mongers to get the troops to tell the home folks how noble the mission is, how pure the politicians' motives are, and how evil the enemy is. Quite often, they also exploit the emotions of the parents and relatives of dead or wounded soldiers. A sacrificed victim won't be condemned by loved ones and his cause will rarely be rejected, however irrational and immoral it was. It's hard for a family to accept the sad truth that they lost a son or daughter for nothing or, even worse, for a politician's political career or for some cowardly and sick dream of conquest, profit, and reflected glory.

Some few parents do see through the lies and ambitions of the politicians. But, if any parent or any person dares to object to unjust or unnecessary war, they will be smeared and condemned as traitors by the politicians and their followers. The war lovers will attack the "peaceniks" and will say crazily that it is those who oppose the war who are responsible for the harm and death that comes from that war. They will say dishonestly that the dissenters are not supporting our boys over there and are literally causing their deaths. They will say that the dissenters are helping the enemy and they will try to shame, imprison, or silence them. Sometimes they will even physically attack their own fellow citizens for not being as murderous and as compliant as they are. War corrupts all motives, reduces all rational judgment to violent, nationalistic hatred. Warmongers always reverse the truth so they can justify their immoral behavior. The fury of their patriotism is caused by their guilt.

When wars end, the troops want to be celebrated for their sacrifice. They return home and are glorified as flags fly and bands play. Many of them spend the rest of their lives reliving glories that never were, lapping up the adoration of the false patriots who stayed at home and cheered them on as they maimed and killed others. After the Vietnam War and still today, some of them went on the attack against such courageous war critics as Jane Fonda, Joan Baez, Cindy Sheehan, and John Kerry. Those warmongers thus keep their self-glorification alive by continuing to wage their personal war against dissent long after the real war has ended. Unable to face the truth of their own viciousness and personal corruption, they try to destroy those who favored peace and human decency. Those warmongers claim to be patriots. They are not. They are traitors.

Here I want to insert some quotes from Cindy Sheehan who lost her son in the Iraq war and became a bitter critic of the Bush administration as a result.

> George Bush has made the Christian faith an obscenity. To rationalize what he's doing in Iraq because God told him to do it or to make Jesus some kind of warmonger is another immorality. And for people in America to buy that?...That is just so hypocritical and wrong beyond anything.

> And I know that the Jesus that I studied about in the Gospels would not approve of what George Bush is doing....

> We have to get our troops home. A Mission Accomplished would be for the Iraqi people to rebuild their government and have whatever system of government they want. Because—you know what?—It's their country. It's not the fifty-first state of America....

> We've made a horrible mess of that country. The people there want peace, they want their electricity back, they want their water back, and they want their jobs. They want America out....

> You can't be successful in Iraq. The generals on the ground have said that. There is not a military solution.... It's insane. Are we fighting terrorism or are we creating terrorism? Obviously, we're creating terrorism and an insurgency by our military presence there.

> We all have lost a loved one in war. I say *lost*, but I don't like that euphemism because Casey wasn't lost; he was killed by George Bush's murderous policies in the Middle East.

> —Cindy Sheehan, interview with David Barsamian, *The Progressive*, March 2006.

Distance of Generals from Battle

In time of war, do common soldiers and the people at home ever notice the ratio between distance from battle and military rank? All the way up front, under the shellfire, are the privates and corporals. Just behind them are the sergeants and lieutenants. At a medium distance back, at company headquarters, are the captains and an occasional major. Most of the majors and the colonels are well behind the front lines, at battalion and regimental headquarters. Except for an occasional drive-through or fly-over by the most daring of the lot, the generals are nowhere to be found. They are far back, in a major city somewhere, at a safe distance from the main line of battle and well protected from enemy attack or much discomfort.

Most of the generals and many colonels are in another country altogether or even at home in the United States directing the "strategic" phase of the conflict from the comfort of their big homes and plush offices (Strategy is accurately defined as vague planning at a comfortable distance by high-level officials). The Joint Chiefs, the Secretary of Defense, and the President sit in Washington in their palaces and their oval and pentagon-shaped imperial suites sending tough messages to the front by long-range communications, waving flags in public, making patriotic speeches, cursing the enemy, attacking "treasonous" journalists who dare to criticize the war, and rounding up citizens who don't want to fight or who think the war is unnecessary or unjust.

Battle of New Orleans

Andrew Jackson's victory in the Battle of New Orleans was one of the few times when American military forces (excepting the Marines) fought bravely and smartly against a superior foe and won. In modern times, the American military wins battles and sometimes (rarely) whole wars by overwhelming the enemy with greater manpower, vastly superior technology, and with a great flood of supplies put in place by an incredibly expensive logistics system extending half way around the world.

When it comes to fighting face to face on the ground, however, Americans usually lose and, when the war is a guerilla war supported by the population, the Americans always lose. The American Marines are an exception. They almost always win their battles because of their spirit, pride, and leadership. However, there are not very many of them and they cannot win whole wars by themselves.

In spite of the general incompetence of the American military, the generals, the politicians, and the old soldiers incessantly pump out a completely imaginary version of the country's military prowess and its success in wars. Many of them, for example, claim that the United States military saved France and all of Europe from the Germans in the two world wars. There is no truth to this at all except that the United States did indeed supply the allied forces and those wars (especially the Second World War) probably could not have been won without the American supplies.

In the First World War, the American troops entered the war very late, after the bulk of the fighting was over; at that point, a stalemate existed and the fresh American troops did tip the balance to the allies. In the Second World War, it was the Soviet army that fought the largest part of the German army and inflicted most of its casualties. The American and English forces were the "second front" and, while many of them fought bravely and won a number of battles, the war was decided, for the most part, on the Eastern front. The Soviets killed most of the Germans, about eighty percent of the total, and took most of the casualties. They lost between 25 and 30 million of their citizens in the war, the Americans about 300,000.

America's fake patriots do a lot of bragging about themselves and go to great lengths to downgrade the contributions and the suffering of their allies and the competence and bravery of the enemy. It's too bad they don't understand just how deeply immoral their phony patriotism really is. It does them no honor.

Reagan's Militarization

The Reagan administration simply threw trillions of dollars to the military to do with as it chose. The military was not streamlined or made more accountable or more efficient as a result nor was it made more powerful or more effective. It was simply made larger, richer, and softer. With its new riches, it bought more creature comforts, more staff luxuries, and more ineffective and inoperable war toys to play with. It hugely increased its own bureaucracy and its administrative waste. It became fatter and lazier in every way. It bought more useless contrivances and gee gaws, prettier uniforms, shinier shoes and buttons, bigger bases and more comfortable barracks, higher salaries, more expensive housing and support services for dependents—in other words, more welfare and more hardware.

No great new weapons were invented during the Reagan years. There were no important technological advances. The military was not reformed and no new tactical or strategic systems were initiated. In fact, the military system was not changed in any serious way at all. It simply bought more and the more it bought was not useful or useable. Like all excess, it was pure waste and had no sensible purpose beyond its propaganda value. It was never used and never could have been used. It was a substitute for patriotism and an excuse for ignoring the real needs of the American people.

Invasion of Vietnam

It is surely no surprise that those who want independence and self-rule for their country should kill those of their countrymen who collaborate with colonial occupiers and who enrich themselves by accepting money and position from those enemy aliens. This is what happened in Vietnam.

The United States invaded Vietnam and imposed a whole series of military dictators on the people there. It established an infrastructure to support its military machine and bought the loyalty of various Vietnamese in Saigon and in the villages. Naturally, the people despised the traitors and sometimes killed them. The overwhelming majority of the people—north and south—opposed the occupation and wanted the invaders out. The Americans knew this very well but kept on attacking anyway. They kept insisting stubbornly that the issue was communism, but it was not. The issue was the right of the people of Vietnam to choose their own form of government and their own rulers. They were fighting for their independence from French colonialism and then from American dictatorship.

The Americans claimed they were saving the people of South Vietnam from a bloodbath but, in fact, they were themselves carrying out a bloody assault against the Vietnamese. The invaders killed from three to four million people according to Robert McNamara, injured many more, and destroyed the homes of one third of the sixteen million people who lived in South Vietnam. The total killed in the two halves of Vietnam was five million. Yet, the generals claimed they were being restrained unfairly, that they weren't killing and hurting nearly enough people, and that they were being forced to fight a "no-win" war by the politicians at home. These were the exact same things they said about the Korean War.

It was the conservative Republicans who originated these lies as a part of their fanatical devotion to their ridiculous anti-communist crusade. Anti-communism was a conservative opiate and it led the United States into a sick addiction never equaled by the effects of any ordinary drug. This craze to kill communists led to the vast atrocity of the war against the people of Vietnam.

Forcing Democracy

If you really believe in democracy, or at least in democratic elections, you have to accept that you can't get what you want in places like Vietnam, Iraq, Syria, Lebanon, Palestine, and Israel. The people in most of those countries live lives enflamed by fundamentalist religions and, except for Israel, they aren't going to vote for George Bush, American corporations, or the US military. Although they haven't been on offer during this country's recent aggressions, they aren't going to vote for American liberalism or secularism either.

In truth, Americans themselves don't vote for liberalism or secularism anymore. Instead, they embrace the Republican hatred for democratic and secular government here at home and overseas too. And they vote as well for an ill-defined and so-far incomplete theocracy being put in place every hour of every day under the cover of the Bush administration's Christianizing policies.

Astonishingly, the Democratic Party and the establishment media both refuse to recognize that Bush and his cohorts are fascists and tyrants of the most obvious kind. To claim that the Bushes are sincere democrats trying to spread the American word by military invasion and occupation is worse than crazy. Only lunatics believe you can spread democracy by force. Democracy is free choice by definition and you can't force people to make free choices. Furthermore, the Republicans aren't democrats in Iraq or anywhere else.

Real democrats don't claim that absolutely no law applies to them and that they can arbitrarily arrest anyone they want to arrest, make no charges against them, tell them nothing about their supposed crimes, allow them no legal representatives, abuse them and torture them, convict them without any evidence or any proper defense, allow them no appeal, and then render them or execute them, all of this without any oversight by Congress, the courts, or the American people.

Democrats don't run massive and surreptitious surveillance systems either, or at least they didn't until Barack Obama became president and began to imitate George W. Bush, and they don't win elections by corrupting the electoral machinery, by suppressing the voting of minorities and others unlikely to vote for them, by viciously smearing opponents with the most incredible accusations imaginable, or by hiding behind an enormous collection of extreme, insistent, aggressive, and bizarre lies about false enemies such as the Iraqis, the Iranians, and the Palestinians.

There is nothing democratic about the Republican Party or about the DLC Democrats and "liberal hawks" who nestle up to Bush while expressing a vile and sick hatred for anyone who opposes Bush's brutal and illegal wars. Perhaps the most disgusting thing about the rise of George W. Bush and his twisted reign is the fanatical support of tens of millions of people who call themselves Christians but who nevertheless voted for and insist on policies and practices so sadistic and bloodthirsty that they far surpass the indiscriminate evil of bin Laden's attack on this country on September 11, 2001. That such people claim that they are emulating Jesus is fantastic and perverted. They are the enemies of everything Jesus ever stood for or said. They are not Christians at all and neither is George Bush.

Bush's Version of Democracy

Trying to impose democracy on a country is like trying to impose virginity on a whore. It can't be done. And yet a collection of self-described liberal hawks praise George W. Bush for trying to force his fake democracy on the Muslim and Arab world. By the way, the term "liberal hawk" is as much a corruption of language as is the term "virginal whore." Decent liberals are doves, not hawks.

Bush doesn't believe in democracy. Neither does anyone else in the Republican Party, least of all the neoconservative imperialists and their allies, the "liberal" hawks. The Bush administration adamantly opposed elections in Iraq because its members knew the Shia (allies of Iran) would win but the threat of massive opposition by the Shia leadership forced them to stage an election, which they then tried to corrupt. That election decided nothing and was not democratic but it pleased a lot of superficial people and it allowed Bush to pose as a democrat.

It really ought to be self evident that you can't force a choice on anyone. An occupied and manipulated country can never conduct "democratic" elections and, of course, the election in Iraq was conducted entirely by the occupier and its agents. The occupier had all the power and all the guns, made all of the rules, and pre-approved all of the candidates. And, when there are large self-interested factions in a bitterly divided country as was the case in Iraq, any election is bound to be about control, not about any level of free choice.

The Bush gangsters are engaged in a self-deluded contradiction: they are supporting a faction that they oppose. I mean the Shia. As for the Kurds, they too were engaged in a contradiction. They were cynically voting to destroy the country they were determined to separate themselves from. They were merely helping Bush create an illusion of orderly progress so they could stand aside and observe the carnage sure to emerge from the fraud. The only people fooled by it were those in the U.S. electorate.

Bush has completely destabilized Iraq and the whole Middle East. No American attack against Iraq could possibly have resulted in anything other than disunion, disorder, and disaster. You can't compel a voluntary union of separate peoples whose goals all contradict and oppose one another. As for democracy, it was never an honest goal by Bush or any of the players in the ridiculous charade they arranged for Iraq.

When Bush spoke of "democracy," he was falsifying his aims, disguising the real purposes and beliefs. Republicans simply don't believe in democracy. In unguarded moments, they publicly rage against democratic government and complain bitterly about the "rights" of the people. How many times did Reagan express his hatred for the democratic government of the United States? How many attacks have the Republicans made against civil rights and human rights? How often have they told us of their contempt for working people and their unions, of their disgust with every public program and every public institution. How often have they tried to privatize everything public and democratic in existence? When have they ever supported any plan or any intention by government or even civil institutions to advance the welfare of the people of this or any other country? The answer is never.

No, the Republicans don't believe in democracy and no one should be foolish enough any longer to think that they do. In one way or another, they corrupt every election, use the vilest kind of slander and false accusation against their Democratic opponents, especially the dwindling fraction who still dare to call themselves "liberals" or "progressives." Quite plainly, the Republican Party is un-American and it dehumanizes and corrupts everything it touches. And the DLC Democrats are no better.

Lying About the Taliban

Why do so many journalists fuzz up the facts to make it seem that there was something legitimate about the Bush administration's determination to widen the guilt and the "war" itself to include people who had nothing to do with the September 11th attack against this country. Paul Starr wrote in the January/February issue of The American Prospect that "The legitimate objectives after September 11 were the defeat of the al-Qaeda network of terrorists who had attacked us, the overthrow of the Taliban regime that harbored them, the elimination of other enclaves where terrorists could train and organize, and the strengthening of moderate Islamic forces that could combat Muslim extremism." This kind of fuzzy and over-complex thinking is just what enabled Bush to launch a world war against millions of innocent people. Neither the Taliban nor any other Muslims, other than al Qaeda, had anything to do with the September 11th attack.

Were the Taliban bad guys? Yes, because they were religious extremists who oppressed their subjects but the world is full of such people and we have plenty of them right here in the United States, including George W. Bush. Did the Taliban harbor al Qaeda? In a very vague and indirect way, that charge holds a little water but not much. The Taliban didn't exist when bin Laden and his Arab gang came to Afghanistan. It was the Reagan administration that put al Qaeda in those caves, armed them, and supported them along with the rest of the Mujahideen. After that, the Taliban themselves came into existence on the borders of Afghanistan in a group of schools created by Arabists in the maelstrom of refugee enclaves set up as a result of Reagan's anti-communist proxy war. The schools that trained the students who became the Taliban were Wahabist, a violent Saudi sect supported by the US right along with the other Mujahideen forces supported and celebrated as freedom fighters by Reagan.

When the Taliban overthrew other murderous elements of Reagan's collection of "freedom fighters" (the Northern Alliance) with the backing of the Pashtun people, bin Laden gave them money. You might call it rent. The

Taliban didn't know a thing about the al Qaeda attack; they played no role in it at all. If a rat gnaws off your big toe and you're sane, you don't ignore the rat, then grab a gun and start killing all of the monkeys in the neighborhood in the stupid belief that the monkeys are in cahoots with the rat or that they are "harboring" him.

The Bush administration launched a general war against the people of Afghanistan, including the Taliban government. It was a distraction. The attack should have been directed like a laser beam against the real enemy, bin Laden and his al Qaeda gang. The US could have won that "war" very quickly. It could have exterminated al Qaeda almost entirely.

Furthermore, the whole world would have supported that goal, including just about the entire Muslim world. But that was not what Bush and Cheney wanted. They wanted a much wider war. They wanted a war that would keep them in power for another term, one that would give them near total power over the American people as well as the entire Middle East and the oil there. That's why they then very quickly attacked the wholly innocent people of Iraq. This was no war against terrorism. There was no worldwide attack by Islam extremists and there was no clash of civilizations. The US had very few serious enemies in the Muslim world but Bush and Cheney created hundreds of millions of new enemies all around the world, including most Muslims. And the United States will regret the instability Bush created in the Middle East, especially in Palestine, Syria, Iraq, Iran, Egypt, and Turkey.

Crazy Generals

The trench warfare of World War One was obscene and ridiculous. Here were two mighty armies facing one another from long holes in the ground from which the shooters had to protrude their guns and their heads to shoot at the enemy, usually to no effect. From time-to-time, just to satisfy the goofy generals on one side or the other, the troops on one side would emerge from their holes and charge directly into the gunfire of their hidden enemy on the other side. These charges were suicidal and served no purpose whatever.

When the charging units did manage to breach the barbed wire and get some of their troops through the heavy gunfire and into enemy trenches, they were usually outnumbered by the enemy in the trench and were immediately shot at close range or bayoneted to death. Once in a great while, the attackers actually succeeded in seizing a trench or two from the enemy and thus gained a few yards of completely useless land that was of absolutely no strategic or tactical value.

These trench battles were fought without sane objectives or any hope of winning anything and the side that always had most of the casualties was the aggressive side. Time and time again, absolutely moronic generals made senseless attacks out of false pride and arrogant impatience and without any regard at all for the lives of their underlings. One can understand battles and even whole wars of movement and tactical cleverness but no one can understand battles or wars of mutual, irrational, self-induced slaughter.

Punishment and Crime

Everybody, it seems, believes that severe punishment is the solution to criminal behavior. It doesn't occur to them that punishment is one of the prime causes of criminal behavior in the first place. Unless you believe that some people are inherently criminal, then you must believe that they behave badly because they are treated badly. Surely it is no stretch to believe that vengeful, resentful, embittered, angry people are more likely to commit crimes than are fulfilled, satisfied, nourished people.

The prisons are full of poor and uneducated people. Sure, there are some middle-class and upper class people there but not many. Conservatives would like us to believe that this is because some are inferior to others, that the lower classes are inherently unfit. For these conservatives, the capitalist economic system is a kind of barometer that measures the fitness and unfitness of people. Thus, having money and status is proof of your fitness; not having them is a good predictor of unfitness and probable criminality.

It's very strange that conservatives believe they can make the unfit fit by beating them up and throwing them in jail. How can you possibly help people or reform them by hurting them? But then again maybe the conservatives just want to incapacitate or exterminate everyone who isn't useful or profitable to them. When you believe that people are unreformable, then it's easy to disable or do away with them.

Censoring Displays of Violence

It's truly absurd to claim that the display of violence in movies, on television, or in songs literally causes people to commit violent acts. No doubt there is some vague correlation between the depiction of violence and the presence of violence in a culture but it does not follow that the first causes the last. It makes much better sense to say that the prevalence of violence in a culture causes storytellers and songwriters to depict what they see around them in their creations. Without much question, American culture is among the most thoroughly violent in the history of mankind. It didn't get that way because there is too much freedom of expression. Artificial representations of violence do not cause the real thing. No, there are other causes.

American culture is extremely aggressive and acquisitive and everyone is armed. In one way or another, people in America take what they want and they are invariably praised for their initiative, enterprise, and success in doing so. Capitalism is a way of exploiting and using others for personal gain, of victimizing them. Climbing over the bodies of other people is what rapacious capitalism does. Favorite terms used to describe this syndrome are "individualism," "competition," "free enterprise," "free-marketism," etc. Turning people into economic predators is hardly a formula for harmonious cooperation and nonviolence.

Christianity is also predatory. Evangelizing is a way of attacking other people for the purpose of converting them into believers. Of course, the idea always is to pressure these impure people until they cleanse themselves by agreeing entirely with the belief of the crusaders. You see, their own beliefs are considered dirty and evil and entirely unworthy of respect or tolerance. The idea is to save them from themselves and from some competing religion or ideology.

Intolerance of others and disapproval of their way of life are characteristics of evangelizers. These religious predators are very energetic and very aggressive in their attacks against the beliefs and the behavior of others. Throughout the history of Christianity, they have been on the attack. In fact they and their colonialist enablers have killed millions in their quest for converts.

One such evangelizer, Billy Graham, has spent his entire life traveling the world for the sole purpose of converting others to his belief system. In the process, he regularly condemns and chastises all of those who do not absolutely share his dogma. Public conversion display is his one goal in life. He even counts them up like dollars in the bank. He claims to be working for god but it is only his particular god that he approves of and tolerates. He is not a man who believes in tolerance for different others or cooperation with them. He wants to change every one on earth so that they become just like him in what they believe. Otherwise, they are sinners and god is going to punish them with an utterly brutal torture in a chamber of horrors called hell. In short, Billy Graham is a predator and an avenger for his god, just like our commercial masters.

Nature of Censorship

What's astonishing about those who want censorship is how little they understand the nature of the repression they favor.

If you stand outside a culture and look at all of its expressions in music, literature, painting, speech, and the like, you might think that certain of those expressions are obscene or otherwise unworthy of acceptance. If you censor those expressions, then none of your fellow citizens can ever see them, hear them, or even know of their existence. They cannot know anything about those things you have shielded from their senses and, therefore, they can make no free choices of their own. In other words, they are entirely dependent on your decisions about what they can hear and see and say. You are thus automatically superior to them in knowledge and free choice and you are their absolute ruler and controller. Such an environment is not just intolerable but also totalitarian.

Perhaps there are sincere people who want to censor things but, if so, they are deeply ignorant and recklessly intolerant. They do not respect the freedom of others or trust them to lead their own lives and make their own choices. The worst of this lot are the sexual puritans and the political conservatives. They don't care about the freedom of the people; they only care about the triumph of their sick dogma.

The Gun Frenzy

In 2008, the five Republican justices on the Supreme Court ruled, in *District of Columbia v. Heller*, that the right of individuals to bear arms protected them from firearms regulations in federal enclaves. Then, in June of 2010, those justices ruled, in *McDonald v. the City of Chicago*, that the *Heller* decision extended to states and cities. In that decision, Justice Samuel Alito insisted that the right to bear arms was a "fundamental" right. These rulings are obvious distortions of the plain language of the Second Amendment of the Constitution. For something like two hundred years, the meaning of the Second Amendment was understood by everyone, including all Supreme Court justices, to refer to a militia only. The court is now resorting to radical and extremist rulings that have no precedent in American history.

The Second Amendment says, "A well regulated militia, being necessary to the security of a free state, the right of the people to keep and bear arms, shall not be infringed." This does not mean and cannot mean that every individual citizen has a right to keep and bear arms.

When a sentence begins with the words "A well regulated militia, being necessary to the security of a free state" and then, after a comma, follows those words with "the right of the people to keep and bear arms," no sane person can throw away the initial words and jump to the never stated or even implied conclusion that the sentence is about an individual and an absolute right that has nothing to do with the initial words. This is simple grammar. Those initial words are not extraneous; they qualify the words that follow and limit those following words to the initially stated conditions. In other words, they refer to a militia and only to a militia and not at all to an individual right standing alone and outside the bounds of a formally established militia.

The Founding Fathers were not stupid men. They knew how to say what they meant. Had they meant to establish an absolute right to bear arms, they would have said so without any reference to a militia or to security. They would have left out the first twelve words of that sentence and it would have said, "The right of the people to keep and bear arms shall not be infringed." They clearly did not establish an absolute and unqualified right for every citizen to bear arms. As usual, the five Republican justices are corrupting the words of the Constitution to make them agree with the extremist views of their political party. They do not believe in the literal or original meaning of the words of the Constitution as they pretend. Indeed, they are incapable of reading a simple sentence and understanding what it says.

Some have argued that the word "militia" means the whole people. It cannot be so. Unlike life under a divine king, the people have a right to change governments by voting. They don't need to do it by force. When voting is corrupted and there is no fair voting (as is the case right now, in 2015), there might well be a moral case for violent revolt as in the American Revolution. However, it makes no sense to say that the government has given some armed citizens its permission to use arms to overthrow the rest of the people.

A government cannot give some citizens the right to overthrow it by force. Such a view is utterly senseless. However, if some are treasonous enough to want to overthrow their elected government and they cannot do it by voting or some peaceful method, then they must resort to armed force and take their chances. They don't need nor does it make any sense to say that they have the advance permission of the government to overthrow it.

The National Rifle Association represents a huge collection of arms manufacturers and sellers. It has enormous amounts of money, it controls the Republican Party completely, and it has great influence in the Democratic Party. Its methods are immoral and anti-democratic. It lies and manipulates without conscience. It twists and distorts the meaning of the Second Amendment. It corrupts elections, all to guarantee the massive profits of arms makers and sellers. It enables and causes levels of murder and mayhem that in total hugely exceed the deaths from war. Unfortunately, many decent citizens support this immoral lobby because they have been deceived into believing that there is an absolute "right to own and bear arms" in the constitution.

If you can't understand that it's foolish to make it much easier to kill people by randomly giving large numbers of guns to people whose natures and inclinations you cannot know in advance, then you're far out of touch with reality. That millions of NRA supporters should deny this is fantastic. The NRA argues, in effect, that the total elimination of guns would result in a massive number of deaths by gunfire. The other end of their argument is that one hundred percent ownership of guns by the population would eliminate all deaths by gunfire. As starkly incredible as this belief system is, it is precisely what the NRA types believe or say they believe. Right now, there are almost as many guns in the United States as there are people and some conservative politicians want to make gun ownership mandatory for all citizens, including children, criminals, and the demented.

In 1996 in Port Arthur, Australia, a gunman killed thirty-five people with a semiautomatic rifle. The people of that country then passed a law that made it nearly impossible for anyone to get assault weapons and large ammunition clips. There are now very strict permit laws for all firearms, and dealers are required to register sales. People were encouraged to sell their guns to the government; 700,000 were bought and destroyed. A Harvard University study shows that there were thirteen gun massacres in the eighteen years before the law and, in the sixteen years since, there have been none at all. Gun related homicide dropped by fifty nine percent and gun suicide dropped by sixty five percent.

The U.S. homicide rate is 747 times higher than Norway's and five times higher than Germany's. Australia's, after the gun law, is 142 percent lower. You are forty times less likely to be killed in Australia, with a murder rate of 0.09. Singapore had a murder rate of 0.02; you are two hundred times more likely to be killed in the U.S. than in Singapore. In the U.S. in 2012, the national average of people killed per 100,000 was ten. In Connecticut, it is four per 100,000. In Louisiana, it is twenty per 100,000 and, there, forty five percent of all households own guns. In 2012, 20,000 people in the U.S. used guns to kill themselves; 8,000 veterans did so, in most cases using a gun.

Some have many guns and some have only a few or none. However, if the guns were distributed evenly over the population, then eighty percent of Americans could own a gun, reports the U.K.'s *Guardian* newspaper. In Japan, it's less than one percent. In the U.K., it's roughly six percent.

Gunshot wounds and deaths cost Americans at least $12 billion a year. A study by Ted Miller found that gunfire deaths and injuries cost $32 per gun. In 1992, medical care for a fatal shooting averaged $14,500. In 2010, it went up to $28,700. Miller also found that Medicaid covered twenty eight percent of admissions for firearms injuries, thirty seven percent of hospital days, and forty two percent of medical costs.

This is a violent and crazy country. Some towns are considering a local ordinance to make gun ownership mandatory. Augusta, Maine, was considering such an ordinance in 2013. In many places, there are laws allowing, even encouraging, teachers to bear arms in their classrooms. A number of cities and states allow guns in schools, even in the hands of children, and in bars and restaurants as well. The federal government has now opened up national parks and forests to gun bearers.

There are 7,000 U.S. gun dealers within 100 miles of Mexico. From the end of 2006 to April of 2010, the Mexican army seized 31,946 handguns and 41,093 assault rifles. Of those that could be traced, eighty percent came from the United States. Needless to say, massive numbers of people are being slaughtered every day in Mexico by American guns. In May of 2010, Felipe Calderon, the Mexican president, all but begged the U.S. Congress to stop the flow of assault weapons into Mexico. Nothing at all has been done.

Fanatical gun love is a perversion, a sickness. Male gun lovers love their guns more than they do their wives and children and much more than they do their country. Now, even many women have caught the macho disease and are proudly arming themselves against their fellow citizens. They all think that "liberty" is defined entirely as the love of guns and as a bitter hatred of the democratic government of the United States for even mentioning any regulation whatever of guns and magazines.

CHAPTER 8. THE REPUBLICAN COMPLEX

Clear Definitions

When speaking of the Republican complex, clear definitions are hard to come by. Whether the Republicans are a part of a conservative complex or the conservatives are a part of a Republican complex is not easy to decide. If a conservative complex is the big tent, then it includes quite a few Democrats. On the other hand, the Republican Party excludes those Democrats at least as formal members but includes them as voting partners on conservative issues and on propaganda forays. So it must be said that, in politics, there are a number of overlapping sects arranged in confusing and self-contradictory patterns.

Though conservatives and libertarians claim to see a great difference in them, republicanism and democratism are the very same thing. Theoretically at least, both support majority rule and, in America and Western Europe, both support a bundle of minority and individual rights that trump the sometimes-oppressive attacks of majoritarian aggressors. Originally, Jefferson's liberal party was called the "Democratic-Republican Party." The word "Republican" was dropped because it was redundant. When a new, largely abolitionist party was formed just before the Civil War, it called itself the "Republican Party." In a short time (1876), it changed its policy drastically from abolitionism to acceptance of Southern discriminatory segregation, under a "Southern Strategy" which continues today. At roughly the same time, the Republican Party became the big business party. Its covering philosophy was social Darwinism and Eugenicism. Thus, the Republican Party is not today republican or democratic, whatever nuances the conservatives try to impose on the two terms.

And it doesn't end with Republicans, conservatives, and libertarians. There are the neoconservatives, for example, and there are many religious and commercial groupings that have their own ideological and faith dogmas to push into the political sphere. The libertarian movement has superimposed itself on the Republican Party very effectively. The neoconservative movement itself is largely Zionist and always intensely pro-Israel. It dominated the foreign policy actions of the Republican Party during the Ronald Reagan and the George W. Bush administrations, and it has near-total control over both parties on all issues touching Israel and the American war against the Muslim world in Israel's interest.

Then, there are large numbers of religious groupings that, under Republican force, have been pushed into the political and ideological mix against the secular traditions of this country. In other words, the Republicans have forced religion blatantly into election and issue campaigns and have quite deliberately undermined democracy itself for, without a firm secularism, there can be no true democracy or any religious freedom. The Republicans have done this cynically and without conscience because it gives them political advantage. They want to rule and they don't care how much they have to corrupt this country in order to grab and keep political power for themselves and their corporate clients.

Christianity itself consists of a group of organizations that can only be described as corporations, in fact specially privileged corporations. The Christian religions are vastly but not exclusively conservative and Republican. This is true with a vengeance of the evangelical and fundamentalist Protestants and the Catholic traditionalists. Since the rise of the "moral majority" in support of Richard Nixon, the Christian religion has become a big player in the political game. Except for the Christian attacks against Thomas Jefferson in the 1800 election, this was not often true in the past in this country. Most politicians in both parties used to leave religion out of their political campaigns because they believed that government should not be religious and that religious freedom depended on this neutralism.

The Republican Party is the corporatist party in America and it has drawn the conservative religions into its corporatist maw and, in the process, has redefined the political function almost entirely to the considerable consternation and confusion of the Democrats. Because the Democrats refuse to name or openly confront the corporatist (that is, fascist) nature of the Republican Party, they simply will not fight back and they persist in an astonishing effort to court the Republicans by surrendering to them on nearly every issue, frequently by compromising their own fundamental principles almost out of existence.

Republican Intransigence

Democrats have no taste for combat. The Republicans know they are always willing to bow down submissively and so they take trenchant and unyielding positions as a matter of course. What is amazing about this is that truth and constructive political endeavor are almost always on the side of the Democrats and yet they seem always to give in. Truth ought to defeat lies in a political fight but, sad to say, that rarely ever happens in this country anymore. The Republicans win almost every battle precisely because they are unreasonable, furiously negative, and utterly dishonest. Lies and accusations always win, it seems. An important segment of the American population is endlessly gullible and easy to fool. Accusatory attacks by the followers of McCarthy, Nixon, Reagan, the Bushes, Rove and Gingrich work every time.

Because of its false religiosity, its racism, and its conservatism, the South has become a key element in the political success of the Republican Party. When Lyndon Johnson passed the Civil Rights Act of 1964, he remarked that he had just lost the South to the Republicans for a generation. He was right but the shift seems to be permanent. The reach of the Democratic Party was hugely reduced by the Southern Strategy of the Nixon, Goldwater, and Reagan campaigns. Religion and racism were a big part of that strategy and continue so today. Republicans adamantly deny that they are racist; but, whatever their personal pretensions may be, their political and issue behaviors are racist all the way. The Republican Party owns the solid South and the religious right. It is enough to win most elections. This amalgamation of politics, commerce, and religion is an especially potent brand of fascism, one that served Mussolini, Franco, and Hitler very well in an earlier context.

Democratic Submissiveness

The Democratic Party can have no effective future until it screws up its courage and begins to expose the Republican Party for what it really is: namely, a force called "fascism." There is an unpleasant goody-goody quality in the Democratic Party that makes it ineffective in political campaigns. The mainstream media shares this goody-goody quality and rarely ever tells the unvarnished truth about anything political or religious. In a very straightforward way, politics really is a battle between constructive, helpful behavior and destructive, negative behavior. You might well call this a battle between good and evil. Republicans just bitterly hate democratic government and don't want it ever to do anything good and useful for ordinary people. As much as they hate the government, they still want its power in their hands so they can cripple it and use what's left to pay off and benefit corporate interests, including religion.

Republicans are right in thinking there is an inverse relationship between the power of democratic government (public power) and corporate power (private power). Thus, they tell us bluntly that they want to destroy democratic government or at least reduce it to irrelevance—except for its military and police power, of course, which, until quite recently, they always embraced warmly but which they are now privatizing at a furious rate. They want all of the power and privilege in private hands. However, they do not want anarchy. To the contrary, they want every citizen under the very tight control of corporate and religious powers effectuated by policemen and soldiers. Quite clearly, they want a soft despotism based on an abundance of consumer goods but very little real freedom and no serious dissent, disorder, or disobedience. They value citizens as workers and consumers (that is, as mules and garbage disposals) but not as actual citizens with minds, opinions, and needs of their own. Republicans want everyone and everything to be pliable and exploitable. To them, it is all about their position, privilege, money, and control.

The Republican Party and its many adjuncts always behave in the same way in political campaigns. Its entire purpose in every election is to construct a story line that arouses fear and hate and creates mass hysteria in a significant portion of the electorate. To do this, they relentlessly spew out an incredible collection of lies, most of them incoherent, internally contradictory, and bizarre almost to the point of lunacy. In this way, they manufacture movements hostile to their enemies: the Democratic Party, liberalism, democratic government, and any foreign enemies, however imaginary. It doesn't matter how absurd or fantastic these lies are. They work. They win elections. Accordingly, this is not a democratic country anymore. When just about every election is decided on the basis of a huge flood of lies and distortions, then the electoral process cannot be called democratic. When lies win, tyranny wins. Inequality, unjust wars, and predation follow. Inequality and war always lead eventually to economic breakdown and impoverishment.

The Media's Even Steven Stance

The mainstream media helps the Republican Party do its dirty work. Even when a few commentators criticize or even ridicule the preposterous nature of the Republican propaganda, the counter arguments they offer are usually weak, naïve, and hesitant. Media apologists say they have no responsibility for correcting lies and explain that both sides are equally "extreme" and that they should both move to the middle. They use the sixties as a time when, they say, the left was running amok and performing all manner of violent and disruptive acts. They're talking about the civil rights, the free speech, the anti-poverty, and the anti-war movements. Almost all of the people hurt and killed in those times were movement people, not the authorities. I don't think those movements can be equated with McCarthyism, the cold war, or the anti-terrorist wars nor indeed with the concealed destructiveness of corporatism. The arguments between Democratic and Republican partisans are not "even-Steven." Yes, Democrats do trim the truth but Republicans lie blatantly and their lies are fantastic, bizarre, and frequently violent.

Nearly every media outlet is a corporate entity. To listen to mainstream media reports is to listen to pablum, if the squishing of pablum can be heard. Most of it comes from official sources or from trusted military and business "experts." The idea always is to level down the language to make it neutral sounding and inoffensive. They can't or won't say that Bush and Cheney were responsible for the abuse, rape, torture, "rendering," persecution, degradation, exile, and mass slaughter of millions of innocent Iraqis. These words are absolutely accurate; the broken, suffering, expelled, and dead bodies are still there for everyone to see; and they will always be there in the memories of their families and friends. The victims had names and families and their destruction is a matter of undeniable record. The broken stability and order of Iraq, for example, is once again, in the summer of 2014, flaring into a violent civil war between the Sunnis and the Shia. Things are much worse there now than they ever were under the brutal dictatorship of Saddam Hussein. The blowback of American interference has once more led to disaster for innocent others.

Yet, these words are never used by the mainstream media to describe the atrocities committed under the cover of a massive eruption of extreme lies. In fact, they can't even bring themselves to call Bush and Cheney the liars they clearly were and are. There is always a new lie on top of the old lies. The reason they won't say these things is because such words would upset Republicans and cause turmoil and counter attacks.

Covering for Clinton and Bush

When Bill Clinton continued H.W. Bush's sanctions and bombing campaign against the innocent people of Iraq for eight bloody years—a campaign that killed over a million Iraqis, half of them children under the age of five—there was likewise hardly a word of condemnation in any media outlet. It isn't just Barack Obama who doesn't want to "look back." Nobody in the United States does, least of all the media. This country doesn't ever punish or even seriously investigate and expose the criminals its political system produces at the highest levels of government and among the generals and secret police agents. Those criminals walk among us now and are being honored and praised as celebrities, their crimes forgotten.

Bush and Cheney were far worse than Saddam Hussein. Saddam was a brutal dictator put in power by this country and kept there by Reagan-Bush while he was gassing his own people and waging war against Iran for eight long years. More than a million people died in that war and Reagan-Bush cheered him on and gave him billions of dollars of credits and secret information about Iran. As brutal as Saddam was in his own country, he was attacking Kurds and Shias who were trying to overthrow his government and kill him. Incredibly, Reagan-Bush, even while they were openly supporting and arming Saddam, were also secretly selling American arms to Iran, sending them through Israel to the Iranian leaders; this criminal plot, known as the Iran-contra scandal, was, of course, exposed by a Middle Eastern newspaper, not by the clueless American media. Then just a few clicks later, Bush-Cheney launched a completely unprovoked and indiscriminate attack against twenty-five million Iraqis, people who were not our enemies and had no desire or any ability to attack us. Not a single one of them was a terrorist. They had nothing to do with the September eleventh attack against us. It's always a slimy deception when a powerful country attacks a helpless population and claims it is an attack against their dictator, especially when their dictator is really our dictator and not an enemy of our country at all.

Even the number of people Bush–Cheney killed is massively downgraded by the media. There is little question but that the figure approaches a million and may well exceed that. Bush himself claimed he killed only thirty thousand. Bush's Shiite dictator claims it was eighty-six thousand. Only a couple of years into the war, *Lancet*, a highly respected British medical organization, estimated the number, at that point, to be far above those numbers. Contrast the George W. Bush claim (thirty thousand) with the figures from his father's six-week-long war against Iraq. The Census Bureau reported a figure of 158,000 dead in the H. W. Bush attack against Iraq. So George W. Bush killed only 30,000 in a seven-year all-out war but his daddy killed 158,000 in a six-week-long very limited war that never even reached Baghdad? What kind of media publishes this kind of drivel?

George W. Bush is now being praised by the so-called mainstream media. They say he cautioned the American people not to blame "all" Muslims for what some of them did on September 11. Bush did indeed say such words, once in a while, but only among a large mass of other words that roundly blamed the people of Iraq and Saddam Hussein for the attack. Furthermore, Bush blamed an "axis of evil" meaning most Muslim and Arab countries. He also called his war a "crusade" and said that his god ordered him to invade Iraq. Cheney said he and Bush were going to wage war against fifty to sixty terrorist countries. Guess who. Nor should anyone forget that many of the top people in the Bush administration were oil people and many of them were very close to "certain" Saudi and other Gulf Coast Muslims. So of course Bush, Cheney, and Rice didn't want to accuse their buddies and business partners, that is, not "all" Muslims.

Bush said he was attacking Iraq because he was "attacking terrorism." That's why the troops in Iraq went wild in their rush to punish the people Bush and Cheney had convinced them were responsible for attacking the United States. The Bush–Cheney lies enflamed the American troops just as the Johnson–Nixon lies enflamed the troops to commit atrocities at My Lai and elsewhere in Vietnam. Following suit, the conservative media has invented an even more fantastic demand: Obama should thank George W. Bush for "winning" the war in Iraq just as Ronald Reagan "won" the cold war and didn't get the praise he deserved, apparently for launching a sneak attack against tiny Grenada, that mighty communist outpost off America's shores, and for huffing and puffing and blowing the Berlin wall down with a big puff of wind. This is absolutely astonishing stuff but it doesn't seem so to the media.

Attacking Obama

The utterly fantastic and irrational attacks on Obama consist of claims he was born in a Muslim country, is not a real citizen, and cannot be the real president of these United States. The Republicans just can't accept seeing a black man in "their" White House. It seems incredible to them. In addition, they say he is not a real Christian as all of the evidence shows; instead, he is a secret Muslim just waiting to impose Sharia law and betray us all. Lately, Romney is referring to him as "foreign" and "strange," this from a fake Mormon with beliefs that defy reason and credulity. In other words, only Obama is illegitimate and "un-American." Are Romney and the Republicans referring to his color? You're damn right they are.

They also say he is a socialist, apparently having worn out the word "communist" in their previous attacks against Democrats over the last century and more. Here is a socialist who helped Bush give trillions of dollars to Wall Street bankers and financiers, who then "bailed out" large corporate auto companies, and gave billions to the states to pass along to private corporations and companies for use in improving the infrastructure. Still worse, he passed a health insurance plan that requires thirty million citizens to buy health insurance and drugs *from private insurance and drug corporations* thus putting billions and at last trillions of dollars in their hands. Since when did socialists start lining the pockets of corporations? Like Bill Clinton, Obama is a grow-the-economy, trickle down man. He is, in fact, a dedicated Friedmanite and a lover of capitalistic private power, not to mention his full embrace of fundamentalist Christianity. He is, in fact, an overt and enthusiastic predatory capitalist and a dedicated Christian Zionist as well.

The absurd attacks against Barack Obama and the Democratic Party have undermined democracy in this country and have damaged the reputation of the government and its attempts to improve life for many Americans. The lies have wiped out the credibility of the Administration and have dragged down Obama's popularity. It appears nearly certain as of this writing (September of 2010) that the Republican Party will take control of the Senate and the House in the coming elections and Obama looks more and more likely to be a one term president. (In fact, since this was written, the Democrats did just barely retain control of the Senate but lost the House by a big margin) The media represents the tea party attacks against Obama and the Democrats as a genuine populist movement based on legitimate grievances. In fact, the grievances were entirely manufactured. Indeed, the tea party movement itself was invented and nurtured into being by a rich corporatist family, the Koch brothers; the Kochs may not be card-carrying members of the John Birch Society but they are dedicated Birchers all the same. In fact, their father, at first a follower of and employee of Joe Stalin, was one of the original founders of the John Birch Society, an organization that was deliberately imitative of the Communist Party. This entire hate campaign is a fraud and a treason, one arranged and executed by the Republican Party and its adjuncts.

Here is a quote from a syndicated newspaper column by Leonard Pitts on August 25, 2010:

> The situation has been vexing for years, but the last two summers, with their birthers and Ground Zero mosques and their death panels and town hall shouting matches and guns at rallies and rocks through windows and threats of Quran bonfires and charges of socialism, Nazism, terrorism, and a general sense of end-times bacchanal, have been especially disheartening.

Here are some additional quotes from an article by Michael Tomasky in *The New York Review of Books*, October 28, 2010:

> Once again, as was the case after September 11, and has so often been the case recently in American politics, the Republicans have succeeding in branding the Democrats as not merely elitist but somehow alien and un-America, and the Democrats, from the President on down, have had almost nothing to say about it. One had thought... that the Democrats would not let themselves be so represented again. But here we are....

> Whatever emerges, one thing is not in doubt: if the Republicans win the House, they will launch a series of investigations into the Obama administration, quite possibly leading to another impeachment drama....

> Much of their [the Republican] base already believes that Obama is probably not an American citizen and therefore is an illegitimate president. In a Harris Poll from March, 24 percent of Republicans even agree that Obama "may be the Antichrist."

Here's a letter to the editor reprinted in the *Asheville Citizen Times* of February 17, 2015— "While in Florida recently, I read the following letter to the editor in the local paper:

> Many of us Canadians are confused by the U.S. midterm elections.

> Consider, right now in America, corporate profits are at record highs, the country is adding 200,000+ jobs per month, unemployment is below 6 percent and the U.S. gross national product is the best among the countries in the Organization for Economic Cooperation and Development.

> Also: the dollar is at its strongest level in years, the stock market is at near-record highs, gasoline prices are falling, there is no inflation, interest rates are the lowest in 30 years, U.S. oil imports are declining, U.S. oil production is increasing, and the deficit is rapidly declining.

> America is leading the world once again and is respected internationally—in sharp contrast to the Bush years. President Obama brought troops home from Iraq and gave the order that killed Osama bin Laden.

> So America votes for the party that got you into the mess Obama just dug you out of? This defies reason.

Fawning Calves

The Republican attacks against Obama are preposterous and yet, like Bill Clinton, he snuggles up to his Republican attackers like a fawning calf. Bill Clinton has become a great pal of H. W. Bush despite a Bush/James Baker smear attack that claimed Clinton was a communist traitor who tried to defect like Lee Harvey Oswald. Obama has embraced George W. Bush as if he were a long lost brother. In fact, when there are state functions to which all living presidents are invited, Jimmy Carter gets elbowed aside while the Bushes cling together with Clinton and Obama like members of the same family. I think Carter is coldly treated because he believes in human rights and they do not. Carter did not approve of their attacks against the innocent Iraqis and he also criticizes Israel for its brutal abuses of the Palestinians. Obama obscenely hugs George W. Bush at every opportunity and calls him "a good man," the very last thing he is. He is, in fact, an abuser, torturer, exiler, and killer of millions of innocent people including women and children.

First Clinton and now Obama are true successors to Reagan and the two Bushes. Two things they all share is a vast genocide against the people of Iraq as well as massive support for the Zionist genocide against the Palestinian people. Obama has, in many ways, multiplied the G. W. Bush spy and surveillance program and continues Bush's phony and misdirected "war against terrorism." Although a far better president, Obama is no more principled than Ronald Reagan, Bill Clinton, and the two Bushes.

PART TWO. FALSE GODS

CHAPTER 9. WORK AND RELIGION

Supervisors of Work, Masters of Belief

I think that work and religion are the two most dominant organized forces in human history. All economic systems are about work, its products, and its uses. Religion is about belief in some intangible being or spirit. Religions have dominated all known civilizations; and religious differences have been responsible for an enormous amount of the world's superstition, strife, discord, war, oppression, and cruelty.

It's rare for religious people to tolerate one another even a little bit. Religious leaders insist on their "right" to seek converts by any means they choose. However, if differing believers are to live together, they have to tolerate one another or fight one another. If they choose to live with or near different others, they and their leaders have to give up their drive to dominate and convert those other people, that is, people whose religions they do not like.

Strong beliefs in certain economic systems, such as communism and capitalism, are commonly referred to as "ideologies." Believers in such economic systems can be quite as fanatical and aggressively hostile to one another as are the religionists. Thus, the supervisors of work sometimes oppose one another and sometimes merge their economic concerns with their religious concerns. The fights between capitalists and communists were not much different from the fights between Catholics and Protestants, Muslims and Christians, Zionists and Palestinians, etc. These hostilities not only create confusion about religious matters but also about the nature of work and the methods used to supervise work. These days (especially in the United States) "free market" capitalists are even more fanatical and less willing to cooperate with others than are any of the other ideologues and religious believers. Some of them are now even calling themselves "free-enterprise Christians." They and the fundamentalist Christians, Muslims, and Zionists are determined to smash their enemies and punish all deviations. For these reasons, I believe the masters of religion and the supervisors of work are both enemies of ordinary people. They want to dominate the peoples they have placed themselves above and they do this in the interest of their own dogma, privilege, and profit.

Thus, I think the common definition of religion is too narrow and I think that capitalism and communism should both be treated as "religions." They are both intense, even fanatical in their beliefs, they are both absolutist, they both proselytize with all their might, and they both live by a set of rigid dogmas that they apply forcefully to the world and to their own followers. Furthermore, they both regard their property and wealth as sacred and worthy of something like worship. Communism is asleep now, perhaps even dead, but something aggressive is likely to replace it. Capitalism rages on, conquering everything in sight, celebrating what it imagines was a great victory over communism. Its implementers even imagine that history has ended and that they rightfully own everything and have a right to it all. Capitalism always was far more aggressive and assaultive than was communism. Though much bloodier toward their own citizens, even Lenin, Stalin, and Mao weren't as far-reaching and aggressively ambitious as the Americans. They did not have a Supreme Court to sanctify their invisible and intangible collectives and to turn them into actual living human beings with rights and privileges (corporations have been ruled legal "persons") far beyond those of any other beings.

> *Homo sacralis* (aka *Homo sapiens*) will not be without gods....Buddhist philosopher David R. Loy says that the capitalist market is functioning like a religion, issuing its commandments from its own Olympus and its own Sinai, superseding the increasingly dysfunctional major religious traditions....the market religion is booming, binding all corners of the globe into a worldview and a set of values that we think is secular but it is functioning with religious fervor. Traditional religions, eat your hearts out; you have never matched the missionary zeal and success of this divine pretender.

> – *Free Inquiry*, 2014 October/November issue, Essay by Daniel C. Maguire, "Christianity Doesn't Need God."

Obedience to Absolutist Religion

When it comes to requiring absolute obedience to higher authority, religious leaders go beyond the mere supervisors of work. Under the spell of religion, you are often required to sacrifice your own life for some superior figure in your church or mosque as in the crusades and jihads imposed, as a matter of faith, on believers. Religion is very much a matter of zeal and fanaticism. The Christians and the Muslims in particular are expected to die for their god or to kill for him on orders from above. The ones issuing the orders rarely volunteer to go first. Apparently, their own lives are too precious to waste and they certainly don't want to get blood on their hands or flesh in their teeth. From the very start, both of these religions grew and got rich by forcing themselves on others and by stealing from the weak. A central and all-important part of the duty of each Christian and each Muslim is proselytizing, bringing others and their property into the faith by any means necessary. God requires you to hunt them down, rob them, and convert them, the religious bosses say.

Nearly every war has had a religious element in it somewhere. Chaplains and jihadist preachers carry their holy texts into battle with them and almost all national leaders declare wars, or launch them, with god on their lips. We and other Western powers have long dominated and manipulated the Muslim and Arab peoples in the Mideast. We have made hundreds of millions of new enemies there. Our generals here in America tell us that our "god is bigger than their god." One resentful enemy, Osama bin Laden, attacked us in an indiscriminate rage and killed nearly three thousand innocent Americans. In response, George W. Bush attacked the wrong people: twenty-five million innocent Iraqis, none of whom had anything at all to do with bin Laden's attack against us. Bush told us he was conducting a "crusade" on orders from his god and that anyone who wasn't with him was against us all. He even called up versions of Gog and Magog from his bible for our inspiration. Then, he proceeded to abuse, rape, torture, degrade, shame, persecute, render, exile, and murder millions of completely innocent Iraqis because, he said, god told him to do so. As always, he confused up with down.

All the major religions and most of the minor ones have been massively violent and domineering throughout their times in power. All preach gentleness, compassion, and peace but none pays the slightest attention to his and her own words when they decide to conquer something or someone. The supervisors of work and the masters of belief are always on the hunt for something to grab or someone to kill. They work together to support one another when it helps the bottom line or their dogma and they attack one another over the spoils when their greed exceeds their loyalty to one another.

Is Christianity Christian?

Christianity began with an obscure Jewish prophet named Jesus. Early on and especially after the Roman emperors Constantine and Theodosius paganized it, this religion became powerful and viciously tyrannical. From then on, its philosophy and practice had very little to do with the supposed words and peaceful character of Jesus Christ. As time passed, it became increasingly hierarchic and rigidly monarchist. It claimed to be exclusively holy, absolute, and unchallengeable. It was totalitarian by every measure and it ruled the Western world for nearly two thousand years. Its ruling system very much resembled the ruling systems of capitalism and communism. In truth, the Christian religion is not really Christian at all.

Chapter 10. The Road to Damascus

Three Factions

A "Christian" sect known to the Jews as the Nazoreans (Nostrim) or the Nazarenes came into being in Palestine in the first century A.D. At its center was the belief that a man known as Jesus of Galilee was the longed-for Jewish Messiah prophesied in the Hebrew Bible. Jesus never claimed to be the founder of a new religion nor did his followers make that claim. He told a Phoenician woman, "I have been sent to the lost house of Israel." He selected twelve disciples who were to sit on twelve thrones and rule over the twelve tribes of Israel. He told his disciples to tend the lost sheep of Israel and to keep away from the Gentiles and the Samaritan villages. There was thus a substantial Nazorean movement in Jerusalem and it sought to advance the Jewish gospel, not to establish a new Christian religion.

After the death of Jesus, there were soon three factions of "Christians." The original and authentic one consisted of the relatives and friends of Jesus gathered together in Jerusalem under the leadership of James, the brother of Jesus. Peter the Apostle and Jude, the second of Jesus' four brothers, were members of this group. No Gentiles or uncircumcised people were allowed to be members of the Jesus faction in Jerusalem. It was for Jews only.

Two other competing factions emerged, one in Rome and the other in Asia Minor. The faction in Rome was loyal to the state and, at first, consisted of both Gentiles and Jews. The faction in Asia Minor was very much the creation of one man, Saul (Paul) of Tarsus. Paul was a Jew and a loyal Roman subject. Indeed, he was, at first, the enemy of the Nazoreans and persecuted them for the Roman state and its loyal Jewish officials in Jerusalem. These three factions might well be called the "Jesus church," the "Roman church," and the "Paul church." Ultimately, the Roman church incorporated but rewrote the writings of Paul and excluded the beliefs of the Jesus church entirely.

Paul and Peter

Paul never saw Jesus or had any association with him at all. He was intensely ambitious and egotistical; he thought he was the best candidate to be the Jewish Messiah, not Jesus. According to his own claim, he was on the road to Damascus, sent to punish Christian followers there, when he was blinded by a bright light and was, in this way, converted to the Christian religion. Some biblical scholars speculate that this conversion experience was the result of an epileptic fit. Thereafter, he claimed to be a humble follower of the teachings of Jesus but he also claimed that his views of those teachings were superior to those of Jesus' relatives and followers in Jerusalem. He even invented an argument holding that the truest understanding of Jesus' teachings came directly to him in the air from Jesus up in heaven and not from the people on the ground who actually knew Jesus and were his closest friends and relatives. To make his argument even more bizarre, he charged that the Jesus faction in Jerusalem was not Christian at all but merely Jewish, a convenient fact. Naturally, the Jesus faction saw him as an enemy and a subversive out to undermine them and their Jesus movement. And he was surely guilty of that in the long run, since the Jesus movement was ultimately expunged entirely, leaving not a word or a trace behind.

This man used his Roman name, Paul, instead of his given Jewish name of Saul. His father was a Roman citizen and a man of some means. Paul came from Tarsus in Asia Minor but he was educated in Jerusalem. There, he studied the law under Gamaliel the Elder, grandson of the famous scholar Hillel and president of the Sanhedrin. Paul was a zealous Roman nationalist and probably a Pharisee. The Pharisees were one of two Jewish religious and political parties; they were opponents of the Sadducees who called them "separatists" or "deviants." They insisted on strict observance of the Jewish law but did not support the revolt against Rome in A.D. 70. Paul was always a loyal Roman. He was a tentmaker by trade but, of course, his dominant activity consisted of missionary work and the writing of quite a few "epistles" that formed the basis of the Christian dogma adopted by the early Roman church. Much of the New Testament text came from Paul's pen but, of course, the Roman church shaped and amended it to fit its own purposes.

Some three years after his conversion, Paul spent fifteen days in Jerusalem where he met Peter and James, Jesus brother, but none of the other apostles. After that, he spent perhaps ten years performing missionary work in Syria and Cilica, on his home ground. When the Antioch church started accepting gentiles as members, Paul became a zealous supporter of opening up the movement to all people including the uncircumcised. Without this policy, the Christian religion would almost certainly have disappeared from the world.

Apparently, the Apostle Peter was a wishy-washy character. When he visited Paul in Asia Minor, he ate with the uncircumcised gentiles there, an unclean act, and agreed with Paul's and their view that traditional Jewish practices were not necessary to the Christian calling; but when he was at home in Jerusalem, he agreed with James and the Jews there that only the circumcised were real Christians. Some Rock! The ambivalence of Peter's loyalty to James and his occasional bowing to Paul brought criticism from the followers of Jesus.

The Roman Church

Later on after the deaths of both Peter and Paul, the Roman church used this ambivalence to pretend that Peter supported Paul and not James and the Jesus faction. This is how the Roman church appropriated the allegiance of Paul's Christian followers in Asia Minor and exploited a pretended connection to Jesus through Peter without at all including the real, Jewish followers of Jesus in Jerusalem. In this way, the Roman church was also able to use the writings of Paul as a basis for its early dogma. In those early days, there was no bible or any accepted writings except Paul's for the Roman church to rely on and develop to its taste. Needless to say, it gave no consideration at all to the contributions of James and the apostolic Jews, that is, to the real followers of Jesus. Instead, it launched a bitter attack on the scattered Nazoreans in the name of Paul and the Roman state.

It appears that the Jewish revolt against Rome played an important part in the formation of the dominant Roman Catholic Church. It set the Roman church and the state against the Jews for good even while the church was opportunistically embracing Paul and Peter as the "founders" of their now almost exclusively Gentile religion. These maneuvers also resulted in the exile and disintegration of the Jerusalem faction, which included the only true followers of Jesus. The members of that faction fled Jerusalem and disappeared from history altogether. They left no writings behind or any accounts of their time with Jesus. Thus, the Roman Catholic Church was not really Christian at all.

The great irony is that a collection of Jewish reformers, including Jesus, his brothers, and his disciples, and, perhaps, most of all, the outrider, Paul of Tarsus, were claimed to be responsible for the birth of an enormously powerful anti-Semitic religion headed by the Roman Catholic Church. It is quite insane that great masses of Catholics, and later Protestants, should claim to love and worship Jesus and his followers with such fanatical devotion while, at the same time, they violently hated and persecuted Jews and all of their works with such fervent bitterness for nearly twenty centuries. Adolf Hitler, himself a life-long and devout Catholic, provided the hardest blow.

What the Church Became

In the end, the Christian religion became a mixture of Old Testament (Jewish) myths, Paul's dogmatic inventions based not at all on the teachings of Jesus, and on old Roman, Greek, and pagan mythology. If the Gospels can be believed, Jesus was an extreme pacifist who believed it was impossible for rich people to get to heaven, that is, if Jesus ever really existed at all. There is still considerable doubt. Those early Nazoreans expected the world to end soon and they thought the Jews would be the ultimate winners in a final struggle for peace and justice as they saw those virtues.

The various deceptions and manipulations of the Roman church officials were deeply immoral and unjust. There are even suspicions that church officials may have played a role in the crucifixion of Peter and the beheading of Paul there in Rome. Leaning on Paul's beginnings, the Roman church invented its own history and mythology and finally its own highly suspect bible. It took several centuries for it to get its story and its dogmatic culture in place, and it was able to do that only because the Roman state needed a single belief system to unite it in its struggle to survive and prevail over the dissenters within and the barbarians at the gates.

Note: The above account was taken in large measure from a book entitled, *Those Incredible Christians*, by Dr. Hugh J. Schonefield.

CHAPTER 11. TWIN MAGICS: CAPITALISM AND CHRISTIANITY

Churches *are* Corporations

Religions were among the first corporations. Each of the mainline religions is organized as a top down business, a corporation. Indeed, all are in the money-collecting business and each owns great swaths of land and many buildings, businesses, and material goods. In the two previous centuries in this country, corporations built entire towns for their employees. Remember the robber barons and their way of erecting numerous coal, textile, gold, copper, and steel towns. Those towns aggregated and completely controlled workers and their families. The owners hired preachers, built churches, and imposed morality on their employees. Henry Ford had a "sociology" department that policed the moral behavior of each family. Everywhere there were religious requirements and pressures. The corporations were not religion-free by any measure. The pretty picture painted by right-wing ideologues about these arrangements is false.

As corporations got larger, they had to become more diverse. To find enough workers, they had to hire people of different religions, nationalities, races, and genders. Narrowness was not convenient or profitable. The motivation had nothing to do with tolerance, secularism, diversity, or democracy. Rather, it was profit and indiscriminate control over the working lives of employees that mattered to the corporatists. However benevolent some of them may have seemed or pretended to be, these arrangements were, nevertheless, tyrannical constructions and arrangements.

Churches and corporations today are all modeled on the tyrannical ruling systems of long ago; that means pyramidal systems of supervision based on rank and obedience. The model came from systems of divine royalism, aristocracy, and military rank going all the way back to the invention of agriculture, the resulting end of nomadism, and the beginning of permanent settlements. The narrow ownership of land and water followed and some were able to grab more land and greater access to water than others. Hierarchies evolved based on the ownership of such property. Those with land and water could grow food and store it. They could thus control those with little or no ability to feed themselves and their families. This resulted in supervisory arrangements and servanthood or even slavery. This is how capitalism began. Religion followed the same path.

Oligarchs and Missionaries

Capitalism is about the use and supervision of work by an oligarchy made up of property owners and bosses as well as priests and preachers. The end purpose of this arrangement is profit and privilege for the members of the oligarchy. In this arrangement, the generals and the police chiefs are the enforcers and the punishers of reluctant and dissident citizens. In the Western world, the Christian religion has long been an arm of this concoction of repressive forces.

Both capitalism and Christianity need external enemies that they can scapegoat as a part of their effort to spread themselves across the world. Both of these isms—capitalism and Christianism—are proselytizing ideologies. They need to spread and conquer in order to survive and flourish. They both claim to be on a quest to save others from the sin and error of their ways. The enemy is all of those out there who have not yet been conquered.

Historically, this drive for dominance expressed itself as missionary colonialism. Today, it is less obviously territorial and more deeply ideological. Even so, the advancing wave still consists of military invasion accompanied by economic and religious conversions. Quite often, the corporations arrive before the military but there is always a lurking armada somewhere near. And there is always an arrangement of treaties, bankers' tricks, monetary rules, and religious dogmas for everyone to live by, or else. These paperwork aggressions are as violent as military attack.

Although there are still plenty of Christian missionaries scattered about, the religious proselytizing is less fierce than it used to be. However, the religious message is inherent in the economic and military messages. In truth, the merger of Christianity and capitalism is far advanced. Many proselytizers today call themselves "free-enterprise Christians" and many generals and CEOs carry their bibles into battle. At headquarters, in the United States and England in particular, all of the politicians are "born again" and love Jesus. Religious propaganda is as widespread and as deceptive as commercial advertising.

Fascist Amalgam

This incredible amalgam of capitalism, Christianity, politics, militarism, and police statism can only be called fascistic. Benito Mussolini, the inventor of the term, said that fascism should be called "corporatism" since it consists of a "merger of state and corporate power." He also said, "fascism is a religious concept." Nowadays, of course, the merger includes the Christian religion and all of the military and police power available. It is now pretty much a one-world system and the leading force is globalism. This kind of capitalism is much stealthier than direct military attack or a massive Christian conversion campaign as of old.

Yet, the United States is too impatient to let the twin magics of capitalism and Christianity work their miracles on the unsuspecting world. And so, military attack has become routine, especially when Republicans are in office. The Democrats also do a lot of attacking but mostly to placate and calm the Republicans who are forever accusing the Democrats of being weak, cowardly, and treasonous as a way of forcing them into action against some barely-real or fully-invented enemy such as monolithic communism, creeping socialism, or raging terrorism. Clash-of-civilizations rhetoric is always a good motivator for the cowardly.

The phony world we live in now was invented by Christian capitalism or capitalist Christianity, take your pick, and it has all been hyped and pushed outward by our burgeoning military and police agencies, all of them now being privatized in the interest of greater profit and less democracy. Liberal democracy is the great bugbear of capitalism and Christianity, in fact their number one enemy, much more so than any imagined or exaggerated communism or terrorism.

Attacking Democracy

What is going on in the United States, under the imprimatur of the Republican Party and its Christian followers, is a vast attack against democratic government itself. In truth, there is very little democracy left now although a big mask has been fitted over the ruins; the shards are under our feet. Oblivious, the American people think that they live in the best of all possible worlds, that is, under a system of "democratic capitalism," an impossible combination of words.

Capitalism cannot be democratic. Working for a boss is not democratic; it is antidemocratic. Capitalist systems are made up of owners and bosses and their servants, that is, their workers. The owners don't just own the premises, the equipment, and the raw materials; they own the work too as well as the workers. If you work for someone, you are a servant or perhaps a slave. You are certainly not a free agent or a voter in any of the economic or religious decisions being made all around you and above you. You don't even own your own job and you have absolutely no rights your owner and your bosses and priests are bound to respect. You are a cipher and a tool, nothing more. Hierarchic systems cannot be democratic. Thus, the very language of capitalism is a self-concealing lie and a sham. So too is the dogmatic absolutism of the Christian churches.

Eventually, in the life of any organized society, there will be a drift toward tyranny and it will be impelled by efforts to merge the powers of commerce and/or religion with the power of government. When commerce and government come together in a big way, the result is fascism. When religion and government merge, the result is theocracy. The only type of government that can exist for long without a close alliance with some kind of religion or commerce is a firmly democratic and secular one.

Ideologies with strong "faith" systems based on fixed dogma (including such systems as Soviet communism and American capitalism during the cold war, for example) are essentially religious in that they command intense and irrational loyalty from their followers. Both of those isms claimed to be about commerce and belief only but both try to swallow up government. Thus, ostensibly secular government cannot be democratic if it adopts the dogmas of either of these isms any more than it can be democratic if it too-closely embraces traditional religions such as Christianity, Mohammedanism, Hinduism, Zionism, or Judaism. Separating government from the dominance of such competing faith-systems is the only way to assure a democracy that tolerates the belief and faith of all citizens. This is also the only way to insure stability and mutual respect.

Civil Society and Secularism

So-called communitarians like to talk about "civil society" as a cure for too much government. The trouble with civil society is that it consists almost entirely of private organizations under the control of religion or commerce. These organizations are thus hostile to government by definition. They might be temporarily helpful in bringing down a tyrannical government but they can never advance democracy in any meaningful way because of their own narrow self-interest. The only way to advance democracy is through the establishment and maintenance of a strong secular government that opposes the abuses of commerce and religion.

Secular government has to have dominant control over the polity, or democracy cannot rise or survive. A true democratic government is elected by the people and must represent all of the people against any opposing powers. Religion and commerce must be entirely separate from government but those two powers must be regulated by the government in the interest of the freedom of the people. Individual citizens must be left free to make their own private choices and government must guarantee this freedom especially against the aggressions and suppressions of religion and commerce. This does not mean tyrannical repression of religion and commerce by government but it does mean that religion and commerce have to be made to respect individual freedom and have to refrain from subversive attacks against the democratic system.

Democratic government cannot be defined as majority rule alone. Some matters—such as the election of democratic representatives—must be subject to majority vote but there are many personal rights that must never be subject to majoritarian control. These rights include those in the Bill of Rights, in the Freedom Amendments, and elsewhere in the constitution. They also include the right of all citizens to lead healthy, secure, un-coerced lives as well as the right to be free from every form of religious persecution and abusive commercial exploitation.

Chapter 12. The Founders and Religion

Jefferson and Adams

The Christian religionists in America in colonial times hated Thomas Jefferson. Today, they try to claim him and all of the other founders as their own. With Tom Paine, Jefferson spoke out against the tyranny and superstition of organized Christianity. Most of the other founders were also deists and religious nonconformists like them, but they did not very often make public statements about their skepticism and disbelief. Some of them went to church at least some of the time, and, in public, they professed to be members of one or another of the established churches. In private and to one another, however, they expressed their dislike of religious orthodoxy and its repressions. Some of them thought that public piousness was good for public morality and for their careers. Luckily, they were not all that careful about their disbelief and there is ample evidence of their private words and thoughts, many of them bitter and contemptuous toward Christianity.

The Danbury Baptist Association asked President Jefferson to declare a day of thanksgiving. In his January 11, 1802 letter refusing their request, he said:

Believing with you that religion is a matter which lies solely between man and his god, that he owes account to none other for his faith or his worship, that the legislative powers of government reach actions only, and not opinions, I contemplate with sovereign reverence that act of the whole American people which declared that their legislature should 'make no law respecting an establishment of religion, or prohibiting the free exercise thereof, thus building a wall of separation between church and state.

In his *Notes on Virginia*, Jefferson said:

Millions of innocent men, women, and children, since the introduction of Christianity, have been burnt, tortured, fined, imprisoned; yet we have not advanced one inch towards uniformity. What has been the effect of coercion? To make one half the world fools and the other half hypocrites.

The Enlightenment caused the rise of deism and Unitarianism in Europe and these unorthodox systems of belief spread to America and influenced Jefferson, Adams, Washington, Madison, Franklin, Paine, Ethan Allen, and many others. The French Revolution destroyed the divine right of kings thus delivering a blow to illegitimate political power and rank religious superstition at the same time. That revolution established a democratic idea in the place of those two evil forces. Soon, Napoleon became the dictator of France and so no stable democracy was established just then. However, the seed had been planted and not just for France alone. Along with the American Revolution, the French Revolution was an enormously important breaking point in Western history.

In 1776, Virginia state laws imprisoned for three years those who doubted the trinity and required the execution of those guilty of heresy. With help from James Madison and George Mason, Jefferson halted tax support for the Anglican Church and got a statute on religious freedom passed; it eliminated punishments for disapproved beliefs.

In the election of 1800—called by some the cruelest in US history—the Federalists (Alexander Hamilton in particular) along with many preachers denounced Jefferson as an atheist. Speaking of the clergy, he vowed, "eternal hostility against every form of tyranny over the mind of man." He said, "I am not afraid of the priests. They have tried upon me all their various batteries, of pious whining, hypocritical canting, lying and slandering, without being able to give me one moment of pain."

Jefferson prepared his own bible by extracting Jesus' best sayings and collecting them together for his own use. He described the rest of the Christian bible as "so much absurdity, so much untruth, charlatanism and imposture" and said it was full of "vulgar ignorance, of things impossible, of superstitions, fanaticism and fabrications." He did not believe in the divinity of Jesus but did consider him a great moral thinker.

David McCullough's recent admiring biography of John Adams represents Jefferson as the iconoclast but says that Adams was a devoted Congregationalist who attended church twice on Sunday. Allen Guelzo of Eastern College says that Adams' private belief was much the same as Jefferson's and that the letters between them show a "mutual contempt" for orthodox Christianity. In a letter to his brother-in-law Richard Cranch, dated October 18, 1756, explaining why he did not want to be a preacher, he said, "The frightful engines of ecclesiastical councils, of diabolical malice, and Calvinistical good-nature never failed to terrify me exceedingly whenever I thought of preaching." In a letter of December 3, 1813, to Thomas Jefferson, he said, "Indeed, Mr. Jefferson, what could be invented to debase the ancient Christianism which Greeks, Romans, Hebrews and Christian factions, above all the Catholics, have fraudulently imposed upon the public? Miracles after miracles have rolled down in torrents." As president, he also signed a treaty with Tripoli, passed without any dissent at all by the US Senate on June 10, 1797. It said, in part, "The government of the United States is not, in any sense, founded on the Christian religion."

Washington and Madison

In his private journal in February of 1800, Jefferson wrote, "Gouverneur Morris, who pretended to be in his secrets & believed himself to be so, has often told me that Genl. Washington believed no more of that system [Christianity] than he himself did." Historian Barry Schwartz has said, "George Washington's practice of Christianity was limited and superficial because he was not himself a Christian. He repeatedly declined the church's sacraments. Never did he take communion, and when his wife, Martha, died, he waited for her outside the sanctuary.... Even on his deathbed, Washington asked for no ritual, uttered no prayer to Christ, and expressed no wish to be attended by His representative."

In 1776, Jefferson and Madison got the legislature to disestablish the Anglican Church in Virginia and cut it off from tax support. In 1784, Patrick Henry helped the clergy try to reestablish the Christian religion by giving tax money to all such churches. Jefferson and Madison called it "government-enforced religion" and defeated it. You see, Virginia was much more liberal then than it is now. Later, this principle of separation of church and state was written into the First Amendment of the Constitution.

As president, Madison vetoed a bill giving land to a Baptist church in Mississippi and another incorporating an Episcopal church in the District of Columbia because, he said, those acts violated the principle of separation of church and state. He also criticized the Congress for hiring chaplains to pray at legislative sessions. In an 1803 letter, he said, "the purpose of separation of church and state is to keep forever from these shores the ceaseless strife that has soaked the soil of Europe in blood for centuries." He also said, "Ecclesiastical establishments ... have been seen to erect a spiritual tyranny on the ruins of civil authority....They have been seen upholding the thrones of political tyranny; in no instance have they been seen as the guardian of the liberties of the people."

Franklin and Paine

Benjamin Franklin called himself "a thorough Deist." He complained that, because of his own writings, he was "pointed at with horror by good people as an Infidel or Atheist." Dr. Joseph Priestly, a Unitarian minister, wrote, "It is much to be lamented that a man of Dr. Franklin's general good character and great influence, should have been an unbeliever in Christianity, and also have done so much as he did to make others unbelievers." In "Poor Richards Almanac" in 1758, he wrote, "The way to see by faith is to shut the eye of reason." And elsewhere, "Lighthouses are more helpful than churches." And again, "Revelation has no weight with me." And still again, "I looked around for God's judgments, but saw no sign of them." In "An Essay on Toleration," he wrote, "The primitive Christians thought persecution extremely wrong in the pagans, but practiced it on one another. The first Protestants of the Church of England blamed persecution in the Romish Church, but practiced it upon the Puritans. These found it wrong in the bishops, but fell into the same practice themselves both here [in England] and in New England."

Theodore Roosevelt called Thomas Paine a "filthy little atheist." In fact, Paine was born a Quaker but soon became a deist. In *The Age of Reason* in 1794, he said, "All national institutions of churches, whether Jewish, Christian or Turkish, appear to me no other than human inventions, set up to terrify and enslave mankind, and monopolize power and profit." And also from *The Age of Reason*, "Priests and conjurers are of the same trade," and "Whenever we read the obscene stories, the voluptuous debaucheries, the cruel and tortuous executions, the unrelenting vindictiveness, with which more than half of the Bible is filled, it would be more consistent that we call it the word of a demon than the word of God. It is a history of wickedness that has served to corrupt and brutalize mankind," and "I do not believe in the creed professed by the Jewish church, by the Roman church, by the Greek church, by the Turkish church, by the Protestant church, nor by any church that I know of. My own mind is my own church.... Each of those churches accuses the other of unbelief; and for my own part, I disbelieve them all." He also said, "Belief in a cruel God makes a cruel man," and, "The age of ignorance commenced with the Christian system," and, "One good schoolmaster is of more use than a hundred priests."

Christian Denial

Against all of the evidence, Christians like to pretend that the founders of this country were Christians just like them and that this country was founded as a Christian nation rather than a religiously free nation. Yet, in October of 1831, one of their own—Episcopal minister Bird Wilson of Albany,

New York—said, "Among all our presidents from Washington downward, not one was a professor of religion, at least not of more than Unitarianism." No one with an ounce of intelligence or any honesty can possibly believe the Christians' nonsensical claims. With few exceptions, the founders were deists and Unitarians. The Christians of their time frequently called them atheists and unbelievers.

A country cannot be both Christian and free. Christians do not believe in religious freedom and, really, not in political freedom either. All of the Christian religions are proselytizing religions; they all seek to convert everyone with a belief different from theirs, and they do this because they are certain that their religion alone is right and all others wrong and sinful. Thus, any Christian with power must use his power to force the conversion of others. It is his god's will that he do so and anything less is sinful. All of the Christian sects are tyrannical by nature and, to one degree or another, they all insist on a theocratic government, one that compels belief or, at least, does everything in its power to spread the faith by force of law and political and social pressures.

The founding fathers did all they could do to prevent the use of government for religious purposes. They feared religious wars and the loss of freedom. They were right. Those today who keep pushing their religion at others through public and political institutions are courting vast dissension and persecution and they are disloyal to the basic principles of their country. Christianity is not a monolith; it is a horde of scuffling sects all of them with quite different beliefs and different definitions of both god and sin. The wisdom of Thomas Jefferson and his fellow founders must prevail now and forever if this country is to remain free.

CHAPTER 13. GODLESS SEX

Religion's Control Over Sex

To some, it may seem odd to treat sexuality, including reproduction and marriage, as religious concerns, but, in fact, religion has governed the sex and reproductive lives of citizens throughout modern and perhaps all of human history. Even when rules about such matters have been incorporated in civil law, they were invariably placed there by religionists and their political supporters. Asceticism, marriage, divorce, homosexuality, celibacy, virginity, abstinence, abortion, rape, and sexual abuse have all been and continue to be highly emotional and intense religious issues. It has been religion that sought, and often gained, control over the sex lives of citizens. Repression, punishment, extreme self-denial, shaming, and even rape and killing were the results. Thus, I think it is appropriate to include discussions about sex and reproduction with discussions about the religions themselves.

In the main, it has been religion rather than just commerce and politics that has influenced and controlled the sex lives of the citizens of this and every other country. Sex is the strongest and the most consequential of all drives. That is why religionists have always tried to control and often to suppress it in the name of some god or other. Organizations that can effectively control and direct the sexual behavior of citizens have a powerful tool to use as a way of enhancing their power. If all of the rules of your sex and reproductive life are under the control of priests and preachers, you are their servant. When they manage to present themselves as their god's sole moral representatives on earth, they can manipulate even lords and kings and generals.

As Freud showed, sex gets into and hugely influences just about everything. The priests learned long ago that the more you suppress sex, the stronger the countervailing urges become and the easier it is to direct them into useful channels. If you can manipulate the sex and reproductive lives of an entire population, you can dominate them in most other ways too. Guilt is a powerful tool as are rape, jealousy, shame, seduction, and romantic yearning.

Kings and Popes

Throughout history, kings and high priests have jointly ruled over most nations. At times, of course, they competed with one another and quite often they became enemies. Popes have raised themselves above kings and, at times, have issued edicts and moral rules to be enforced by political authorities. Religious leaders pretended to be sacred, pretended to speak to god and to hear back from him. Kings had armies and wealth and dominant control over the populations in their hands but they were often under the control of the religionists. Finally, democratic liberalism and science pretty much put an end to royalism and the divine powers of kings; presidents and priests still rule today, but with weaker hands. Among the tools still at use are sexual constraints and demands for purity and abnegation. Even in democratic countries, the religionist still set the rules of sexual behavior and the politicians implement them and enforce them.

Natural Urges

Celibacy is unnatural and turns humans to violence, repression, and fanaticism. In fact, all forms of fleshly denial are unnatural and inhuman. The theory of religious extremists the world over has been that abstinence somehow purifies the body and pleases god. Quite the opposite is true. Abstinence poisons and harms the body and certainly displeases any decent god. The hunger for food, the thirst for water, and the desire for sex are all absolutely natural. To deny any of them is to pervert life and religion. Nothing is more abnormal than a refusal to allow the human body to function as its inborn tendencies direct it to do. Temporary denials and restraints are sometimes necessary for purely practical, usually economic, reasons but, even then, they are harmful to the body and psyche. Freedom from want and the full expression of inborn appetites are the natural and moral conditions of humankind. Those who restrict the freedom of others to function normally are tyrants. Those who restrict themselves for no practical reasons are fools.

Censorship

Suppression of dirty pictures and words is not possible without censorship. In the end, all censorship must become total. There can be no such thing as a little censorship. To allow censorship at all is to give absolute power to the censor. The victims of censorship cannot know what the censor forbids them and thus surrender all choice to him. By the very nature of his function, the censor may suppress anything he chooses to suppress and his subjects can never know what he has screened from their view. They can only know what he allows them to know. There is no tyranny any worse than this, no suppression any more complete. Given the power, of course the censor will define everything as pornographic so he can hide it all and control it all.

In the end, there can be no useful argument about any definition of pornography. Those who sincerely attack pornography delude themselves; it is not pornography that they oppose but freedom. They should ask themselves some questions. Why do they have such an insatiable lust to rule the bodies and senses of others? Why do they insist so fanatically on trying to dictate the private lives of everyone else? Did they never hear of the right of people to make their own decisions and govern their own lives and their own bodies?

The greatest perversion of freedom is censorship. Liberty cannot coexist with censorship. The would-be censors want to keep the rest of us locked in total darkness forever. Those who fear dirty pictures and words and want to suppress them only help the tyrants; or more likely, they *are* the tyrants.

Conservative Sex

There is nothing more obscene and corrupt than sexless love, the kind displayed in the Hollywood movies of the forties and fifties but, for some reason, not in those of the twenties and thirties nor in those of the sixties and thereafter. Sexless love consisted of a pretense that romance was somehow pure and spiritual, that it was platonic and Christian and never involved the body at all. This weird kind of love was raised up by the myths of medieval knighthood and by cloying lies about those flowers of Southern womanhood. What was so obscene and corrupt about it all was the pretense and hypocrisy, the separation from reality, the substitution of romantic lies and evasions for the real, mucky thing. No wonder the kids of the sixties were disgusted by the phoniness of their parents and revolted against their fairy tales.

The conservative "moralists" among us are still preaching the lies and corruptions of this sick mythology and, of course, it is always presented as the very essence of Christianity and patriotism. For example, the truly slimy attacks against Bill Clinton were fanatically dishonest and they were based on the crazy notion that Clinton's sex life was not only unusual but demonic, deeply perverted, and treasonous. He was supposed to have dirtied the oval office and betrayed his country by being a sexual being. Those who accused him—nearly the entire membership of the Republican Party and most members of the establishment press corps—pretended that they themselves didn't have sex organs at all and had never done anything sexual. They thought they had a right and even a duty to judge him harshly and a moral calling to destroy him, his family, and all of his associates. They actually thought or pretended to think that they were on the side of morality and that they were protecting children against some monstrous predator and abuser. It was all horse shit, of course. The real scum were the accusers, not the accused.

Because Clinton had evaded and obscured and even lied a little about the minute details of his sex life, the conservatives accused him of being an extreme liar and perjurer. In fact, he was more honest than they were and he was nowhere near as dishonest as Nixon, Reagan, and the Bushes or even as dishonest as Lyndon Johnson and Dwight Eisenhower.

Clinton was not a paragon of virtue but he was of better character than his enemies. That he was impeached over a total triviality was one of the great disgraces in American political history. The Republican Party has once again proven itself to be the McCarthy party. How any decent American could vote for a Republican is beyond me.

Children and Sex

Children are not the sexual dolts and ding-a-lings their parents think they are. Though they may get the details comically wrong, even the very, very young know all about sexual desire and the pleasures of their own body parts. Sex is not evil and a knowledge of it is not damaging to the minds and morals of the young. On the contrary, it is ignorance, shame, fear, and guilt that are damaging and even debilitating. Parents harm their children terribly by loading their own shame and guilt onto them.

The real child abusers are the suppressers and the fanatical moralists, in short, the parents and the idiot preachers and priests who have convinced them that sex is evil and that all knowledge of it must be locked away from the eyes, the ears, and the entire bodies and minds of the young. Such ignorance and superstition have maladjusted millions of people and made them miserable and twisted throughout their lives. Christianity and capitalism together have made greed, repression, and exploitation high moral values and sexual expression low and disgraceful. Can there be a worse perversion of life or of the lives of the young?

Nature of Homosexuality

I don't think that homosexuality is a mental illness and I don't think it's a choice, because I can't imagine anyone freely choosing such a life. I do think that homosexuality is abnormal in the sense of its being unusual and comparatively rare. Homosexuals are certainly not like the great majority of people, at least in their sexual behavior and perhaps in some other related ways. It really doesn't make much sense to pretend that it's perfectly "normal" for a man to behave like a woman or a woman to behave like a man. And it strikes me as absolutely coo-coo for anyone to pretend that sexuality is just a political or social construction.

I also don't think the word "perversion" is inaccurate when it is used without malice to describe homosexual behavior. What homosexuals do sexually is certainly a deviation from "normal" sexual behavior; in fact, such behavior is so far from the norm that it seems incomprehensible to most heterosexuals. I myself can't imagine how anyone can get pleasure out of another body just like his or her own. Nevertheless, there is no reason for anyone to hate homosexuals and no one should suppress them, oppress them, or reform them. Their sex lives and their personal habits and customs are their own business and there is no rational reason to interfere with them or reduce their rights.

If you could push a button and end all heterosexual behavior, then all life would end with the deaths of those now alive. If you did the same to homosexual behavior, nothing biologically important would happen. No life would end and no species would be changed. This is surely an argument for the normality and necessity of heterosexuality and the abnormality and triviality of homosexuality. This is not a moral judgment, just a practical and logical one.

It's really not possible to conclude that homosexuality is perfectly normal biologically or that it has no negative consequences. Homosexuality is sterility; it produces nothing biological. It is not life enhancing and it offers nothing biological to the human species; in fact, it subtracts from human possibility because it smothers out and misdirects the life force in every involved human being. There is simply no way to raise homosexual behavior to the same biological level as that of heterosexual behavior. This is not special pleading; it is simply factual. I am talking about biology here, not about the right and naturalness of humans to love one another in whatever way they choose without being persecuted by governments or religions.

None of this is an argument for abusing or persecuting homosexuals. God knows, they must suffer enough just from being different and for being persecuted because of their difference; but they exist and they have every right to be treated as full human beings with the same rights and the same respect as anyone else. However, this does not mean that their behavior, whether chosen or inbuilt, is normal and natural.

Gay Pride

What homosexuals deserve is indifference, benign neglect if you will. They certainly don't deserve the attention they demand for themselves or the concentrated political power they seem to seek for their movement. Why should anyone try to make his or her sex practices into a movement anyway? Sex isn't or shouldn't be political. Of course, there are plenty of suppressers and punishers out there and they take a special and fanatical interest in the sex lives of other people. No one should allow them any power over others but that is no argument for the politicization of homosexuality. Sex ought to be kept out of politics altogether.

It seems to me that homosexuals are extremely stupid in their efforts to become players in the political game. They must be about three or four percent of the population. They can never win any majority vote on anything without depending on the tolerance and cooperation of heterosexuals. Their perpetual, sometimes aggressive, and often comical political actions gain them nothing but disdain and resistance. In fact, their political antics have hugely damaged the Democratic Party and liberalism and have probably put Republican conservatives in office in a good many elections.

The Anti-Abortionists

For a long time, the Catholic hierarchy has believed that both abortion and birth control are murder and that the sexual impulse is dirty, unholy, and sinful. Even thinking about sex is thus a crime against their god and his church and only abstinence is truly moral and upright. This condemns all of humankind though the priests and nuns and other religionists pretend that they don't have sexual thoughts or ever have any kind of sex at all. They are all liars, of course. If sexual desire is evil and forbidden, then why did the gods embed it so deeply and unshakably in the human body and mind? Could there be a god so utterly vicious and silly? Everybody has sex and uses birth control these days though the Pope and his legions continue their strange pretense of abstinence and purity.

The big issue is abortion. Until the rise of the moral majority and the Protestant fundamentalists a few years ago, nobody in America but the

Catholics ever believed that abortion was murder or worried about it at all. Then, there was a political alliance and a whole crew of fanatics emerged from the religious slime to claim they were on the side of the so-called unborn. They began attacking and killing people in the name of mercy and compassion, a fairly routine practice by Christians since that religion began.

To prop up this murderous theory, these Christians argue that life begins with conception, a change in thinking that more or less trivializes their former belief that birth control was also murder. Now, they pretty much concentrate on stopping abortion and leave complaints about birth control to such people as William Bennett, Jesse Helms, Henry Hyde, and the Pope. They still object to all sex except their own but they ordinarily won't kill you unless you threaten the "unborn." Strangely, they claim that the unborn are already alive but they don't extend the same courtesy to the un-conceived.

To believe their hocus pocus, these Christian conservatives have to believe that life is created anew every time a man impregnates a woman. This is an odd departure from their claim that god created human life originally about six thousand years ago, and it is a massive departure from the scientific story that says the life spark came into existence somehow through evolution several billion years ago and then developed into other life forms and eventually into human beings. The anti-abortionists reject evolution, of course, but even their own shorter version of the story that has god creating human life originally out of mud, a bunch of ribs, or some other handy substance is a flat contradiction of their claim, now, that abortion is murder in some special sense that is fundamentally different from other methods of avoiding conception and birth. You see, aside from squeamishness, there is no difference in the end between terminating a fetus and refusing to conceive in the first place.

If human life began long ago and if the spark has been carried ever since in a long succession of copulations and ejections into ovarine crevices, then abortion does not end life in any final and irrevocable sense and it cannot be considered murder, that is, unless all abstinence and any damming up of sperm and waste of ovum without conception is also murder. In short, if the aborters are killing the unborn, then so is the Pope, all of his priests and nuns, and any other holy refuseniks who pour out their seed on the ground or leave their ovum unfertilized and the life in it dead. Thus, the virgins and celibates are killing all of the life in their loins and bellies and the various anti-sex brigades can't have it every way at once. Carried to its natural conclusion, their theory of the creation of life requires every human being to maximize the potential life in his or her body irrespective of age, convenience, practicality, consequence, or any marriage vows whatever.

In other words, it is everybody's duty to copulate all the time so none of our seed or any of our eggs is ever wasted. Short of that, we are all killing the unborn in the billions and it is the celibates, virgins, and eunuchs who are the guiltiest of all. Now, if anyone is willing to support the idea that everyone must have the maximum number of offspring possible, then maybe—just maybe—they have the moral right to call abortion murder and birth control sinful.

Anti-Abortion Frenzy

Why not have a law requiring that every egg be fertilized? Why not a death penalty for masturbation and even for wet dreams? If abortion after conception is murder, then so is abortion before conception. The egg and the sperm are as alive as any fetus.

To waste any of them must be murder. The pro-life tyrants aren't pro-life at all. They abort their own arguments and try to arrange nature to suit their own biases and conveniences. They are dishonest, hypocritical, and self-serving in everything they say and do. They care nothing for the lives of "unborn" children or anyone else.

With a few exceptions, the pro-lifers are the conservatives who love war and hate the poor, the sick, the hungry, and jobless. They are always moralistic about sex but never about the exploitation, injury, abuse, and death they so viciously visit on others in the name of their empty, corrupt morality. Hate guides their anti-abortion brutality as it does every other facet of their gory conservatism. They are not the children of god; they are the vomit of Satan.

Saving Vegetables and the Un-conceived

I think the absolutist positions taken by the animal-rights activists and the anti-abortionists are similarly irrational and unreasonable. If science is right that all life on earth came from one original spark two or three billion years ago, then that might *seem* to give some validity to the claims by the two groups that both animal and human life are sacred and must not be ended arbitrarily. However, the two groups only argue for the protection of their own selected clients and not anyone else. In fact, the anti-abortionists, to a considerable degree, believe in blowing people up and killing them to "protect the unborn." In other words, they don't value life at all. The as-yet unconceived and the already born are often the targets of their irrational inconsistency. Though not fanatically violent like the anti-abortionists, the animalists don't argue for the rights of plants, least of all vegetables, and not for the rights of bacteria and other microscopic life forms either.

If all earthly life came from just one original spark and if all life is, therefore, precious and equal, then it must be equally wrong to terminate or prevent life in any of its forms. However, if such a moral policy is followed to its natural end, than all life must end now or soon. We are all predators. We must eat something and what we eat must have come from something now or once alive. We cannot live without using other life forms for nourishment and even, in the case of bacteria, for protection against assaults by other bacteria or germs. Each of our bodies contains within it billions of other life forms and we use them for our survival. Life consumes life. Human beings could never have come into existence at all without destroying other life.

The eggs in a woman's body are alive as are the sperm from a man's body. In a narrow sense, a particular piece of life is, indeed, ended by abortion but it is also ended, even more completely, by celibacy and virginity. Celibates, especially religious celibates, are usually permanent life deniers and baby-killers. To refuse all sex for all time is to destroy completely all of the life in your own body. Unless you are willing to make a baby every single time it is possible for you to do so and without regard for age, marital status, economic condition, health, or even mutual attraction, then you are an aborter. In other words, we are all aborters including especially the Pope, his priests and nuns, and all of those in the antiabortion brigade.

What this means ultimately is that the arguments of the animalists and the anti-abortionists are moral baloney. Their arguments are inconsistent and hypocritical at their core and on all their edges. Killing animals for truly useful purposes and terminating pregnancies or practicing birth control for practical and sensible reasons are not cruel practices by any rational measure. In fact, they are absolutely unavoidable if humanity is to survive at all. And so, finally, the question is where to draw the line. Absolute prohibitions won't work and aren't rational or moral. Both the animalists and the anti-abortionists are dead wrong and their attacks against others in the interests of their dogmas are unethical in the extreme.

Spark of Life

Some argue that a fetus is a recognizable human being. Well, it does look a little like a human but so does a Mandrake root. What makes a human being is the spark of life, not a shape and a form, and that human spark exists as much in every egg and every sperm as it does in any fetus. Human life does not begin with conception or at birth. It began several billion years ago when the spark of life first kindled. Life is continuous and universal, not intermittent and particular. At some point in the history of life, humanity began, but no one can say exactly when that was. There are those who consider human life sacred and all other life degraded. There is no basis for such a belief. We all came from the same original spark and all life forms are our brothers and sisters. To kill any one is as murderous as it is to kill any other. As a practical matter, however, it is not possible to avoid killing some life forms in the ordinary course of living. Mere breath and movement take lives. Life devours life as a matter of course.

It is not immoral to use the lives of others for our own survival or even for lesser purposes if those purposes are essential and ultimately life affirming. It *is* immoral to waste life and to kill wantonly as in aggressive war, commercial exploitation, and gun proliferation.

Abortion Alternative

The pro-lifers are every bit as murderous as the pro-choicers and then some. Typically, pro-lifers have been warmongers, religious persecutors, racists, and sexual puritans. With few exceptions, they have supported every national war, no matter how irrational or viciously murderous it has been. Their sexual repressions deny life at every turn and they try to impose their morality on everyone else. They are usually bad people but that does not mean there are no valid arguments against abortion.

For me, the major argument against abortion is that it trivializes life. In truth, all a pregnant woman gives is her time and a little pain, all of it a result of her own behavior and her own or her partners' carelessness. Why not bring every pregnancy to its natural end: birth? Then, let society or the state find a home for the child somewhere. The woman can then go her own way without penalty or further pain. That would be no great offense against her choice or her freedom.

Abortion and Choice

The quotation just below backs up a view that I have held for at least forty years but, until now, have never seen expressed anywhere else. About fifteen or twenty years ago, I wrote the essay below exploring the origins of life but no one would publish it, including local newspapers in the last three cities in which I have lived. Even the free choice supporters of abortion rights turned up their noses at this essay. I suppose they thought it might weaken their arguments for abortion although, as the essay shows, I am very much in favor of "choice." The quotation is an extract from an article in the *Skeptical Inquirer* of January/February, 2014, by Dr. Elie A. Shneour titled, *When Does a Human Life Begin?* followed by my long-ago essay.

The quotation:

> Without resorting to arcane considerations, it is possible to argue that life does not begin at conception, as defined by the fusion of an

egg with a spermatozoon. The plain fact is that both the egg and the spermatozoon before emerging are already living entities. That horde of competing spermatozoa engage in a remarkable race until only one of them is left to reach and fertilize the female egg. The rest of that multitude perishes....One female egg is delivered each and every lunar month during a woman's reproductive years, but most of those ova are also lost and die unfertilized as well.... Very few acorns become trees, the vast majority of them dying by the wayside. Life does not begin at conception because it never stops.

My essay:

Even many liberals dislike my argument that life does not begin just with impregnation but, in fact, began a billion or so years ago when the life spark first kindled into being somehow and inhabited the first resulting sentient creature, the father and/or mother of us all. No one knows how or just when this first spark of life came into existence. Science says this and says that the life spark that kindled then has continued in a whole series of material forms made sentient by its presence. These ever-evolving forms carried the spark on through time until the human race itself arrived with that original flame of life still inside those human receptacles.

In short, human life does not suddenly begin when a male plants his seed inside a female and when one of his sperm penetrates her tumbling and also living egg. One life spark thus merges with another life spark to design a whole man or woman child. This is an act of transference and combination, not an act of origination. Anyone who is rational and believes in the findings of science must accept this argument.

Thus, both contraception and abortion are interferences with a natural reproductive process and, because of this interference, early Christians and some other religionists, opposed it. However, this leads inevitably to the conclusion that abstinence, celibacy, and virginity are also abortions of a kind. They all smother out and destroy the life spark in every unused female egg and in every one of the disarmed billions of sperm that swarm in every man's semen. Thus, most of a man's sperm is fated to die by the workings of biology or, as disappointed religionists might say, by the hand of a wasteful god. Believers must conclude that their creator god is also a destroyer god, an aborter through clumsily accidental and irrational means.

Some Buddhists believe that all life is holy and that even the smallest creatures are sacred including germs, viruses, and all of the other forms of life that float in all air and swarm across the face of the earth in multiform abundance. Such believers walk carefully and wear masks to avoid crushing or breathing in and destroying the life that exists everywhere in the environment that surrounds them. This respect for life is admirable but far too extreme to be practical or remotely effectual. These views of the holiness of everything and the duty to fully protect it all certainly seem like a dead end to me.

Some of us die that others may live. We all feed on one another. We are all predators. Enormous numbers of life forms live inside of every human body and those life forms fight one another, some seeking to kill us, others fighting to save us. Our very bodies are battle grounds on which a struggling morass of tangled, opposing forces work in unseen and unknown ways to make us what we are, to keep us healthy and alive, to keep us safe from infection and diminution, sometimes to destroy us. We know not what they do or why. They too must live and perform their purposes.

As far as I know, my arguments about—in favor of—abortion in limited and truly necessary ways are entirely unique. I know of no one who agrees with what I say. Even liberals who believe in "choice" are unwilling to credit my argument presumably because they think it concedes too much to the anti-abortion forces and because my arguments make a hash of the pretense that life can be lightly and justly canceled without loss or damage. In all of its forms and at all of its stages, life should be respected and should not be snuffed out carelessly and too swiftly.

However, at the end point, I believe that humans must not deny individual choices to those trying to live their lives within their own personal environments and circumstances. Governments and religions have no business making these decisions for women and for their partners. I am much in favor of individual, unashamed, and un-coerced choice. It must be remembered that abortion, in one form or another, is all but universal. Clinical abortion is but one of the many forms of abortion. In one way or another, we all perform abortions, regularly and routinely. Not to use our eggs and sperm is abortion as much as any clinical procedure. The Pope, the priests, the nuns, the preachers, the mullahs, biology or god himself are all aborters.

Yet, there are alternatives. Better systems of humane and respectful financial support for pregnant women coupled with governmental and societal systems of adoption are alternatives. Effective, safe, and universally available contraception is another excellent way to reduce clinical abortions. Abstinence is an ineffective and silly pretense, nothing more. Humans are sexual beings and they are going to do it in some fashion no matter how sinful the religionists say it is. Until the religious dogmatists accept human nature and its complications, there will continue to be misery, fear, shame, injury, and death waiting for women around every turn in the political mood and inside every bedroom.

Repression

It is apparently impossible for Americans to give up their puritanism. Even supposedly liberal and enlightened feminists rage against pornography and the sex act itself as fanatically as Cotton Mather ever did. Almost all Americans think there is something evil about sex and that everyone must be protected from it, most of all children.

Most of the sustained interest that children have in sex comes from the great mystery grownups wrap it in as they try to "protect" the children from any knowledge of it. It's hard to see why anyone the least bit rational should think that children can possibly be harmed by the sight of a "dirty" picture, a naked body, or even a vision of two live bodies copulating. Despite their lack of experience, children are not idiots and they do not imitate everything they see. Children are sexual beings but they are not ravenous and they are not likely to prey on one another gratuitously.

Obviously, there has been and there will always be sexual abuse in the world but there has been far more economic, political, religious, and social abuse. Those who want to abuse others always strike at vulnerability and weakness and, quite obviously, sexual repression by society has made everyone sexually ashamed and vulnerable. In cases of sexual abuse, it is shame that is being exploited, the shame created by a society pretending to shield children from evil, in effect, from themselves. What makes the threat of sexual abuse especially potent is the natural desire of the potential victim and the way that desire has been distorted into fear and shame by the repressions of society.

Ignorant people are the most vulnerable, especially children. Those who have been hiding their sexuality all of their lives are terribly afraid of their own natures and the uses to which others may put their inclinations. Most of the fear is self-generated and artificial. Those who fear sex are ruled by it.

Marriage for All

Republicans are trying to protect the "sanctity of marriage" by suppressing marriage among homosexuals. They think marriage is a sacred institution. In fact, it isn't an institution at all but, rather, a contract between two people. That doesn't mean it shouldn't be taken seriously but it does mean that the contract is only binding on the two people involved and on nobody else. I don't think an unmarried person can commit adultery at all. The persons who made the contract are the only ones who can violate it. Nevertheless, people ought to keep their agreements, they ought to comply with their contractual obligations. The two people involved can have an understanding: they can alter the terms of the contract as they choose. It's nobody's business but their own. Why shouldn't all people, including homosexuals, have these same rights and worries? None of the people involved have any institutional obligations at all. They have every right to live as they choose and to institute and end their unions when it is no longer mutually beneficial and satisfying. In fact, either party, with or without the consent of the other, has or should have the complete right to terminate the contract. Property settlements and the custody of children are proper civic matters judicable under law.

It's absurd to say that religion and the state have a right to force people to marry or to prevent them from marrying. Forced relationships and separations are tyrannical and they always come to a bad end, sometimes a violent one. Children are not better off living under the tyranny of a coerced marriage. No doubt children are better off in a stable family situation but that does not include forced marriages nor does it exclude the right of homosexuals to have or raise children. Forced marriages and separations only serve the interests of the institutions that compel them and those institutions are always acting out of arrogance and tyrannical self-interest. There is nothing sacred, democratic, or decent in raising institutions above the welfare and happiness of the people whose interests they are supposed to serve.

Abstinence

George Bush and the Republicans have ginned up an abstinence movement of considerable size and influence, and they are handing out hundreds of millions of dollars of the taxpayers' money to push it and advertise it.

The crazy Christians have children swearing under oath that they will refrain from any and all sexual activity until they marry. These Christian sex-nuts claim to believe that children don't have sex organs at all or powerful sex drives and refuse to admit that all normal human beings regularly have sex of some kind starting at or even before puberty and extending all the way to the edge of their graves. They are denying the very existence of a drive that is at least as powerful and as natural as the hunger for food and the thirst for water. These false moralists are teaching a perversion that is bound to result in blighted lives for millions of innocent people.

The puritan fanatics who advocate this nonsense are themselves sexual beings and every one of them indulges in secret sex routinely. Those who don't have sex with some other being or object turn to masturbation. In fact, masturbation is a universal practice. I doubt that there is a single person in this or any country who hasn't masturbated. Those innocents who try to resist in the name of godliness have wet dreams and live guilty, agitated lives. Just about every biologist and doctor knows this as do all other sane people, even including most Republicans and Christians if there are any sane ones left. Lying about your sex life doesn't mean that you don't have one.

In the middle centuries of the Christian era, some twisted church rulers made sex into a taboo and tried to force abstinence on everyone not married under their rules. Many of the officials of the church, ordered to be celibate, took this fake moralism seriously and were driven crazy by their unrestrainable urges. They punished their own bodies for refusing to obey the commands of the church. To prove their obedience and their purity, they flagellated themselves cruelly with sticks and whips and chains and knives. Some of them castrated or otherwise maimed themselves in revenge against their sinful bodies. They wore sackcloth and thorns, beat and injured their flesh, went filthy, sickened, and suffered so greatly that they became addled and simple-minded. A Catholic clique called Opus Dei still indulges in this system of self-flagellation today and its members carry on their persons instruments of self-torture. It is said that our most punitive and authoritarian Supreme Court justice ever, Antonin Scalia, is a self-torturer and carries around such a device.

Some of the extreme nuts killed themselves and were made into saints so the church could point to them as good examples of chastity and holiness. It was crazy stuff and the sensible people, in the church and outside it, went right on having sex with one another and ignored the absurd behavior demanded by the religious hypocrites. Many a child was fathered—or mothered—by priests and nuns, some even by bishops, cardinals, and popes.

Most people realized long ago just how ridiculous this experiment in lunacy was and just how dangerous it was to the lives of those who were damaged by it, that is, by everyone except the "true" Christians. Now, the religious cuckoos are in charge again, at least in this country, and their dogmas are as bizarre and twisted as were those of their degenerate forebears.

Chapter 14. God's Version of Sex, A Little Myth

(Extracted from an unpublished novel, *Man of Light*.)

Of course, it was god who invented men and women and everything else too. He didn't have anything to do one day and so he began shaping up and refining a lot of random objects and essences just to amuse himself and the other gods. It was a kind of doodling, and it was a little bit careless. You see, god made a lot of mistakes when he created men and women. He did a pretty good job on all the other animals, and the plants, and on the minerals and gases too, but he just couldn't get the physical and especially the mental and emotional sides of the humans just right. As we said, he made everyone else first and then he made people, so you would think he had some good examples to go by for his very last creation. But god was not like you and me. He didn't learn anything through repetition and practice because he was already perfect to begin with and didn't know how to add to his great store of knowledge and skill. And to make matters worse, he got bored real easy, and it was repetition and hard work that bored him the most and made him nod off. He nodded off a lot when he was working on his original human beings, and sometimes he forgot what he had already done and confused it with what needed doing. Consequently, he left a lot out, he unintentionally did some things two or three times, and, of course, he never did any of it exactly the same way twice in a row. The results were lots of flaws, a fair number of incompletions, and quite a few inner and outer contradictions.

To be completely honest, god really made a mess of us human beings; and the rest of the creatures on earth, including the minerals and gases, were real disappointed. They had hoped for something better. When they found out that humans were very dependent and parasitic and just couldn't make it through life without leaning on everyone else for heavy help and sustenance, they were pretty bitter. I mean, right away the humans began breathing in, swallowing down, stomping on, elbowing aside, pulverizing, using up, harnessing, exploiting, enslaving, injuring, and killing everybody and everything else. It wasn't very fair, and it made life unstable and unpleasant for everyone. It also made everyone just a little bit mad at god, human beings most of all.

Just about the biggest mistake god ever made was his version of sex. There in his workshop one day, he divided some partly-made humans into two groups for no particular reason at all and began welding on a spigot down between the lower legs of each of the incomplete creatures in the first group; of course, the purpose of the spigot was to drain off any excess liquids and impurities that might collect in the human body through normal wear and tear. You see, the spigot was a safety mechanism. About half way through, god nodded off and, when he awoke, he forgot just what he had been doing, but he remembered enough to know he had been working on the drainage problem. He continued with the second group, but this time he just carved holes down there where he had been previously welding on spigots. The hole was a valve for draining off excess liquids and impurities. You see, god had solved the same problem twice without meaning to. God didn't ever correct his mistakes because he was a very proud entity and didn't like to admit that anything of his making ever went wrong. And so about half of his people were stuck with spigots between their legs and the other half with valves.

God was very good at using his earlier mistakes to make still worse ones later on. He did that with the spigots and valves. He wanted his new creatures to get a little pleasure out of life. Of course, it occurred to him as it does to just about everyone that the spigots fit right into the valves. It takes a lot of preparation and loud panting, a little wriggling, a lot of horizontal contortion, and some pushing and pulling, but it does work. Sometimes, it *is* necessary to use a little Vaseline, some butter, or perhaps some whipped cream to get things started, but just about all of the spigots will fit comfortably and pleasurably into all of the valves. Of course, god built in the pleasure part of the equation after making his unacknowledged manufacturing mistake and after then noticing the good fit among spigots and valves.

Most people don't understand the natural laziness of the immortals and especially not that of god and his brothers and sisters. Efficiency is the capitalist name for laziness, but the gods aren't capitalists and they wouldn't understand that definition. Satan would, though, for, you see, hell is just a big capitalist factory, a kind of foundry or steel-making plant. Anyway, god wanted people to die off one-by-one so they wouldn't get bored with life or take it too much for granted, but he didn't want the whole human race to disappear right away. He was pretty good at arithmetic, and he knew that

that was just what would happen if death was common place and he didn't add some more humans to the population from time-to-time. Because of his laziness and because he didn't want to be a capitalist, he just couldn't put himself in the people-making business throughout all of eternity or even through enough of it to give the humans time enough to use their free will to polish one another off a few million at a time or perhaps, at last, all in one big conflagration. Therefore, god decided to use the spigots and valves of humans for another purpose other than just the disposal of waste and the titillation of sex. He decided to let human beings propagate themselves by purposefully and pleasurably meshing their spigots and valves so the male could shoot some seed from his spigot through the female's valve and into her stomach where the seed could grow and be safe until it became a little person and gained enough will and vim and vigor to hoist himself or herself out of the female's stomach through her valve and into the light of the larger world. And so god unthinkingly mixed the pleasure of sex with the result of propagation, and this dual function confused the conservatives into believing that pleasure is a sin and new life a tainted punishment for doing it without a religious license and a strong sense of guilt and shame.

But, despite what conservatives believe, sex is a perfectly natural and indeed essential function. Its multiple purposes still confuse some people but only the ones cursed with an excess of stupidity, religion, arrogance, and resentment at the pleasure of others. In their confusion and self-love, conservatives intensely dislike poor people, especially the colored ones, and don't want them to have any kids. Therefore, conservatives object to sex for both of its purposes. They dislike pleasurable sex for everyone except themselves and want to prohibit reproductive sex by everyone different from themselves so they can limit their populations, cancel out their voting power, and keep them subordinate and useful as pack animals and servants. The reason conservatives so much dislike pleasure in other people and try so hard to control it and even to suppress it entirely is because they believe in privilege for the few and hard work for the many. They just can't see how the economy or anything can work at all unless there are stern absolutes to stop easy pleasure and require hard work for the great majority. You see, conservatives love the idea of leisure for themselves and work for everyone else. It's their one and only world view. The funny thing is that their intense and angry efforts to control everyone and everything lead them into all kinds of perversions, sterilities, blocked passions, greedy obsessions, and misguided actions that rob them of the ability to enjoy anything normal or function humanely in the presence or with the participation of others. They actually believe that those who take pleasure in one another and have kids of their own are committing sins and crimes against them. They even make thousands of laws and invent entire religions to stop sex by the wrong people. It's too bad conservatives can't relax and enjoy life like the rest of us often do. Perhaps the cause is a long-lasting virus, a programming mistake, or a warped gene or two. I certainly don't know for sure why conservatives are twisted in these odd ways, and I'll bet a bowl of garum you don't know either.

And so god created some confusion when he invented sex in just the way he did and compounded the problem still more when he allowed the conservatives to emerge and seize control of sex, journalism, religion, and politics. Throughout history, conservatives have plagued others with their rigid absolutes, their fixed dogmas, their police raids, their military attacks, and their loud, moralistic screechings. They are a real pain in everybody's ass and nobody likes them at all.

Just about the worst thing they have ever done in the United States, at least with respect to their inappropriate mixing of sex and politics, involved their virulent hate campaign against King Billy because of the way he almost deployed his spigot against an intern in the service of his country. It is not a pretty story, or a serious one, but it dominated all the news cycles in our noble country just the same. You can find various accounts about this historical event on the Internet and sometimes on a Big Screen show. Look under "The Impeachment of King Billy" if you want to know the details.

CHAPTER 15. FORCED SCHOOL PRAYER

What's Wrong With Forcing Children to Pray?

When, on June 26, 2002, the Court of Appeals for the Ninth Circuit outlawed the phrase "under god" in the pledge of allegiance, what it was really outlawing was *forced prayer*. The 1953 intrusion of those words into the pledge made it impossible for any citizen to honestly declare his or her allegiance to this country without also embracing the monotheist god of the Christians. As always, the court's affirmation of the right of a citizen to be patriotic without being a Christian caused the Christians once again to express their bitter hatred of "liberal judges" and their utter contempt for the very idea of religious liberty and the prospect of showing some small respect for the rights and the consciences of other people. Toleration and civility are not among the Christian virtues.

The court said that the words "under God" were an endorsement of monotheism. Those words also quite clearly refer to the Christian god. Other religionists do not commonly use the name "god" to refer to their deity. The Muslims call their god "Allah," the Buddhists worship the Buddha, the Hindus Vishnu or Krishna, and the Jews refer to Yahweh or Elohim or refuse to name their god at all. There are as well numerous deistic and pantheistic gods as well as polytheistic ones not to mention the millions of people who believe in no god at all. Does anyone doubt that the Christians would foam at the mouth and march on Washington if anyone required them or their children to pledge allegiance or pray to Allah or Vishnu or Yahweh?

Make no mistake: The Christians do not like non-Christians and want to isolate and harass them by forcing them to publicly identify themselves as non-Christian over and over and over again; then, knowing their names, the Christians can label them as sinful and disreputable people in need of correction. The Christian objective is to force conversions through public embarrassment, shaming, insult, threat, and outright violence. Coupling a patriotic pledge with a declaration of belief in the monotheist god is a way for the Christians to tar disbelievers as unpatriotic and even treasonous. This McCarthyite tactic is especially brutal when it is directed against vulnerable children.

Historically, the Christian effort to force daily school prayers out of the mouths of children was only partially successful and so, fifty years ago, they snuck their god into the pledge of allegiance as a step toward establishing their religion and supporting their preposterous claim that the United States is a Christian nation. They want to exclude non-Christians from citizenship altogether and they want to take names and deliver punishments. As always, being cowardly, they make school children their number one target.

What's wrong with "voluntary" school prayer or a godly affirmation concealed in the pledge of allegiance? Well, to begin with, it can't be voluntary. Approved prayers ordered up every day by the authorities, conducted by them on public property, and involving a captive audience of children with private beliefs and differing backgrounds cannot be voluntary. Announcing to a gathering of such children that they can avoid saying those prayers, or hearing them, by leaving the room is absurd. It is only a way of embarrassing and coercing children who may not share the religious beliefs of their classmates and teachers.

To apply this kind of pressure to a child every single day of his or her school life is offensive and cruel in the extreme. Can anyone possibly doubt that believing teachers, classmates, and parents will taunt and criticize those who are different from them? It happens now to Jewish, Muslim, and atheist children, especially in backward places like Alabama, Mississippi, Virginia, West Virginia, Oklahoma, and the Carolinas.

No teacher and no other school official has any right to say a single word to a school child about his or her religious belief or disbelief. Even children—especially children—have a right to guard their private belief against the prying eyes and ears of government officials, including teachers. People of any age or station have the right to absolute privacy regarding matters of conscience and belief. To demand public words and acts that reveal the heart of a child, or a grown-up, to would-be religious molesters like the Christian fanatics so intensely determined to lay their forced prayers on every child every day is barbaric and vicious.

Every school child and every other citizen should be taught as a civics lesson that he or she has an absolute right of conscience and privacy with regard to matters of religious and political belief. And each child should be taught that those who try to pry open the minds and reveal the beliefs of children, or anyone, for the purpose of pressuring or converting them is guilty of a tyrannical and unacceptable act, an act of child abuse, an act of oppression and bad faith, an un-American and un-Christian act, indeed an act that ought to be made criminal and ought to be punished by imprisonment.

The Viciousness of Christian Threats and Coercions

For a long time now, non-Christians have been persecuted by Christian fundamentalists, especially in the South. Only a few years ago, in Alabama, Governor Fob James whipped up persecution and religious bigotry just as former Governor George Wallace used to whip up racial hatred. Inspired by his governor, state judge Roy Moore dishonored the Bill of Rights in his courtroom and posted the Ten Commandments in its place. This was done in defiance of a federal court order against forced school prayer which Moore called an "unconstitutional abuse of power." This stirred up zealous Christian students in De Kalb County and they marched on city hall and "their" school to protect Jesus from federal attack. Of course, this is what the governor and the judge wanted them to do. Southerners always use their children in their racists and religious attacks against others.

At that time, De Kalb county schools regularly conducted sectarian prayers and bible readings by preachers and school administrators in classrooms, at athletic events, and during commencement exercises. Students were required to pray together and out loud in class. As an alternative, a few teachers required students who did not want to pray to appoint surrogate prayers whose prayer sessions they were required to attend. Gideon bibles were handed out in classrooms.

A teacher in the school system named Michael Chandler brought suit to protect his child from the Christian bigotry there. He said, "I don't want the government involved in the religious upbringing of my son. The state has no business telling my child when, where, and how to pray." As a result, he was shunned, insulted, threatened, and smeared. Newspapers all over the state slandered him and urged others to treat him with contempt. He said of this hate campaign against him, "I have been demonized."

Rhonda Weaver, parent of a child at the school, said the case "stinks" and forbade the school from allowing her daughter to have any contact with the tainted Chandler, one of her teachers. Weaver falsely said of Chandler, "He doesn't believe in God." In fact, he was raised as a Baptist and still went to church occasionally. His wife and son were Methodists. Both Governor Fob James and Attorney General Bill Pryor attacked Chandler in political speeches. Pryor said, the Chandler case "cuts at the heart of all that is good in America and brings shame on our nation." He didn't think that Christian attacks against children were shameful or un-American.

In Pike County, also in Alabama, four Jewish children were tormented and abused by school officials because they chose not to participate in the ubiquitous Christian rituals practiced every day and everywhere in the public schools there. In those schools, Christian prayers and devotionals were incessantly broadcast over the public address system, preachers were brought into the schools to preach to captive children, and both teachers and principals regularly led prayers at assemblies and in class rooms.

The Jewish children were forced to attend Christian sermons in school. Sarah, a sixth-grader, was angrily ordered to pray a Christian prayer by one teacher and another teacher physically forced David, a seventh-grader, to bow down to Jesus. Snarling her Christian dogma, another teacher told Sarah she was going to burn in hell unless she embraced Jesus, after which the child was led, crying and shaking, from the assembly hall. The Vice Principal forced a ninth-grader, also a Jew, to write an essay on "Why Jesus loves me." The principal forbade still another Jewish student named Paul from wearing a Star of David and told him it was nothing but a "gang symbol." Of course, many children in this pious place often wore Christian crosses in class.

These Jewish children were frequently persecuted with vicious anti-Semitic insults and were physically assaulted. Their possessions were defaced with swastikas and they were bombarded with crude cartoons celebrating the Holocaust. When the parents complained, school officials told them if they didn't themselves act to save the souls of their children, then the school would have to do it for them. When the parents complained to the school administration, they were told that the harassment would end if the family converted to Christianity. These are the fruits of forced school prayer in the schools.

Meanwhile, in Mississippi, a federal court had to intervene to protect Lutheran children from being forced to say Baptist prayers and attend Baptist bible readings at school. In Lexington, a fifteen-year-old student was expelled from Sheets Memorial Christian School because he prayed the rosary. The school's administrator said, "The Baptist doctrine and teachings do not complement the Catholic doctrine and teaching." In Woburn, Massachusetts, Reverend Chris Pledger of Anchor Baptist Church promised pizza and basketball games to hundreds of poor children from public housing projects, enticed them onto buses, took them to the church, prayed over them, told them to undress and put on robes, and then dumped them into a tank of water and baptized them against their will. Most of these children were Roman Catholics and at least one was Buddhist. The minister said, "Jesus told us to go into the world and preach the gospel."

In the state of West Virginia, Christian prayers are regularly read over the public address system at Nitro High School and children are also required to pray at graduation exercises and at football games. The same practices are widespread in the Carolinas. These are only a few examples of the tyrannical impact of forced school prayer. There are, in fact, an enormous number of such abuses of religious freedom in America and quite a few have been violent.

In the 1980s, Ronald Reagan greatly aroused the Christian totalitarians and cheered them on as they intensified their efforts to force prayer and other religious activities into the schools and indeed into all areas of the life of the nation. In short order, the ACLU stopped the teaching of creationism in Arkansas and Louisiana, defeated "voluntary" school prayer laws in Massachusetts and Louisiana, and blocked "silent meditation laws" in Tennessee and New Jersey.

Little Axe

At the Little Axe School in Oklahoma, teachers monitored and participated in morning prayers for children conducted by the Son Shine Club. Two mothers, Joan Bell and Lucille McCord, objected to the harassment of their children by classmates for not attending these prayer meetings. Robert McCord said, "They accused me of being a devil worshipper, they did stuff like put an upside-down cross on my locker." The mothers sued the school. In court, clinical psychologist Vernon Enlow said that the prayer meetings tended to "polarize" children into factions—"those who go and those who don't go." The school board claimed that morality could not be taught without religion. One member said, "Go to religious services. That's the best way to become a moral person."

When a Little Axe mother named Carlee McGuire opposed the prayer meetings, she got a phone call with the voice of a little girl crying, "Momma ... Momma" followed by an adult voice saying, "Next time it might be your daughter." Carlee McGuire then received fifty to seventy-five anonymous phone calls threatening her life and the lives of her children. She didn't join the lawsuit "because I'm afraid."

The two plaintiffs, Joanne Bell and Lucille McCord, were driven from their homes. McCord received more than a hundred threatening calls. "Most would call me an atheist or a communist. They'd ask why I didn't believe in God. One said that if I didn't drop the lawsuit, I would get it." She received her own obituary in the mail. In fear for her life and the lives of her children, she moved to nearby Harrah but the harassing calls continued. Little Axe school board member Elizabeth Butts called McCord's landlady there and made derogatory remarks and accusations against her.

Joanne Bell was physically assaulted by a school employee when she fled to a parking lot in response to a false bomb threat. The school refused to discipline the employee, who then took out an ad in the local paper to thank her friends for their assistance. Board member Elizabeth Butts told a newspaper reporter, "If people play with fire, they will get burned." Bell then received a number of anonymous death threats and warnings that her home would be burned if she didn't drop the lawsuit. Then, her home was destroyed by a fire described by officials as an act of arson by unknown persons. The Bells moved to Harrah. Joan Bell said, "We are Nazarenes and the Gideon bible is our bible. I have four children and, when they reach a certain age, I give them their first bible. But we don't want it passed out to the children at school. That's an intrusion."

State Representative William Graves tried to get the case dismissed because the plaintiffs' children no longer attended Little Axe School—having been driven out by the school prayerists. ACLU attorney Michael Salem replied that a dismissal "would allow vigilante justice to prevail. If we allow these defendants to escape responsibility for the violation of the constitutional rights of my clients, all you have to do is to drive people from the community in order to defeat a claim. Mrs. Bell and Mrs. McCord have a right to have a government free of religion."

Three months later, Judge Thompson put an end to prayer meetings at Little Axe School and then he too was smeared as an atheist and a communist.

Local Bigotry

A letter to a local paper here in Western North Carolina said, "Is not asking Christians to be silent not denying us the right to practice our faith? ... God asks me to evangelize the world. Romans 12:1 says present my body a living sacrifice." The writer thinks that she and all Christians have a "right" and even a duty to put their religion on everyone else no matter what it takes, no matter how intrusive, how harassing, and how assaultive it is. These are the words of a fanatic, a "Christian soldier" out to conquer others for Jesus by any means necessary including even murderous violence and suicide ("a living sacrifice"). There is really no difference among the true believers whether Christian, Muslim, Hindu, or Zionist.

A preacher here (in Asheville) named Runion frequently writes similar letters in which he bitterly attacks "separation of church and state" and claims that Christians have a right to pray and preach on all public property and that no one has a "right not to hear." He believes that all of the ears and senses of other people belong to him and his jealous god and that no government and no citizen has any right not to be perpetually proselytized and hustled by Christian shouters, finger pointers, accusers, insulters, and threateners.

He claims that Christian prayers in schools, in government buildings, in the streets and parks, in shopping centers, at football games, and everywhere are "spontaneous" and "voluntary" and that they are, as well, an expression of religious liberty. Of course, he does not extend this same freedom to Muslims, Jews, communists, atheists, agnostics, peaceniks, new ageists, witches, liberals, and other such sinners against his religion and his god. Incidentally, the daily newspaper here refuses to publish any effective answer to this preacher's ravings including even quotations from the nation's founders.

All over the Bible Belt, anyone who complains about this sort of religious bigotry and persecution is routinely ostracized, harassed, cursed, and threatened with physical assault and death by their Christian neighbors. Christian Congressmen like Ernest Istook of Oklahoma, Nut Gingrich, Ronald Reagan, and members of the Bush family try constantly to amend the Constitution so as to legitimize forced school prayer and Christian violence against non-Christian children. These are the direct results of the conservative attack against the Bill of Rights, including especially the rights of privacy and freedom of conscience.

*

The above material was written thirty or forty years ago. Of course, as you can see, it dealt with forced school prayer in the United States (?) Little did I know that as of June 2014, an emboldened group of five Catholic Republican Supreme Court justices have extended the same bigoted idea to all municipal meetings in this country. The below recollection is my reaction to that strike against those of us who do not share the bigotry of their Christian religion.

A Childhood Experience

When I was thirteen years old, I moved from the Southern Appalachian Mountains to River Rouge, Michigan, with my Uncle Clarence, my Aunt Bessie, and her son, Wayne. My aunt Bessie was a mild racist (if it's possible to be a mild racist). She didn't want her son or me going to school with black kids. I didn't care and I don't think Wayne did either.

At any rate, she sent us to a Catholic school named St. Andrews and Benedict where there were no blacks. I was in the eighth grade and Wayne was in the seventh grade. Our family was more or less Protestant. I really wasn't anything, though I never said I wasn't a believer. I wouldn't have described myself as an atheist though, because in those days atheists were considered evil in the Southern mountains (and probably just about everywhere else in the South and perhaps in the entire nation). In fact, my surrogate family never went to church at all except for marriages and deaths. Neither did I.

We lived in the projects, cheap row houses built to provide shelter for the mountain people ("hillbillies" to the Michiganders) who came to River Rouge during the war to work in the defense plant there. We hillbillies came from Western North Carolina, East Tennessee, Eastern Kentucky, and Southwest Virginia for the most part. The Catholic school Wayne and I went to was about a mile away from us, in an attractive, leafy middle class neighborhood. All the kids in the school were Catholics and their families were an economic and social cut above us. Wayne and I were aliens, oddities, and curiosities there. We didn't dress like them or talk like them but we hillbillies did have indoor toilets, radios, and cars.

The school had an hour of religious study every day as well as mass every morning in the chapel. I don't remember if I balked or what, but Sister Benedict told me I could leave the classroom and sit out in the hall during the religion classes. So I sat in the hall for a year. And, of course, I didn't attend mass.

Now, years after I wrote the above material about forced school prayer, the five Catholic Supreme Court justices who are Republicans have issued a decision (*Greece* v. *Galloway*) approving Christian prayers at municipal meetings everywhere in this country for the first time ever. Justice Kennedy said, in his decision, that those in the meetings or gathered in the room to transact business with the municipality who didn't like it should just "get out." His words remind me of my experience long ago when I had to "get out" to avoid forced prayer and forced Christian instruction in a private school in River Rouge. But, of course, municipal meetings aren't private but they do have the power now to isolate, identify, label, and define all of the people asked to "get out." I wonder if the court will next revisit forced school prayer to massively impose one of its attack decisions against private belief or the lack of it on children in public schools. If they do, they will be able to label and isolate just about everybody in this country. Then, of course, it will be easy for the Christians to "deal with" and test the qualifications for public office or public anything for living life in the land of the free.

This is a sad day for democracy and religious freedom. The justices have imposed a religious test on all public officials and have told them that they must publicly label themselves as alien believers or unbelievers by getting out; that means that none of them can ever run for political office without answering to those Christian voters who disapprove of their belief or lack of it. Does anyone seriously believe that any atheist or any Muslim can escape the label the court has burned on his and her backs? These same people have told us that corporations are real people, that their spending of political money is free speech, and, now, that political meetings are somehow Christian and not public and thus free of religious bias as the founders wished.

Do these jurists remember when Adolf Hitler required all Jews to wear a yellow star so they could be identified and dealt with by his government and his followers? Hitler was, like them, a lifelong and dedicated Catholic who imposed school prayer on children and included Catholic priests in his government. He also said the values he was imposing on his country came from the Christian god, more specifically from the Catholic god.

CHAPTER 16. ASPECTS OF RELIGION AND SCIENCE

Religions

A central part of the Christian and Muslim faiths is an intense belief in the holy rightness of their dogma and a duty to impose it on others. The Christians call their intrusions "witnessing" and they are driven to conquer and overcome all resistance to their sect's right to dominate, to have a special privileged position and status in the world they live in. They don't just seek acceptance; they demand the triumph of the call they claim to hear from their maker and they are certain they have the right to force you or at least pressure you endlessly and massively toward their idea of salvation. They want to save you from yourself and from the devil in you that misleads you and causes your resistance to their gospel, their good news. This missionary and proselytizing urge is the most dominant part of both the Christian and the Muslim belief systems and, at its worst, it has led them to holy rage, forceful conquest, and often to mass murder.

"Crusade" and "jihad" are the names of their most salient behaviors throughout the histories of these two religions and in all of their many sects, especially including their most dominant ones. This missionary drive is the enemy of democracy, secularism, and tolerance toward others. It rises above everything else in the most agile and aggressive of the Christians and the Muslims. Throughout history, they have been the great enemy of the rest of us and they have been responsible for much, probably most, of the strife, war, atrocity, and genocide in the world. There are plenty of exceptions, of course, but the dedicated ones are a bloodthirsty lot and they will imprison, torture, and kill you if you get in their way or seriously impede them in their militant march toward their god's tyrannical rule over everything and everyone. The Hindus and, least of all the Buddhists, have had their moments of missionary urge too but, even then, they have been the most tolerant of the zealots.

The Christians say they believe in one god, even if he is a triple god—father, son, and Holy Ghost all wrapped in one. In truth, none of the Christians believe in just one god. Maybe the Muslims do but they are, arguably, even more violent, ignorant, superstitious, and aggressive than the Christians. The Hindus have thousands, perhaps millions, of gods. The Buddhists have no god at all but virtually worship the Buddha. There are many other religions and most of them have a whole host of gods.

The Roman Catholic Church was the original Christian church but it wasn't very Christian at all, that is, its members weren't at all faithful to the supposed words of Jesus in the gospels. Instead, they embraced the rest of the Bible, with its murderous commands, irrationalities, superstitions, and bizarre descriptions of the natural world. In fact, it was far more pagan than Christian. It had four big gods if you include the Virgin Mary, the mother of Jesus, who was not raised up to godhead until later in the churches' manipulations of its organization chart. It had as well an infinite number of little gods though it preferred to call them saints, angels, and miracle workers. The church also invented many "orders," essentially little churches inside the big church, each order devoted to some divergent emphasis, idea, mission, behavior, or world of narrow belief. These were much like the little gods of the pagans and like the believers and worshipers clustered around them in their particular circle of worship. The Roman church was just continuing the old pagan patterns but was giving the figures and groupings new names. Today all of this has been obscured and the various Christian sects have invented fantastic and bizarre constructions, rites, rituals, dress, rules, requirements, heavens, hells, and theories to explain their duties and purposes.

The Protestant Reformation tried to clean up the corruption, arrogance, and tyranny of the Roman church but only succeeded in giving huge amounts of power to ignorant, uneducated and self-appointed preachers left free to invent their own private fiefdoms and to ensnare gullible deviants out to find a place in the broken fragments of their old masters' religious empire. Untethered, these seekers came up with lunatic constructions lifted out of the weird tales and garishly painted pictures in the Old Testament and especially from the muddled fantasies in the Book of Revelations. The Protestant flocks found these lurid and strange preachments and prophecies inspiring and convincing, even literally true and worthy of worship. Today, these kinds of believers infest and infect the worldview of millions of deluded conservative and fundamentalist Christians and quite incredibly the major portion of the belief system of the Republican Party here in the United States. In England and Western Europe, the former greatest homes of Christian belief, this American religious comedy is dismissed as mostly idiotic and demented.

The Zionists present a special case of aggressive hate and violence. Before Zionism captured the minds and nationalistic urges of the Jewish people, the Jews were intense but insular believers in their set of dogmatic beliefs. They did not, in their entire history of Western victimization, resort to missionary zeal and did not try to impose their religion on others. They were not a militant people. Indeed, they made brilliant contributions to the Christian and Muslim worlds into which they were forced to live as second-class citizens.

But then came the Zionists with their message of hope for a special homeland in Palestine just for Jews, a homeland where they would be safe from the hatreds, persecutions, and exclusions of the Christian nations. It was a pretty dream but, in execution, it became terroristic and vastly murderous especially toward their Semitic brothers and sisters, the peaceful Palestinians.

The Jewish belief system became so muddled by the demands of the Zionists for the theft of their "holy land" from the Palestinians that they now themselves look like their greatest Western Christian oppressors, Hitler's Nazis. The Palestinian people, on the other hand, now look like the Jews so brutally exterminated by the Nazis and so often expelled, over the centuries, by the Christian states. Like the Jews in the western world then, the Palestinians now have no homeland of their own, having had their homeland stolen away by the invading and occupying Zionists with the help of the Americans hell bent on proving that Hitler's holocaust somehow justified the Zionists' grab of a homeland by driving out the helpless and innocent Palestinians so they could establish a racist state there in Palestine for Jews only. Their leaders made it clear from the start that they wanted all of Palestine, not just the fifty three percent given them by their enablers. They are among the worst anti-Semites ever but they ignore the fact that their Palestinian victims are themselves a Semitic people.

From that time forward, the new Israeli state has been trying to exterminate or at least cleanse away the Palestinians now reduced to the status of refugees wandering about homeless in the desert where they have been deposited by the ravening Zionists. The Americans, true to their idiotic dedication to Zionist hegemony, have flooded the Jewish state with gouts of money and modern weapons until it is now one of the strongest military states in the world. Using American weapons and money, the Israelis regularly attack the weak and mostly defenseless Palestinians spilling enormous amounts of their blood and the blood of their women and children in the cruel desert. What is going on there now can only be described as Genocide.

The theory behind the Zionist conquest of Palestine is that the Jews are God's "Chosen People" and that he promised them all of Palestine three or four thousand years ago. Thus, they are entitled to Palestine and somehow, in some bizarre rape of logic, Hitler's Christian holocaust only strengthened their land claim and turned the Palestinians and indeed all Arabs into terrorists and some kind of Nazis out to drive them into the sea from which they came. This odd theory very much resembles Hitler's theory that his Aryans (actually Germans) were God's supermen (chosen people) and that they needed "living space" so they could fully embrace their superiority; thus, they had a right to invade and occupy the countries on their borders (their promised land). And the conservative Americans have their own version of this story. They say that Americans are "exceptional" and that they have a duty to conquer and improve the rest of the world by Christianizing and corporatizing it. Thus, Choseness, Aryanism, and Exceptionalism are all the products of a highly confused collection of religionists of some sick kind.

All of this trouble began when Harry Truman and Joseph Stalin manipulated the United Nations into "giving" fifty three percent of Palestine to the marauding, terrorist Zionist movement without so much as bowing in the direction of the Palestinians they were thereby dispossessing. Truman and Stalin didn't own and had no right to give the land to anyone, least of all to the million Jews who came flooding into Palestine with their Palmach, that is, their Haganah underground army, and plenty of American and European arms and money. They hewed a path of destruction and murder right across the settled lands and seized everything they wanted. They drove more than seven hundred thousand defenseless Palestinians from their lands, off of their orchards and farms, and out of their homes and forced them into a refugee status that continues to this day. Most of these Zionist invaders had never lived in Palestine at all; indeed many of them had never even visited. They came from Europe and the United States and some from the Muslim countries; they claimed they were "liberating" Palestine but the Palestinians knew that they had been driven from their own land and that many of them had been liberated from life itself by the invading Zionists.

For the last sixty-six years, Israel has been viciously attacking the largely helpless Palestinians who are left with no homeland of their own. They have no state, no army, no navy, no air force, no coast guard and, in truth, no way to defend themselves except through a weak and ineffective rocket fire that rarely hits anyone or anything of value. It is clear beyond doubt that Israel is trying to exterminate the Palestinians or at least to cleanse them away and drive them out to the nowhere that used to contain the Jews. Israel wants all of Palestine so they can have an exclusively Jewish state, a racist enclave in the very middle of the Arab and Muslim world that they hate and want to destroy. It is the Americans who created the state of Israel and who are now arming and helping them in their Genocidal assault against the powerless, suffering Palestinians. What kind of American president authors such brutality? Apparently, all of them except Jimmy Carter.

Jesus was a Liberal

There are a great many unstated truths in the American air. An important one is this one: JESUS WAS A LIBERAL. I know this is not good news for committed atheists, even less so for Catholic traditionalists and Protestant fundamentalists, including Catholic Supreme Court justices. It is true all the same.

Jesus was a peacenik. He said, beat your swords into plow shares, love your enemy, turn the other cheek when he strikes you. According to the Gospels, he committed no act of violence except when he drove the moneychangers out of the temple. Earnest Christians describe him as the Prince of Peace and, at Christmas time especially, they sing and shout for peace on earth and good will to men even while they are waging vicious wars against others. Thus, Jesus was a bearded, leftwing radical and a flower child. He was a pacifist and he opposed war and violence. When he drove the moneychangers from the temple, it was much like the Occupy Wall Street movement directed against the bankers and the other financiers.

Jesus was on the side of the poor and against the rich. He said it was as hard for a rich man to get to heaven as it was for a camel to get through the eye of a needle. It's impossible for a camel to get through the eye of a needle and so it is impossible for a rich man to get to heaven. Jesus wasn't kidding, as Billy Graham claims. He also urged his followers to give away all of their possessions if they wished to follow him and he said the meek would inherent the earth. He ministered to the poor, not the rich. The meek are never violent and rarely rich. Thus, Jesus was not only a pacifist; he was also a democrat.

Not much at all is known about Jesus Christ. The words he is said to have spoken, according to the gospels, are very much in dispute even among Christian scholars. Nevertheless, he appears to have been a good and decent man. If his actual words and actions were anything like those claimed, he might be a good model to follow. Unfortunately, today's Christians— especially the fundamentalists—are extremely brutal, destructive, and immoral people and they are secretly contemptuous of everything Jesus believed and said.

Jesus did not believe in family values nor did he spend "quality time" with his own family or very much time at all. He did not hate prostitutes, robbers, homosexuals, lepers, or even those who attacked him. Unlike today's Christians, he was tolerant, humanistic, relativist, communistic, and even secularist. No one knows what he looked like but, if the pictures imagined and painted by his later, supposed followers are representative at all, he was a bearded radical in sandals and dirty clothes and he was a peacenik and a pacifist.

Jesus did not support any Jewish revolt against Rome and he did not oppose Caesar. When the Pharisees asked Jesus if it was lawful to pay taxes to Caesar, he asked to see a coin and asked whose likeness is this? When told it was Caesar's likeness, he said, Render unto Caesar the things that are Caesar's and unto God the things that are God's. Thus, Jesus believed in the separation of church and state and in paying taxes. This is what liberal democrats and secularists also believe — but not fundamentalist Christians.

Jesus said as well, "When you pray, you must not be like the hypocrites; for they love to stand and pray in the synagogues and at the street corners, that they may be seen by men. But when you pray, go into your room and shut the door and pray to your Father who is in secret; and your Father who sees in secret will reward you." The hypocrites are the preachers, teachers, parents, and students who think their desire to force public prayer and their dogma on everyone else rises above the rule of law and even above the words of the man they falsely claim as their savior. I would add that the five Catholic members of the current Supreme Court now raging against religious freedom are also hypocrites of the most obvious kind.

Monotheism

The Christian religion is the largest religion in the world. It has over two billion members, almost one third of the world's total population. Of course, it is not really one religion but many. Few of the sects agree on much of anything at all and very few Christians agree with or obey the supposed words and teachings of the man they claim as their founder. The sects are more various than the seeds in the fields. Sadly, most of them have always believed in holy wars, forced conversions, slavery, economic injustice, political dominance over others, and the worst kinds of cruelty imaginable including torture, abuse, persecution, and outright murder in the name of their sect. They are not an admirable lot but there are a few good ones. Nowadays, the Christians and capitalists have united; many of them call themselves "free-enterprise Christians." Initially, the Christian religion was highly communistic. It seems now to have squared the circle. I don't see any improvement.

The Christian Religion is made up of a huge collection of very different sects. The worst of these are the "dominionists" and this extreme characteristic frequently infests various parts of the Protestant and Catholic religions. I dislike these Christians because of their invariable determination to impose their belief systems on others by harassment and force. I know very well that there are many decent and honorable people among the Christians and probably among those represented by the other major religions as well. The critical words I use to denigrate Christianity are meant for the extremist elements who seek so indecently to attack and subdue everyone different from them.

Wikipedia describes Christianity as "a monotheistic religion centered on the life and teachings of Jesus of Nazareth." This is the way the Christians see their religion but it is a fanciful view. For example, the Christian religion isn't monotheistic. Christianity is as polytheistic as were the many pagan religions in earlier times. The different Christian sects of today have almost nothing in common other than their pretense that they all believe in the same god.

The Catholic religion is made up of a whole horde of gods. The major gods are called the father, the son, and the Holy Ghost and, as impossible as it is, they are supposed to be both separate from one another and united in a sort of three-sided godhead. Then, the Virgin Mary is herself a god every bit as important as the other three. In fact, she is the most important of all to many members of the Catholic horde, especially among the Latins. The lesser gods are called saints; they have powers over particular pieces of the religious pie and can deliver miracles and answer prayers just as well as any of the four major gods.

The Protestants have an enormous variety of gods, usually but not necessarily only two for each sect. No Christian sect believes in just one god as they all pretend they do. At the least, each such sect believes in God the Father and Jesus the Son, and most of them also believe in a vaguely defined Holy Ghost. Some Protestant sects have gods that resemble one another but most of these gods are very different and they require different beliefs and different behaviors from their followers.

For Christians to pretend that they all believe in the same god is absurd. There are thousands of quite different gods under Christianity. The pretense that everyone believes in the same god is just a way of trying to bind people together so they won't attack and kill one another at every disagreement about the nature of their gods. Our world is not monotheistic; it is vastly polytheistic. This fact should be absolutely clear to anyone with an ounce of intelligence. Peoples' beliefs are easily corrupted for political purposes. Accordingly, almost no one ever admits out loud that each separate sect has its own god and that such gods are all different from and antagonistic to one another.

What the Christians choose to ignore is that they are not one religion but many. The different sects have vastly different dogmas, different rules of behavior, and different definitions of their various gods. There is no way they can live together in peace and without trying to "save" the members of contending sects through coerced conversions and militant propaganda campaigns. The Christian sects cannot live together without violence as they have proven time and again throughout their history in Europe and everywhere else.

Forced Christian Prayers at Municipal Meetings

If you are not a Christian, this is what the five conservative Catholics on the Supreme Court have just said to you in *Greece v. Galloway*: From now on, you are required to say a Christian prayer before any municipal meeting; if you don't like it, get out.

The court says Christian prayers don't mean anything anyway because they are only ceremonial and you don't actually have to say the words out loud, you can pretend. They say it's a tradition and it's been going on for a long time; they just want to formalize it and cement it in place so the Christians can smoke you out, identify you, and isolate you so they can deal with you later if you do anything they don't like, such as running for public office or becoming a dangerous public figure who doesn't go to mass or kiss the cross. We will have your number now, they say, and we can tell the world you are not a good Christian or any Christian at all. Now, we will know exactly who you are, where you live and what you believe or refuse to believe. That's useful information for bigots like us.

We don't want non-Christians in the House, the Senate, or the White House and we don't want any public figure modeling anything or secretly competing with or criticizing Christians. You don't have a right to private beliefs, there is nothing in the constitution about privacy or any right to silence or any right to deviate from Christian norms. You aren't real Americans, anyway. Maybe you should convert right now. If you are participating in a municipal meeting as a start to a political career, just forget it. Non-Christians shouldn't be allowed to have public careers anyway; now you will have to pass our religious test to be eligible to even try.

Jesus said pray in your room or your closet in secret. Public political meetings count as closets say the justices. If this arrangement scares you, you can arm yourself so you can protect yourselves from the Christians; isn't that what the Second Amendment is for. The very idea of separation of church and state is ridiculous, at least that's what we Catholics have always believed and we are now in charge of religious liberty in this country and so liberty means what we say it means. It's our job to isolate and identify unbelievers like you as we have always done, and different believers too; but the Protestants are with us, we trust, at least the fundamentalist ones. We hope there won't be any religious wars or riots or public burnings; we don't do those things anymore. Or do we? At any rate, we are numerous and we will always win.

Why are there five Catholics on the court, you ask. Actually, there are six but the other one is a woman and a Latino too so she doesn't count. As for the Jews among the three remaining justices, we've been telling them to get out of our countries for centuries and they have usually had the decency to comply, going most often to the Muslim countries for their helping of religious liberty and tolerance. Of course, Adolf Hitler and his Catholic comrades, Benito Mussolini and Francisco Franco, went a little too far. Don't blame us because Hitler made the Jews wear a yellow star so they could be isolated and identified and so their Catholic neighbors and governments could deal with them properly by harassing them, persecuting them, and killing them.

Root of Christianity

The root of Christianity was in Judaism and, when it split from Jewish belief, it embraced pagan thought and ritual and combined it with old Jewish myths to make the new religion of the Holy Roman Empire. You would certainly have to grunt and strain to find any marriage between the true Jesus movement in Jerusalem and the Christian theology of the Roman Catholic Church. Everything original in the Jesus movement was suppressed by Christianity. Thus, Jesus himself was not really a Christian. Indeed, the followers and relatives of Jesus were driven out of Palestine and nothing was left behind, no writings and no direct contributions from Jesus himself, not even any fresh memories.

Christianity warred against the books, libraries, folklore, rituals, and beliefs of nearly everyone else in the world and wiped out enormous amounts of human knowledge. Christians have always tried to disappear everything that was not Christian. Though their killing power has been reduced, their intolerance and proselytizing militancy continue today, as exemplified by our Catholic Supreme Court.

Christian Repression

Christianity has always been repressive and totalitarian. It has always assaulted nonbelievers, destroyed their churches, their relics, their altars, their images, their books. It has always sought to conquer everyone on earth by converting them, willingly or unwillingly. It has always used coercion, threat, censorship, suppression, violence, and slaughter to force others into the Christian straight jacket. It has never tolerated any difference or deviation it had the power to change into servile obedience.

Today, Christians have less military and police power than they once had but they continue to proselytize and coerce different others, to pressure and punish non-Christians, to grab after political power that they mean to use as a weapon against anyone who does not obey their moral rules and prohibitions. Christians are the bitter enemies of personal freedom. They are severe tyrants by definition and they are out to subvert democracy and destroy the rights of everyone who does not accept their god and obey his orders as defined and legislated by them alone.

Christian Conquest

What the Christians really want is a world in which everything and everyone is Christian. Those things that aren't Christian must be made Christian and those people who aren't Christian must be converted, condemned, or killed. There is no doubt about this. This has always been the Christian way. This attitude comes from the Christian god. He calls himself a "jealous god" and dooms everyone who doesn't believe in him to the pit of hell and eternal damnation. This god is not only jealous but also cruel and unjust. He regularly condemns children and other weak mortals to misery, suffering, disease, and death. In fact, he quite often kills them himself. Christians do not believe in tolerance for non-Christians, not even for the innocent, the helpless, the sick, and the wounded.

Religious Freedom

Freedom of religion has little or no meaning unless it allows citizens to keep their belief or lack of it to themselves. The issue of forced prayer in public schools or forced obeisance to god in the pledge of allegiance and elsewhere reveals the tyranny of Christian conservatives determined to force their beliefs on every helpless school child and indeed, if given a chance, on every citizen everywhere. Forced prayer in school and elsewhere is not about the right to pray which has never been prohibited in or out of school as long as it remains private and unorganized. It is about the power of Christians to cram their religion and their prayers down the throats of everyone else by forcing organized, public displays of their religious rituals on property and activities that do not belong to them personally.

Totalitarian Christianity

If Christians practiced their various religions in their churches, at home, on their private property, and even quietly and unobtrusively in public, there would be no clash between them and those of us who do not share their belief. But this is something they can never do. They are not capable of neutrality or even civility. They are determined to testify and condemn, to proselytize and convert, to rage against and attack the sin they claim to see in the world and in the lives of all of those different from them. They are determined to conquer us all down to the last resisting child. They despise the idea of democracy because it requires tolerance and respect for the private beliefs of all. They claim to believe in religious freedom but they lie when they do so.

Over and over again, endlessly, they tell us that their god is the one and only king of this and every other country and that we have no right to disobey any of his rules as formulated, stated, and interpreted by them alone. They pretend to be humble and meek but they are the most arrogant, bigoted people ever to exist on the face of the earth. They cannot bear the freedom of others, their right to keep their beliefs to themselves, their right not to be bombarded by Christian propaganda just about every hour of every day. They are always on the attack and frequently they are tyrannical and brutal in the name of their unjust, murderous god.

Good People in Bad Religions

I don't accept any of the rigid dogmas of the Christian religion or any other religion. However, I do not, by any means, believe that all Christians are bad people. There have been and there are many good people among the Christians and among those who practice other religions too. I just don't believe that they arrived at their goodness through the tenets of their religions. Indeed, I think that organized religions are bad for people and for society generally. All of them are based on strange and inhumane superstitions.

Organized religions are often cruel, violent, and destructive. It's hard to imagine a more destructive country than the United States, and the greatest drivers of the war spirit in this country are the Christians, especially the Protestant fundamentalists, the Catholic traditionalists, and the Zionist neoconservatives. Aggression is what drives American foreign policy and that desire to control others spills over into American domestic policy, especially with regard to the desire by government and even more so by the corporatists to spy on everyone so as to manipulate and exploit them for a profit and in the name of security and religious dogma.

The proselytizing practices of the priests and the free market corporatists are based on a desire to conquer people, to claim them, body and mind, along with their resources for the church and the corporation. Fundamentalist Christian and the Muslim religions are by far the most violent and the most arrogant of the religions and most corporatists share their immorality. Their exclusionary behaviors are offensive and domineering. They think that their religious and economic beliefs are superior to all others and that anything different cannot be "right." They think that their god is bigger than all others. Even worse, they claim that there are no other gods as good as theirs and that those who disagree are deluded and evil and especially so if they believe in no gods at all.

Thus the "true" and extreme religionists cannot live tolerantly with those who do not belong to their religion. This leads to the frequent belief that different others must be converted by force or exterminated altogether. And it leads to internal purges designed to eliminate deviants and heretics inside their religious sects.

Religions humiliate their followers. The religious world is full of bowers, kneelers, beggars, and crawlers. They are forced to efface themselves, to bow down and kiss the hands and feet of their leaders. They must also crawl before false images, ogle and embrace ridiculous relics, say they believe in absurd and impossible miracles. Their subjects are forced to believe in holy ghosts, phony saints, flitting angels, soul and body possessions, exorcisms, devils and demons and evil spirits. Their world is a world of fear, of terrified submission, of abject obedience, of subordination and surrender of will. Those who endure this rainfall of abuse are trained to be masochistic and submissive. Their awe and fear of their powerful god and his enforcers rob them of humanity, peace, and will.

Religious leaders prey on their subjects, demand money and sacrifices from them, threaten them with god's disapproval if they do not comply. Their subjects are forced by edict to come begging and praying to the thrones of their preachers and priests where they are systematically fleeced and robbed all in the name of god. But, of course, it is the preachers and priests who get the money and they are the ones who spend it, often for political purposes or self-aggrandizement. None of it ever goes to any god, saint, or angel. Pirates and highway robbers are more honorable and less cruel and greedy.

*

Chosen People

No doubt, the Jewish claim that they are god's chosen people is in some way responsible for anti-Semitism. Every Christian sect believes *they* are god's chosen people and that is why such people hate Jews. How dare they claim to be superior to Christians, the real chosen people, the real favorites of god. There is no one as violent as a jealous Christian. Not only was it arrogant of the Jews to identify themselves as superior to others in the eyes of god, but they went a step further and turned god into a sort of real-estate agent in the sky or a landlord who had actually promised them a great parcel of land and had given them permanent title to it for all eternity.

The arrogance of the Jews was thus met and countered by the even-greater arrogance of the Christians. The result was anti-Semitism and generations of hate and persecution. This is the kind of mischief that religious dogma invariably produces.

The Americans went even further than the Jews in *their* arrogance. They concluded that they were an "exceptional" people under the approval of god and set out to conquer the world for democracy, god, and Uncle Sam. Patriotism was a belief in American superiority in all things, especially American commerce. Capitalism was the American religion even more completely than was Christianity. The American captains of industry said that they not only had a right to exploit their own people but a right, even a duty, to exploit others for a profit and for their own good. The American owners and bosses said they were instructed by god to conquer the world so they could rule it for the chosen people of industry and commerce. This fanatical racism was called "Exceptionalism."

Does anyone doubt that capitalism is a stronger and more fanatical religion than Christianity? In fact, the capitalist credo has become a large part of the Christian message. Not only do preachers have their own commercial empires, they are the heads of political factions that represent the commercial bosses against working people. In America, Christianity is merely a part of the capitalist establishment; its interests are identical with those of the money kings and their servants.

The Goy

Why is there no specific term for Jews who hate gentiles? God knows, many Jews, perhaps most, regard Christians and Muslims with contempt. I suppose that is not surprising. When an entire people has been viciously persecuted and demeaned for nearly two thousand years, it is not strange that they should have learned to hate back. And, of course, the same is true of blacks. Hate begets hate. The victim is always eager to get on top and avenge himself.

Still, many Jews and many blacks have persecution complexes and it doesn't make them less hated. They both brag about their world-class suffering and do all they can to rub the noses of white, Anglo-Saxon Christians in it. They each believe they are without sin and that anything wrong that they might do is in reality the fault of their persecutors. They had better get over it, and soon. Otherwise, they are likely to rekindle the old persecution and hate and become victims of it yet again.

Celebrating the Holocaust in Washington

Why is there a holocaust museum in Washington or in America at all? None of the victims or the victimizers were American. That crime was not an American crime. The location of the museum is offensive and inappropriate. It comes across as a kind of Disneyland Holocaust attraction designed for tourists on vacation. The museum should have been located in Israel, Poland, or, most appropriately of all, Germany. Americans don't like to see the history of our country confused with the history of terrible crimes committed by and in other countries and other cultures and against another people.

Why does every American have to have the holocaust shoved down his throat every five minutes? God knows it was a horrible crime, but it was not exclusive or even rare. If the US is going to have a museum in Washington that commemorates atrocity, why should it be a holocaust museum dedicated to the memory of Hitler's European victims? Atrocities were committed on our own soil by European and American tyrants bent on enslaving blacks and slaughtering Indians. Where are their museums? For that matter, where are the museums to help us remember the exploitation, impoverishment, injury, and deaths of so many working people at the hands of greedy owners and bosses out to suppress all resistance to their money-grubbing developmentalism?

The history of humankind is full of such atrocities, some at least as horrible as the holocaust. Modern Jews celebrate their own degradation and victimization as others celebrate their glories and apparently intend to force everyone else to celebrate it all with them endlessly. Well, enough is enough. Wallowing in the ugly trough of Nazi atrocity will not protect the Jewish people from its repetition in future times. In fact, it might even increase the possibility.

Some of the Jews in Israel have become every bit as vicious and murderous as the Nazis, qualitatively if not quantitatively, and quite often they cite the holocaust as justification for their attacks and vilify their innocent Arab victims as virtual Nazis. The Jewish people had better look to their own morals and abandon this bizarre effort to force everyone on earth to pity their superior suffering and celebrate their world-record victimhood. They were not chosen by god to suffer for all humankind and they are not as pitiful and helpless as they like to pretend they are. Perhaps the rest of us should insist on a holocaust museum in Jerusalem for the Palestinians.

*

Science

The difference between science and religion is the difference between the open mind and the closed mind, that is, the difference between accepting something workable based on the best information available and accepting something claimed to be absolute and eternal based on belief without evidence. Unlike religion and ideology, science does not have dogmas and absolutes to believe in, only its method. Narrowly defined, science is the collection of evidence that can be tested and replicated. No scientific "truth" is absolute and eternal. Every such truth is operational; it is forever open to reexamination based on any new evidence. Scientific laws are laws because they work, because they have predictive value. If the context changes or new information emerges, then the laws must be retested, adjusted, and restated. Scientists accept the continuing need to reexamine their findings. Scientific holdings are not absolutes; they are ever improving approximations.

As a rule, scientific claims are coherent and more or less open to testing; religious claims are not coherent and are hard, even impossible to test. Religion is about things that have no material existence in the natural world. Religionists dwell in this magical netherworld. They deliberately couch their claims in language so misty and large that their claims are impossible to test at all. They claim that their god moves and governs in ways so hidden and mysterious that no human beings can ever understand them. No one can read their god's mind, they say; if he somehow transmits impossible and irrational messages in his bible or through the air or causes contradictory or evil things to happen, then the fault lies with the humans' sinfulness and lack of understanding, not with god's bad or inconsistent behavior. In other words, the believers define their god as a being that cannot be defined because of his largeness and greatness. Thus, they define him as un-definable. Their god is beyond reason and science, they say, but we must obey him just the same. It makes little or no sense to argue with such people. They themselves are beyond reason and sense and they say so proudly.

Some people say that science can make no contribution to questions about the origin of life or its ending or about morality. There is some truth in this. I can't really conceive of endless time and space. How can time or space come to an end? Yet, how can they go on forever without any ending? The term "infinity" has no practical meaning for me. I can conceive of my own birth and death but I cannot really understand my own place in that continuum much less the birth and death of everything. Human understanding is a closed system and we cannot get out of it or beyond it. I know there can be no science of everything, no one universal law or collection of laws that explain it all. However, religion has no answers either. Human beings are doomed to quest forever. It is our nature. As long as human life exists, we will still be looking for final answers and we shall never find them all. We are alone in the universe. There is no god to save us or explain it to us. We will go on dying and the world will go on living until, one day, it too will die and only the silent void will be left behind.

Morals are another matter. Science understood as history, sociology, anthropology, astronomy, chemistry, and other studies of past and current human and natural behavior surely can inform us and explain our proper functioning in our differing civilizations and societies. Morals are variable and they certainly can be described, studied, and understood. However, science cannot and should not try to tell people how they should behave in their moral and ethical lives. Science is not dictatorship. It is a search for truth and useful information. Religions have tried to dictate to people and they have made a horrible, tyrannical, and bloody mess of the world. Science must not emulate religion in this respect. Yet, science should test and describe everything it can get its instruments and examinations in touch with including moral and religious claims. Everything possible should be examined and every discovery should be revealed openly and honestly just as new testing should always be welcomed.

What Our Record on Earth Looks Like.

Science is a system of continuing approximations. Every truth is always open to question and reexamination. Science cannot be absolutist. It must always test and retest. It must always adjust its truths to fit the newest findings. Science is an inexact "science." This is how truth grows and improves itself. However, in the United States at least, science is losing the battle for truth and reality to greedy commerce and dogmatic religion.

Many people—especially religious and political absolutists—are uncomfortable with tentative, inexact, and ever changing truths. Such people believe fanatically that their religious and political absolutes are better than scientific evidence. As a result, they frequently make themselves into enemies of the fact-based world and its revisionary character. They do enormous harm to the world and to us all and they are poisoning our history on earth. Indeed, they are poisoning the earth itself. Commerce and religion are our greatest deceivers.

The United States is the most information-laden country in the world. And yet it is one of the most irrational, superstitious, and dishonest countries anywhere. When people are continuously bombarded with great masses of what passes for information but is, in fact, religious and economic drivel, they will certainly be twisted in dozens of different directions. Great swaths of commercial and religious junk get dumped into the heads and onto the nervous systems of our citizenry just about every minute of every hour of every day.

When this happens, the result is the utter corruption of every democratic entity we have left in the public sphere. The private sphere is far worse. The ad men will do anything to force their products into the attention of consumers without ever describing the actual characteristics of the products they are hyping. Television ads consist of millions of flash cards shuffled into view in great splashes of blinding light. Attention grabbers consist of paid celebrities doing something, anything to win the attention and approval of the watchers. Great movement, violent clashes of objects and people, flashes of color, loud, pounding music, dancing figures, and screeching cartoon creatures are all mixed together in senseless gobs of crazy incoherence. Once in a while there is a little vignette or a quick scene displaying this and that product as wonderful and pleasing but saying nothing about its true nature or function.

Standing in the present world, scientists look into the past for evidence about what happened then and what may still exist now. Anthropologists and archaeologists look underground for traces of past events and for the artifacts of lost civilizations like ours. Astronomers look outward for receding images that show traces of the past and its many shapes and pulses. Historians, if they are scientists at all, look at the leavings of times past and at the tendrils and connections of advancing events and causes twining their way forward into our blighted time. What we are depositing now, what we will leave behind for our successors is what we are all watching now on our television sets, what junk we are leaving behind us in the streets and fields and woods, not to mention what we have done to the wounded and war cleated earth and its sun and moon and whirling stars. How much ugliness, wasted sweat, violence, war, hate, and other indecencies have we contributed to our record here on earth?

Limits on Our Search

If you don't believe there is a god, you have to believe that humans are the ultimate beings in existence. That does not mean that we are the source and expression of everything good and real in existence but it does mean that collective humanity is the source of the only meaningful story to be told for and about sentient beings and the natural world. Nevertheless, human knowledge is limited and never can tell the whole story. That means we all must live with uncertainty and without any absolute grounding concerning the final meaning of our existence on earth or the nature of the universe in which we live. Thus, there are no ultimate truths except those we can discover and create for ourselves with our inherently limited faculties and imaginations. Those who seek a resting place in the arms of Jesus or on a heavenly cloud are clutching for straws. There are no absolute havens, dogmatic harbors, or glorious destinations for any of us. The great certainty and the greatest tragedy is that we all must die. Our existence is finite and so is our understanding.

First Life

About two or three billion years ago, first life came somehow from the boiling seas that covered earth with a violent maelstrom of clashing elements combining with one another and transforming intense energies into units of something mysterious, something like life. The nature of that resulting capsule of life, that one-celled phenomenon is not known and perhaps cannot be known. Those religionists who accept science nevertheless claim that some unknown god infused this bit of life into material forms and thus created first life. They cannot prove their claim; there is no evidence. But science cannot disprove it either, at least not yet. Science is always tentative but hopeful in its quest for ultimate truths. But everything cannot be explained.

Infinity, the idea of limitless time and space, is a useful formulation but it cannot be explained in any concrete way. An absolute wall of limitation stands against understanding the eternal flow of time and the endlessness of space; these concepts are not reachable by the tests of science or by its careful calculations. There are limits to what we can know but we must quest all the same. Science cannot be absolutist. Only popes and other dictators can pretend to achieve that level of certainty.

Science must keep itself open to questions and it must test its own findings as long as human life and endeavor exist. Yes, it must examine everything—including religion—and it must report what it finds, however upsetting it may be to the religionists. The successes that civilizations achieve depend on scientific investigation, not on closed dogmatic religious certainty. Faith runs counter to truth; it refuses self-examination and all openness to scrutiny. All too often it is the enemy of science and reason; and, when it ignores or suppresses science, it becomes the enemy of humankind and its forward thrust into the great unknown. Even if ultimate truths cannot be known because of the inherent limits of human capabilities, science must nevertheless continue its journey.

Faith Alone

Most humans are delusional: they see things that aren't there, believe things that aren't true. It's remarkable that we should have lived so long and traveled so far without learning the easy lessons of science and reason. There are millions among us who believe absolutely fantastic things without any evidence whatever. Included are beliefs in angels and devils, witches and unicorns, miracles and virgin births, alien visitations and resurrections, the demonology of Bill Clinton and Barack Obama, divine signs and miraculous cures, dire predictions and conspiracies of just about every description.

Science and reason are the only means we have for reliably describing and predicting anything at all. The rest is bunk. Of course, humans are emotional and instinctive beings and those traits are of *some* importance. When people try to live by emotion and instinct alone, though, they live misguided lives and often become civic menaces. Almost all of the cruelty and fanaticism in the world come from that quarter.

For example, orthodox religion and conservative ideology come from a blind faith in some kind of magic pattern in human affairs. Those who believe in this kind of magic invariably become militant and self-righteous. They frequently want to kill somebody in the interest of their belief system and often do. And they always proselytize and preach. Their manner is fervent, they are full of awe and worship for some wonderful, airy personage, and they have a catechism full of dogmas picked right out of the sky. They incessantly spout slogans and homilies that are obvious gibberish. They all use the same set of nonsensical, trance-inducing words to preach their gospel and they chant those words over and over again stupidly. Their purpose is to convert others through the force of their own babbled belief and through the spells they hope to conjure up with their ritual, ceremony, and prayer.

Immoral Science

Why are conservatives so hostile to scientists? According to their story, just about every scientist who worked on the atomic bomb was a spy and a Russian agent. In recent years, the New York Times has bristled with reviews of books expressing that view. The reason the anti-communist fanatics took out after the scientists was because they suspected all science of being liberal and, of course, it is.

Most conservatives align themselves fanatically with religion, more often than not with orthodox and fundamentalist religion. Their political and social views are usually based on absolutist tradition and they believe in iron discipline for the masses; they think that people will work hard and behave right only if they are forced to obey their master's rules. Relativism, secularism, modernism, skepticism, free inquiry, and tolerance must not be allowed to interfere with the workings of government, capitalism, Christianity, education, and a very upright social life, they say. Conservatives believe that liberals and scientists are in favor of all of these bad things and that they are un-American and immoral because they question and doubt conservative dogma.

You see, conservatives don't understand the open mind or the need to prove things through the use of evidence. It's much easier for them to just believe in their comfortable absolutes and the lessons of their narrow past and to question nothing. Liberals make them exceedingly uncomfortable and threaten the stability of their fixed minds and inbred habits.

Challenging Religion

Sadly, there are scientists who believe that religious dogma provides a system of beneficial social control over the population; therefore, they refuse to conduct serious examinations of religious matters. The reason large numbers of people believe a great many clearly false things is because scientists and rationalists have so often refused to stand up against popular myths and superstitions.

I am not calling for an attack on religion by science. As always, science and reason must be applied carefully—with strong precision; and scientist certainly should insist that people not be persecuted for their beliefs however silly they may be. However, the truth must be told directly and completely no matter how many religionists object. Organized religion is destructive because its adherents almost always attack others for disagreeing with them and persist in trying to force their religion on those others without the slightest respect for them or their different belief or lack of belief. I want to see scientists and other rational people stand up to the religionists and the proselytizers.

The world can be a better, more decent place but not until the majority of people learn the truth about the world they live in, including the truth about the ways in which they are being misled and deceived by religious hucksters. Only science and reason can save people from religious superstition. Etiquette and an exaggerated sense of respect for the religious opinions of the devout cannot.

CHAPTER 17. ATHEISM AND SECULARISM

Atheism is Simple

Atheism is not thick or fat or deep or complicated. There is nothing to say about it beyond its simple definition as a denial of the existence of any god. It's critics say it is empty and cold; they are quite right. It does not warm the heart or offer any consolations. It has no rules or corollaries. It does not provide a magical path to follow or a mystical way to guide anyone anywhere. It has no dogmas or articles of faith. It has no requirements. It has no direct connection to secularism, humanism, liberalism, or any other ism. Atheists can be tolerant, noble, and humane; but they can also be bigoted, low, and cruel. Atheism does not establish a faith; it quite simply tells the truth. It is not a substitute for religion. It is not a moral system. It cannot make you a good or a bad person and it does not seek to do so.

Atheism is simply itself, not some other thing or any organized system of belief. It is not belief at all; rather it is a denial of one belief: the existence of a god. It has important implications for religions, for secularism and humanism, for science and history and journalism, for government and common living. But it does not fully embrace any of them or drive their functioning. They can exist without atheism and it can exist without them. It stands alone in the world. It is not a joiner and it is not a partner to anything else. It is the bare and freeing truth, nothing more and nothing less than that.

Atheists Stand Alone

There is a courage in atheism that doesn't exist in the Christian religion or in any religion. Standing apart and alone is hard. Walking with the crowd is easy. Defying the crowd and choosing the seemingly empty truth over falsely full faith is both dangerous and lonely. Those of Christian faith have ever been violent and vengeful. The blood they have spilled and the flesh they have burned is proof enough. There were and are no atheists among the crusaders or the jihadists. Atheists do not give up their disbelief in foxholes or under Christian and Muslim threat and torture.

Long ago, a mad pope sent the crusading mob off into his god's ether to destroy and kill everyone and everything before them. They killed Muslims, Jews, and other, different Christians in their zeal and lust. They waded knee deep in the blood of their victims and gloried in the massacre, tasting the flesh of their imagined enemies. Pope Gregory sat at home on his royal throne waving his golden scepter, cursing mankind in the name of his bitter god.

Johnson, Nixon, Reagan, the Bushes, Clinton, and Obama are just modern versions of the killer Christians unleashed by the popes. Like the popes, the American warmongers and crusading presidents stayed at home in their white palace making patriotic speeches and thumping their chests. George W. Bush especially celebrated his obscene and premature victory over twenty five million completely innocent Iraqis by dressing up in a military uniform and flying off to a battleship where he ordered the flying of a banner saluting his victory, the playing of blaring music, and the forced cheering of soldiers and sailors.

Then he went home to discover that he had not won after all. The people of Iraq had not surrendered to him anymore than had the Vietnamese people surrendered to Johnson and Nixon; they had just begun to fight back. In his cowardly lunacy, George W. Bush then launched a program of abuse, rape torture, persecution, degradation, shaming, forced exile, and wanton murder aimed at the civilian population including especially old men, children, women, and other innocents. He said he was doing it all because his Christian god told him to do it and he insisted it was a war against terrorism although there were no terrorists at all in Iraq. These were all Christian wars against innocent Buddhists, Muslims, and even some embedded Christians.

Atheists

Some Christians claim that atheism is identical to communism and terrorism and that it is "anti-religion." They tell us about the crimes of communist atheism and identify atheism with Hitler's Nazism as well.

It wasn't atheists who raged about the world persecuting, torturing, and murdering unbelievers. Mostly it was Christians but there were also plenty of Muslims, Jews, Hindus, Nazis, and communists. The Christians want us to believe that the communists were atheists per se and that communism was atheism in action. They seem to think that atheism has dogmas and a program. Well, the so-called communists didn't murder millions of their own citizens or destroy churches and synagogues in the name of atheism or according to any atheist belief whatever. They did it for communism, a religion in its own right, one that very much resembles Christianity.

There is no atheist belief in pogroms, utopias, churches, sects, rites, rituals, dogmas, sacred texts, miracles, prayers, chants, jihads, crusades, saints, angels, gods, devils, heavens, hells, limbos, purgatories, ghosts, after lives, or any of the other detritus of religious faith and practice. Atheism is a disbelief in religion, not a belief in some substitute monstrosity like communism. Karl Marx was a Jew who didn't accept the religion into which he had been born. His evangelical fervor led him to criticize capitalism—still another religion— and, just incidentally, organized religion. Nobody sane can blame atheism for communism or any terrorist attacks whatever.

Atheism is not a program or a political system. It does not have and cannot have any dogmas or goals. It is simply a refusal to accept a dogmatic belief in a god or a system of gods. It is nothing more and nothing less than that. Atheists don't have churches or political parties. They have never tried to organize themselves into groups or enterprises. They have written no manifestos and have no bibles or rules of order. They have never had an army and have never assaulted or oppressed anyone. They are not missionaries or evangelists and they do not proselytize or preach. They do not assert a belief in anything at all as a condition of atheism. Atheism is simply disbelief. Of course, atheists may believe any number of things about the world, good and bad, but none of them relate specifically to atheism nor do they depend on atheism for any support.

Atheism is entirely without content. It leads nowhere beyond itself except to freedom of mind and conscience on religious matters. It cannot nourish or warm anyone nor does it seek to do so. It is not a philosophy to live by and it does not guide people anywhere. The only consequence of atheism is that it clears the mind of religious cobwebs and leaves it free to explore the world without superstition or false pride.

Monotheism

Anyone with even half a brain knows that a belief in one god is a belief in monarchy. That's why god is called king, lord, master, and, in his Jesus form, prince. Throughout history, kings, czars, shahs, emperors, pharaohs, and other such dictators have been worshipped as god on earth. Their rule was absolute and it was blasphemy to question any of their power or to treat any of them with less than abject adoration. A belief in a god is as offensive as a belief in kings and dictators. No democrat ought to be a Christian, a Jew, or a Muslim. They all worship and bow down to dictator gods. They are all slaves to their religion and they are all determined to enslave everyone else in the name of their jealous, intolerant god. Their weapon of conversion is always the sword, not persuasion or reason. History is largely a story of their wars and massacres. Their gods are far from meek; they are murderous and brutal in every measure. Let no one go unarmed to the camp of the believers.

The Religious Model

The religionists have a neat way of arranging things. First, the priests invent a god who is utterly cruel, brutal, and irrational and then they say we can't judge him with human intelligence at all. Thus, they protect their invention from all doubt and maintain its power and dominance by suppressing every question and every examination. What this formula protects, of course, is the power of the priests, not that of any possible god. Quite simply, this is a formula for total and unending tyranny. Organized religion is a vicious and corrupt con game, a method for establishing and maintaining control over the people of the world by deceiving them and scaring them into submission.

Like the money and military systems, the religious system is just a mechanism for subduing and dominating the many in the interest of an elite few. Quite often, those in control of these systems attack one another violently but, in stable societies, they work together to maintain their control and extract their rewards of power, privilege, and property.

It's nonsense to say you can't use reason and science to decide anything moral or ethical but that religion is the right tool for such work. In fact, religion has made a horrible, cruel mess of morality and has killed, oppressed, and injured untold millions in its efforts to impose its idea of morality on the pagan, the heathen, and the unbeliever. Religious certainty is always immoral and usually results in viciousness and irrationality. The history of religion is a history of bloody attacks against others, including scientists. Though science itself has been used for immoral purposes, it has never been the scientific method or process that has led to that misuse but a corruption of it.

Religion has a well-deserved bad conscience. Science does not. With reasonable accuracy, science can be defined as an impersonal and unbiased search for the truth. Religion has never been impersonal or unbiased and no one can seriously contend that it has ever had an interest in any version of truth which conflicts with its self-serving dogmas. As a method, as a process, as a system, science is honest. In every one of those same facets, religion is a fraud and a search for self-justification and power over others. Religion is never disinterested. It seeks always to guard its power and expand it and it rarely ever shows any respect or tolerance for contrary views. Religion is the imposition of ignorance, superstition, intolerance, bigotry, and unalterable aggression against everything different from and independent of itself.

Materialism

Far be it from me to agree with the priests and preachers about much of anything but the ones who have been saying for a couple of millennia that materialism corrupts were right. Consumer America is the best possible proof of that. The conservatives have destroyed democracy in America and the people haven't even noticed. They have plenty of consumer goods and millions of credit cards and so why worry. Keep the goods coming and forget about democracy and all of that other political crap. The owners and bosses can get as rich as they like just as long as something electric or otherwise entertaining trickles down to the masses. But it isn't only democracy these people are rejecting; they are also rejecting the religion they claim to worship.

Defining Atheism Again

The material above is mostly about what atheism is not. It really is a simple disbelief in the existence of god, nothing more. Its enemies have a complicated set of false accusations to direct against it. Unfortunately, its friends try to respond by giving it traits and virtues it doesn't have. Let me say again: atheism has no content, no belief system, no program. It simply is.

*

Secularism

As said above, Atheism is simply a disbelief in a god or a system of gods, nothing more. However, atheism does have natural alliances: with science, with reason, with history, with liberalism. Many but not all scientists, rationalists, and historians lean toward atheism because their occupations and life-views are based on evidence rather than belief without evidence, otherwise known as "faith."

Liberalism is informed by the three systems mentioned above (science, reason, and history) but many liberals are Christians just the same. The supposed words and behaviors of Jesus Christ described in the gospels inspire and inform them. In fact, Christ himself was liberal right to the core

Atheism and secularism are related but not identical to one another. Atheism is disbelief. Secularism is a practice or stance more than a belief or disbelief in anything. The dictionary defines it as religious skepticism or indifference and also as the idea that religious considerations should be excluded from civil affairs and public education. Secularism should be viewed as a stance of civic neutrality and as a necessary condition for an open society, one based on broad tolerance toward public and shared areas of life. Separation of church and state is fundamental to the idea of secularism and essential to any system of religious freedom.

Secularism must also be defined as a counterpoise to religion. Like atheism, it lacks content and has no program beyond the neutrality it offers. No one can worship or even swear allegiance to any secular dogma because there is none. It offers a neutral space for individual choice and decision, a haven for the unreligious and also for those believers who support tolerance for different others. Above all, it is a communal umbrella of protection for all believers and nonbelievers. It asks for nothing except mutual respect and an end of aggressive, invasive, and assaultive proselytizing.

Secularism does not offer an alternative system of belief. Being secularist doesn't prevent you from being religious but it does prevent you from forcing your religion on others. Secularism is not the brother of atheism as many Christians claim. Rather, it is the father of democracy and individual liberty. Although several theocratic states (Israel, for example, and the former Soviet Union) have claimed to be secularist, it is not really true. The Christians even claim that the United States is a Christian nation but that isn't true either. No democratic country can be anything but secularist in its attitude toward religious and political belief; else it is not and cannot be democratic.

Some Critics

In recent years, there has been a disturbing effort (even by some liberals) to smear atheism and secularism as twin evils that inspired Hitler, Stalin, Mao, Pol Pot, and other such monsters. There have even been articles in *The Nation, The New York Review of Books,* the *American Prospect, the New Republic,* and naturally in many rightist publications that vilify atheism and secularism in the interest of the Christian religion. The material that follows is fairly typical.

In an essay in the November 20, 2006, issue of *The Nation,* Eyal Press (a good liberal for sure) says, "But there's also no shortage of secular people who have propagated murderous ideas through the years. Hitler hardly mentioned God, and Pol Pot, Stalin, and Mao never mentioned God at all." Clearly, Mr. Press is not a very careful historian nor does he understand what secularism is. The people he mentioned were not "secular people."

In a book review of January 11, 2007, in *The New York Review of Books*, H. Allen Orr attacks Richard Dawkins for "his war on religion" and says, "Dawkins has a difficult time facing up to the dual facts that (1) the twentieth century was an experiment in secularism; and (2) the result was secular evil, an evil that, if anything, was more spectacularly virulent than that which came before." After condemning Stalin and Mao for persecuting, torturing, and killing the religious, he goes on to say, "But Dawkin's inability to see the difference in severity of their sins—one of orders of magnitude—suggests an ideological commitment of the sort usually reflecting devotion to a creed." Orr himself can't count, measure the magnitude of, or face up to the thousands of years of religious persecution and murderous violence directed against unbelievers and different believers by the religionists. Indeed, aside from capitalism, religion is surely the most murderous force to ever exist on earth. His claim that the twentieth century was an experiment in secularism is simply idiotic. It was, in fact, one more century of religious viciousness; and people like him promoted it and excused it.

In the pages of *The Nation*, October 8, 2007, a Canadian named Ian Hacking, calling himself a Darwinian, spits venom all over atheism and presumably secularism as well. He bitterly attacks "the arrogant religion baiters—yes, Richard Dawkins, but others are worse..." Hacking provides the mildest kind of loving criticism of the anti-Darwinians even while he presents himself as an objective scientist who believes in and loves the Christian religion and thinks it is warmly wonderful in contrast to disgusting atheism. He agrees with a Christian sympathizer named Philip Kirchner that Americans need god because life in the U.S. is "so cruel and competitive...that Americans need extra consolation." He says of this Kirchner, "his heart is in the right place, unlike the current crop of atheist propagandists."

Hacking virtually foams at the mouth in expressing his hatred for the "virulent atheists" and their "loathsome arrogance." He adds "those who think that Genesis is just another old book should marvel that its authors got it right, in the very beginning." He claims to be on the side of "the people" and says, "I do have a lot of respect for popular skepticism" and adds, presumably in support of the peoples' disapproval of atheists, "The people do not trust those who present themselves as elite." His arrogant hatred is a sign of his fanatical devotion to an elite Christian system far out of the orbit of those who believe in the meekness of Jesus Christ.

Contrary to the above sneers and false accusations, Nazism and communism were nothing like atheism or secularism in their structures or their ideologies. In fact, the real source of both of these isms was the Christian religion, not atheism or secularism. Nazism was directly Christian; communism was a Christian heresy. The evidence is clear.

Communism is a religious system. Even if its gods are abstract and diffuse rather than "personal" and objectified, it is based on a blind faith in intense utopian dogmas, not at all on history or anything scientific or objective. Some other religions (Buddhism, deism, pantheism etc.) do not claim to have specific or definable gods either and the ones that do make this claim (Christians, Jews, Muslims, Hindus, etc.) have vague, divided, misty, and inexact gods. For them, the word "god" is a ghostly and rather empty word but it plays a kingly or dictator role in the complicated systems of belief and behavior imposed on gullible religionists by their all-too-human rulers. Communists kept big parts of the Christian belief system intact but threw out the word "god."

There is really no doubt about it. Atheism and secularism simply were not a source of or an inspiration for Nazism or communism. On the other hand, Hitler's Nazism came directly from and was an expression of Christian belief, both Catholic and Protestant, and he and his followers always said so. Stalin's communism very much resembled medieval Christianity in its tyrannical repressions, punishments, enslavements, and violence toward dissidents, deviants, and unbelievers. Communism itself was a heretical religion derived from Christianity and capitalism and it imitated those systems in almost every respect though, of course, it had its own cultural configurations. Like Hitler, Stalin was manufactured by the Christian system.

Atheism and secularism are different things altogether. Neither has a set of dogmas and neither is based on faith or force. They impose nothing on anyone and ask for nothing other than tolerance and neutrality with respect to freedom of belief and expression for all people.

Secular Tolerance and Neutrality

The two words that most clearly define secularism are "tolerance" and "neutrality," though the term "nonreligious" (but not "anti-religious") is also accurate. Fundamentalists in the United States are outraged against secularism because they want always to intrude their religion into everything imaginable (they call it "witnessing"), including especially education, the use of public space, and the acts of government. They think that religious freedom means a right for them to evangelize and proselytize in all space and against anything and anybody not fully supportive and completely submissive to their dogmas and demands. They are themselves most definitely not tolerant or neutral about anything they think does or might touch them or their religion. What they claim for themselves and their religion is outright dominance. Indeed, one branch of conservative Christianity calls itself "Dominionism." This attitude pervades the Protestant and Catholic religions.

They want to dominate the whole world and anything that gets in the way of that quest is unacceptable.

In polls, Christians and probably Muslims identify atheism as their greatest enemy. Secularism is second in their fevered minds. Despite strong criticism of capitalism and the so-called free market, particularly by assorted popes, there is also a strong opposition to socialism and communism that does not recognize that early Christianity was, in many ways, socialist or communistic. Most religions these days have given up direct attacks against democratic government except when government policies impinge on their most cherished practices of the moment. They want to make sure that democracy does not spread too far or threaten their hold on their flocks.

The Christians keep telling us that the United States is a Christian country. They are right only in that most citizens claim vaguely to be Christian but there are hundreds if not thousands of sects that claim implausibly to be Christian. I think that most of those who claim to be Christian are decidedly not Christian if the words in the Gospels said to have come from Jesus are taken seriously or accepted at all in practice.

My view is that true democracy is not possible without a secular government strong enough to prevent religions and corporations from exploiting and abusing citizens and public enterprises devoted to the welfare of the people. Because I think that Christian and corporate forces are much too strong and much too controlling and abusive, I do not think this country is any longer fully democratic. I think it is totalitarian in that it spies on, manipulates, and dominates the activities and even the senses and attention of citizens almost all of the time. Television, cell phones, security devices, and policing instruments are everywhere. Almost everyone is under supervision day and night. Just because the police and the military aren't regularly breaking down our doors, shooting people promiscuously, or silencing them massively as in Hitler's Germany and Stalin's Soviet Union does not mean that we are really free and truly in control of our own lives as so many believe.

I think we are undeniably a police state and a military garrison. Clearly we have a military and police presence in just about every country on earth and we have military bases in about 150 different countries, something like nine hundred of them, I believe. We spend more on our military than the next ten countries combined. Such pervasive military power is certainly not defensive or peaceful. We lock up more of our citizens than anyone else. We are forever at war and our streets are filled with police and security agents all the time.

Since the presidency of Dwight Eisenhower, we have had a declared policy of "political warfare" set up to replace Harry Truman's "containment" policy.

We secretly spy on and subvert every country and we have a surveillance system so intrusive and widespread that it is said to include absolutely every one of our citizens and probably most everyone else in the world as well. If this is not totalitarian and anti democratic, what is?

CHAPTER 18. CATHOLIC INFLUENCES

Divine Lies

The Catholic Church is considered the original Christian church; of all the Christian sects, it is the most highly developed and international; and it is clearly corporatist in its hierarchical and power arrangements. Once Emperor Constantine made the Christian religion dominant, it became an important part of a royal and divine order of kings and aristocrats that engulfed and tyrannized the Western world for most of the last twenty centuries. At times, the popes of the church ruled over an entire network of divine kings and their subjects. Indeed, they were called "King Popes" and, at times, they ruled through networks of "King Bishops," King Princes," and the like. This fusion of titles merely illustrates a fusion of political and religious power. The Pope was the ultimate king and nobody had a right to defy his god given power. Until the Protestant reformation, there was no serious opposition.

All of the kings were considered little gods and they had all of the riches, privileges, and powers thought to belong to god himself. The popes were great delegators being unable, as a practical matter, to rule the whole Western world by themselves. Such hierarchy began long ago when bosses and priests first began to supervise workers and other people, but there was a natural growth from that simple beginning to the later political and religious pyramids of power shared by kings and popes. From the start, there was a division and often a competition between religious and political leaders. At times, one or the other achieved near total power. At other times, power was shared. There was a seemingly natural separation of king and priest. The king ruled the practical world, the priest the supernatural world.

If a king was divine as he and his kind pretended, no one had a right to disobey him, harm him, or overthrow him. If he was god on earth or at least his god's representative, everyone had to bow down to him and kiss his feet. People had to venerate him and worship him just as they would god himself. All of the wealth, all of the property in his kingdom came from god to him and he had a right to keep it all or hand out some of it to his favorites as he pleased; and he had a right to take it back whenever he wanted it back. He could likewise delegate some of his power to a royal class of aristocrats selected by him alone. They shared god's power and property with him and they too had god-infused blood in their veins but no divine right to rule from the throne.

This divine idea was a very sweet lie, one that made kings and popes invincible and infallible (incapable of error). Everything the king said or did was holy. If the people believed this lie, and almost everybody in the world did believe it for thousands of years of human existence, then the people had to accept their lot no matter how miserable or unjust it was. They could not revolt and they could not change the king or his regime. Until very recently, this system dominated most of the entire earth, and, though it has been substantially disestablished by Enlightenment ideas and liberal revolutions, strong traces of it still remain in the power of our own "divine" leaders.

King Ronnie and King George

Peggy Noonan said that Ronald Reagan was divinely anointed; she remembered that, while driving in California, "the sun shone on his head the whole way" and later broke through the clouds to shine on his head when he was sworn in as governor. A friend said, "It was like a halo coming down. It was eerie." Noonan said, "I know it doesn't sound true but it is." Then, in the White House, she said, "I am still searching for an anecdote about Reagan that truly reflects badly on him." She said, "Ronald Reagan loved the truth... it was fresh water to him." Noonan quoted Rush Limbaugh as saying, "There was no image creation. There was the genuine Ronald Reagan." Noonan said that Reagan saved seventy-seven lives in seven years as a summer lifeguard on a small piece of water on the Rock River in Illinois. (Note all of the sevens.) She claimed he kept every campaign promise, including even cutting the federal budget. "Done, done, done, done, done, done, and done," she said. She said he was "by nature a conservationist" and "a feminist." "He came out of a home run by a woman," she said. He "wasn't a racist," she said, "because he once had a black friend in high school." She repeatedly implied that all presidents previous to Reagan were communist appeasers and that he was the man who saved the world from communism.

Dinesh D'Souza claimed that Reagan knocked the Berlin Wall down with a speech and Dinesh thought that this was a "miracle." He said, "The most powerful empire in human history imploded. These were not just accidents. Reagan predicted them. He intended the outcome." D'Souza claimed that Reagan's sneak attack against tiny, unarmed Grenada trumped the Brezhnev Doctrine. He said, "Capitalism and democracy were on the retreat in much of the world" and America faced "the greatest economic crisis since the Great Depression." He claimed that Reagan's many gaffes and misstatements were cleverly designed "as a kind of code to transmit important political messages that would be incomprehensible to a hostile media." D'Souza said the huge deficits Reagan created were cleverly arranged by Reagan to force Congress "to impose limits on the growth of government."

When Reagan's own aides in the White House tried to remove him from office for incompetence, passivity, and disengagement, D'Souza said of Reagan's aides, "Thus, the conventional wisdom must be turned on its head. He wasn't their pawns; they were his." D'Souza said, "He saw them as instruments to achieve his goals.... People would work for him for a decade, then they would leave, and he would not associate with them—not even a phone call." D'Souza first said the Iran–Contra scandal was transacted in the White House without Reagan's approval. But, after that claim was overwhelmed with facts, he then said, "He did it because he empathized with the suffering of the hostages and their families." Reagan himself said, "It was my idea to begin with"; but he denied it had anything to do with hostages until it became useful for him to admit that it *was* about hostages. He said his heart told him one thing and his head told him another. This was why he lied, he said, but, of course, he didn't admit that he was lying. The real story was even more complicated than this and far more devious and outrageous, according to a book by Gary Sick called the *October Surprise*.

Reagan's director of correspondence said, "God put him in the White House for that specific time in history to do what he had to do." Nancy Reagan said that Ronnie was cured overnight of an ulcer thanks to a prayer by a lobbyist from Southern California. Larry Speaks, a Reagan spokesman, said preparing Reagan for a news conference was "like reinventing the wheel." Other staff members said he never changed a time or canceled an appointment or even complained about an item on his schedule. His staff was constantly pushing or dragging him around from place to place and were whispering in his good ear when he was at a loss and needed to respond to something or someone. His chief of staff, Don Regan, said, "I didn't know what to make of his passivity." However, Nancy Reagan had a paid astrologer that she consulted on matters of interest and on Ronnie's schedule before she would allow him to do anything or go anywhere. Apparently, Nancy and her astrologer were running the country, naturally with god's help but with not much help from Ronnie, who was pretty much a rag doll regularly manipulated by his Republican handlers and by Nancy.

George W. Bush was just about as challenged by the job and life itself as was Ronald Reagan; he saw himself as god's instrument and asked for and got the same kind of worshipful treatment from his followers as Reagan did. Peggy Noonan said he was "God-Touched." Lt. Gen. William Boykin said of him, "Why is this man in the White House? The majority of Americans did not vote for him. Why is he there? And I tell you this morning that he's in the White House because God put him there for such a time as this." George W. Bush said, "I've heard the call. I believe God wants me to run for president." At an earlier time, Herman Goering said of his hero, "God gave the savior to the German people. We have faith, deep and unshakable faith, that [Hitler] was sent by God to save Germany."

As president, Bush said of his false war against the innocent people of Iraq, "God told me to strike at al-Qaeda and I struck them, and then he instructed me to strike at Saddam, which I did." He said of his attacks that he didn't "need anybody's permission" and didn't "owe anybody an explanation." This too is remindful of Adolf Hitler, a life-long Catholic, who said, "I believe today that my conduct is in accordance with the will of the almighty creator." Bush also said, "If this were a dictatorship, it would be a heck of a lot easier, just as long as I'm the dictator" and "I'm the decider and I decide what's best." He told the American people, "Either you are with us or you are with the terrorists" and his Press Secretary, Ari Fleischer, warned the people, "These are reminders to all Americans that they need to watch what they say."

Republican Sanctification

The incredible claptrap used to sanctify leaders like Nixon, Reagan, and the Bushes, as well as their progenitors and followers, dominates politics today. Here in the United States, the Republican Party and the conservative movement are the depositories of much of this belief system. Conservatives don't like the enlightenment or its fruit, the French Revolution especially, or, for that matter, any revolutions. They pretend to revere the American Revolution but, in truth, they dislike all of its values and go to astonishing lengths to distort those values to make them seem to agree with their own absolutist doctrine. If they ever openly revealed their hostility to America's revolutionary values and its people, they could never gain or keep political office again. Thus, they have fashioned a mask that conceals the real face of their anti-democratic identity.

A few of the most deluded of this Republican lot (including George Will) claim that the American Revolution was a "conservative revolution," a completely impossible construction. Such people are still royalist and absolutist and they are still pretending that they are "republicans." They believe in their own virtually sacred right to rule and dominate, at home and abroad. That is why they go to such lengths to redefine "communism" and "terrorism" so as to include liberal democrats among those aliens and to tar them as America's enemies. In fact, the conservatives are America's enemies. They detest democratic government and say so in every political campaign. They detest the government's helping and healing power and love its punishing and killing power, all in the name of military aggression overseas and repressive law and order at home. Republicans rarely ever support or vote for anything constructive or useful to the people. They seek to destroy truly democratic governance and seek instead to eliminate all restrictions and all taxes on rich, corporate, and religious power. They also seek to use government force to control the sex and reproductive lives of all citizens as well as their religious lives. They employ surveillance and spy systems to poke into the private lives of citizens so they can know everything about everybody. They want a population of servants bowing down to bosses, priests, preachers, police chiefs, and generals and they want themselves at the top of the heap.

Resisting Divine and Royal Power

The Enlightenment began to question the divine nature of kingly and priestly powers. The American Revolution was the first revolt that overturned both of those powers and established a democratic and secular state in their places. The French Revolution quickly followed and it went even further than the American Revolution in giving rights to citizens rather than to kings and priests. Since then, there have been many revolts against the old absolute and divine order.

Before the Enlightenment and the revolutions in America and France, the world system was a Divine one. When the revolutions against kings and their royal houses arrived, conservatives and aristocrats everywhere complained bitterly when the kings and their heirs were killed. One wonders why royal families should expect to have their power and their lives respected by the common people they and their ancestors oppressed, abused, and killed for so many centuries? If, as the aristocrats claimed, the king's blood was sacred because it was put in his veins by god himself then, according to their own logic, his children and all of his relatives were divine too and had an exclusive right to his throne when he died.

As long as any blood relative remained, there was a god-anointed heir to the throne to take his place. In these circumstances, why shouldn't revolutionaries kill entire families, however cruel that may have seemed? They were destroying divine tyranny and all of the royal and aristocratic claimants to the throne. In other words, they were trying to forestall a counterrevolution in the name of divine succession. Thus, all of the inheritors had to die. The kings set their own traps and there was no injustice in their demise.

There was much resistance to kings and, in our time, the remnants of the old royal system have been forced into a non-royal form. Political power shifted to new hands much faster and much more completely than did economic and religious power. Religion continues to reign but its power is much weaker than it was. Economic power has taken new forms and has, at times, fused with political and even religious power.

The Industrial Revolution massively increased economic power and that power eclipsed or absorbed much political and religious power. The old hierarchical pattern of the kingdoms and the churches shifted to commercial companies and corporations. The communist versions of this new ruling system in the Soviet Union and China became total. In those formulations, all political and economic power was placed under the control of one party. Religion was suppressed but not destroyed. My personal belief (apparently not shared by anyone else) is that communism itself was a religion. But then, I also believe that capitalism is a religion. The fervency of the so-called "free-market" ideology and its proselytizing fanaticism strengthen that belief considerably. Predatory capitalism today has as many fanatics and worshippers (of "sacred" property and corporate personhood) as did the communists and the ancient kings and priests. Corporate capitalism survived communism but the two share very similar ideologies or religions. They both have rigid dogmas and intense belief systems and both proselytize furiously.

This brings us back to the political influence of the Christian religion. I think it has become a very definite part of the diverse political structure of the Republican Party. Most of the libertarians are not religious but they share all of the other dogmas and beliefs of the conservative movement and the Republican Party. In fact, libertarians Ron Paul and his son, Rand Paul, are dedicated Baptist fundamentalists and Paul Ryan is a Catholic medievalist much like the German, Italian, and Spanish fascists. However, all of the conservative libertarians fanatically embrace or at least tolerate religion when it is useful to them. The Republican Party consists of a whole collection of disparate, often self-contradictory parts but they are all fused together in an intense hatred of democratic government and liberalism, including a hatred of European social democracy. Religion fornicates with these political and economic forces as it did of old. Whenever it needs to, it reshapes itself to better fit the mold. Political and commercial life in the United States is shot through with Christian influences and requirements. The Catholic Church has played an important part in shaping this phantasmagoria.

Of all the dictators in history, the popes were the worst because they were the highest, the mightiest, and the most absolutist. They have lost much of their power now but they are still foolishly worshipped by hundreds of millions, perhaps by a billion or more people. There is nothing noble or democratic about royal robes, golden thrones, magic scepters, or dogmatic absolutism. These things are the trappings of an ancient, corrupt, and usually brutal totalitarian system of control over the world's populations.

Remnants of this power infest the Republican Party, in the conservative, the neoconservative, and the libertarian movements: yes, even in the neoconservative and libertarian movements, despite the Zionist core of the neoconservative movement and the pretended atheistic beliefs of many of the libertarians. Members of these two parts of the Republican Party are fellow travelers and collaborationists, allied with the absolutist conservatives who share their loathing of democratic liberalism and the rights of working people and the poor.

I associate the Catholic religion with fascism, but fascism is not exclusive to that religion. For example, Calvinist Protestantism, with its belief in predestination, was one religion that embraced the idea of making money as a holy pursuit (the Wealth Gospel). The Calvinists say that success under capitalism was preordained by their god. This same belief is now embraced by nearly all Republicans.

Thus, the conclusion: God wants you to get rich, *pace* Ronald Reagan. This money-loving belief devolved into the Protestant Ethic, a great cover for predatory Christians everywhere, Calvinist or not. According to them, Jesus was wrong. You *can so* get through the eye of the needle and into heaven even if you are as rich as Midas. Money doesn't disqualify you, so have at it. Catholics have believed in the rich life ever since the Romans made their system into the state religion and made it commendable for Christians, especially popes and bishops, to be rich. But the Catholics are not quite as grossly greedy as the Calvinists or as disinterested in what they think Jesus said about the rich.

I center the Catholic Church in the fascist movement because I see royal aristocracy and the divine right of kings as the first forms of fascism (though not yet so named) and because kings could not become divine without a religion to frame them as divine. Of course, as said before, the Catholic Church is not the only religion to be fascistic; to one degree or another, all the mainstream religions whose members love capitalism are fascistic. Fascism is corporatism but it requires a sacred or awesome force behind it; it must depend on mass belief and devotion to acquire and keep its absolutist power.

Communism said it was anti-religious but it posited a "historical" (somewhat mystical) force behind it and it relied on a vaguely defined "dictatorship" to prop it up. The "communist" countries we think of today were never really communistic in the original sense, and for most of their histories the Soviet Union and communist China were mired in open or incipient civil war. The administrations provided a great deal of economic and social leveling, but they did not allow the common people any political power or influence at all. Even the pretense of being an alternative to predatory capitalism proved to be inexact. This was just another capitalism, state capitalism, as was understood by the original founders and was forgotten later on. In time, there will be many such transformations, including of Western capitalism.

The Catholic Church is itself a corporation, a corporation with a king (the Pope) at its head. Catholicism is still a medieval religion, still divine and royal and intensely hierarchical. It no longer rules the Western world but it still has enormous power and influence. The Protestant religions are only copies. The United States has become the most important center of Christian, corporatist belief. It rules the world clumsily but it has enormous productive capability and great, if indiscriminate killing power. The gross stupidity of its political class is a considerable defect, one that is already reducing the nation's power and exposing its leaders as ignorant, arrogant, and frequently pompous moral frauds. In time, it too will go down without much of a struggle. Its splintering polity is devouring itself right now. Meanwhile, the Catholic Church still sits there awkwardly astride the world, a reminder of its former glory and power. Long ago, it was the fount of corporate fascism.

Rise of the Fascists

It's no great surprise that most of the modern dictators, save the communists ones, were devoted and unyielding Catholics. It is also no surprise that a majority of the justices on the current Supreme Court are Catholic corporatist Republicans devoted to unraveling the American constitution in the interests of the corporations, the military, the national police, and the Christian conservative religions. The Catholic Church is dying a slow death but those who support its tyrannical dogmas are mounting a resistance movement. A great deal of corporate money is backing this rear-guard fight.

Liberal democracy has been greatly weakened by this reactionary assault. The Republican Party is fully corporatist (read, "fascist") and the

Democratic Party is so heavily dependent on corporate money that it too has become effectively if intermittently and weakly corporatist. Religious fundamentalism—both Catholic and Protestant—is on the rise and it has massively infiltrated the Republican Party. So far, American military and police forces have not been regularly used for mass attacks and killings here at home; but those forces have been increasingly used to indiscriminately attack innocent people in other countries for false reasons (Vietnam and Iraq in particular), all in the name of corporatist greed, partisan political power, and religious hegemony. Those who can so easily and indiscriminately torture and kill distant foreigners for "moral," "democratic," and "security" reasons can do the same at home and for the same false reasons. In our future, perhaps in our near future, I think, there lurks the specter of military dictatorship backed by the corporations, the churches, the Republican Party, and the Supreme Court.

At this point, there is a need to once again define the meaning of the word "fascism" and to describe its origin. The name was derived from "fasces," an ancient Roman symbol of the regal power of the state. It was borne by guards, called lectors, before state officials, especially dictators and emperors. It symbolized unity and power. Fasces were a bundle of rods bound together around an axe with the blade protruding. It represented authority, more precisely hierarchical and absolutist authority. Politically, it represented the centralization of authority under a ruler. Religiously, it represented the absolute and infallible authority of a pope or other supreme leader on matters of morals and religious belief. Legally, the Roman Catholic Church today is a corporation and even a state thanks to Benito Mussolini. Commercially, fascist power has come to represent the authority of a property owner exercising absolute managerial power over a collection of servant workers through an abstract legal device called a "corporation."

In the first half of the twentieth century, four newly-named "fascist" parties came into existence, the first in Italy under Benito Mussolini, the second in Germany under Adolf Hitler, the third in Spain under Francisco Franco, and the last in Portugal under Antonio Salazar, the "Little Priest." Though it is often denied by conservative religionists, all four of these fascist dictators were life-long authoritarian Catholics and they made their religion a part of their fascist belief system. Thus, the Catholic religion became the third leg of a new fascist system, perhaps stronger than the state and commercial legs. These dictators were immensely popular with those of their citizens who were not their victims (their victims were Jewish, racial, socialist, atheist, democratic, and liberal deviationists and dissidents) and their popularity lasted as long as their regimes remained powerful and stable. When defeat loomed for Hitler and Mussolini, their popularity collapsed and they were destroyed. However, Franco and Salazar retained their power and got little opposition from their own citizens or from the Allied governments in Europe, England, and the United States.

From that start, fascism has infected the whole world. It has had a strong presence in Latin America, in the Middle East, and in the Muslim world, and the government of the United States has often supported it as an imagined bulwark against communism. Wherever economic, political, and religious power have been combined and paired with military and police power, totalitarian fascism has been the outcome. More and more, the United States itself has become increasingly fascist — especially when the Republican Party controls the government.

A Note on Sources

The ideas in this book were influenced by Thomas Piketty's *Capital in the Twenty-First Century*, Noam Chomsky's *Power & Prosperity*, Daniel Guerin's *Anarchism*, Michael Perelman's *The Invention of Capitalism*, F.A.Hayek's *The Road to Serfdom*, Karen Armstrong's *A History of God*, Hugh J. Schonfield's *Those Incredible Christians*, and by such television programs as Amy Goodman's "Democracy Now" and the "Rachel Maddow Show" on MSNBC.

The Libertarian belief system is at the heart of many of the contrary arguments presented in this book and its baleful influence can be read about and seen in just about any of the writings, presentations, speeches, and gatherings of Republicans. It is, I suggest, the number one enemy of democracy in America today.

Printed in the United States
By Bookmasters